The Brittle Thread of Life

The

Brittle
Thread of
Life

Backcountry People
Make a Place for Themselves
in Early America

Mark Williams

YALE UNIVERSITY PRESS   NEW HAVEN AND LONDON

Published with assistance from the income of the Frederick John Kingsbury Memorial Fund.

Set in Fournier type by Binghamton Valley Composition, Binghamton, New York.
Printed in the United States of America by Sheridan Books, Ann Arbor, Michigan.

Library of Congress Cataloging-in-Publication Data

Williams, Mark, 1948–
The brittle thread of life : backcountry people make a place for themselves
in early America / Mark Williams.
p.   cm.
Includes bibliographical references and index.
ISBN 978-0-300-13922-8 (alk. paper)

1. Granby (Conn. : Town)—History.   2. Land settlement—Connecticut—Granby (Town)—History.
3. Social classes—Connecticut—Granby (Town)—History.   4. Rural poor—Connecticut—Granby
(Town)—Social conditions.   5. Country life—Connecticut—Granby (Town)   6. Ashfield (Mass. : Town)—
History.   7. Land settlement—Massachusetts—Ashfield (Town)—History.   8. Social classes—Massachusetts—
Ashfield (Town)—History.   9. Rural poor—Massachusetts—Ashfield (Town)—Social conditions.
10. Country life—Massachusetts—Ashfield (Town).   I. Title.
F104.G65W549 2009
974.6'2—dc22
2009005784

A catalogue record for this book is available from the British Library.

This paper meets the requirements of ANSI/NISO Z39.48–1992 (Permanence of Paper).
It contains 30 percent postconsumer waste (PCW) and is certified by the
Forest Stewardship Council (FSC).

10 9 8 7 6 5 4 3 2 1

for Myck,
and for Quincy, who missed out the last time

Contents

Preface

I have two stories to tell here. Each revolves around the settlement and growth of a small community in early America. Salmon Brook, in northern Connecticut, had its beginnings around 1680. Settlers first moved to Huntstown, in western Massachusetts, sixty years later. The first families of each settlement came from different ethnic and religious backgrounds, and they and their successors in each place lived within distinct social and institutional environments. Two stories—and yet, in many ways they are one. They unfold separately here, but standing together as a single micro-history, they reveal how people of the lowest ranks of early American society—backcountry people—insisted on a place of independence and respectability for themselves, and in doing so played an important role (as important as that of their more famous contemporaries) in pressing a democratic stamp onto the new nation's political and social landscape.

I chose to write about these two communities after poking around the hill towns of New England for several years, puzzling over old cellar holes, mill seats, stone walls, and even various dirt- and rust-encrusted items that I pulled out of my back yard. A project adviser in a graduate program had once suggested that I do a community study of my hometown of Granby, Connecticut, applying the techniques of what was then called the new social history. Eventually, I wrote a narrative history of the town, and in the process discovered some exciting things about its little-known eighteenth-century background (when it was called Salmon Brook). In contrast to the story that proud descendants and locals have told of the town's beginnings in genealogies and local histories, I found that its early inhabitants were mostly poor and disdained people often at odds with their civil, ecclesiastical, and mercantile leaders, and they could become quite disrespectful and insistent when they did not get their way. What was more important was that their so-called betters could not overrule or ignore them, but usually had to meet them at least halfway. This discovery seemed to me to have important implications for issues of class and privilege, equality and social mobility, and the tensions and conflicts that developed when incompatible visions of social order clashed in early America.

As I explored the early years of other settlements in the hill country of Massachusetts as well as Connecticut, I became convinced that people on the fringe in early New England were creating communities outside the region's mainstream, and their relations with the nearby social and political elites were quite different from the "monarchical" relations that are supposed to have characterized early American society. One might view the dynamics of this relationship as an ongoing "negotiation": in exchange for defense and extension of the English frontier and a degree of orderliness, otherwise neglected people won land, respect, and independence. They remained on the outside for some time, yet were always insisting on a place on the inside. Consequently, we should place them on the inside of early American history, for their struggle helped shape the new nation's ideals.

Tracking down the lives and activities of these rough-hewn people among the hills of New England and constructing their stories from registers of land transactions, town meeting minutes, church records, material culture, and the surviving elements of the landscape they created has enabled me to discover a people who seem to have had little to say to posterity, but who actually said a lot in their own worlds. They have had much to say to me as well, and what they said and how they said it have both amused and impressed me—which is a lot more than they did for those of their day who wanted to hear nothing but deferential awe and gratitude from them. We are fortunate that their "betters" did hear what they wanted to say, and even deferred to them.

This has been a long and involved project, and I owe much to many. I am grateful for all the encouragement and helpful suggestions provided by John Demos, Harry Stout, Keith Wrightson, and Joanne Freeman of Yale University, Tracey Wilson of Conard High School in West Hartford, Connecticut, and Christopher Rogers and Phillip King of Yale University Press. In Granby I have enjoyed the support of local history patrons and enthusiasts Seth Holcombe, Carol Laun, and Bill Vibert. Courtesy of their organization, Salmon Brook Historical Society of Granby, Connecticut, Chapters 1–4 of this work contain some segments from the early pages of the book the society commissioned me to write called *A Tempest in a Small Town: The Myth and Reality of Country Life, Granby, Connecticut, 1680–1940*.

When I worked in Ashfield I was welcomed and beneficially instructed by Nancy and Lester Garvin, Alden Gray, Lou Ratté, and Grace Lesure of the Ashfield Historical Society. Nancy Garvin, in particular, has been most helpful in reading drafts of the chapters on Ashfield. At The Loomis Chaffee School, Bob Andrian, John and Lou Ratté, and Russ Weigel have been most supportive. Tony Diaz of the Hampden County Registry of Deeds was always helpful and a bright spot in a subterranean cavern. In fact, all of the people in archives in Hartford, Connecticut, and Boston, Massachusetts, the Hampshire County Court, deed registries in Bristol, Worcester, Plymouth, and Barnstable Counties, Massachusetts, and town clerk and probate offices in the towns of Simsbury, Stafford Springs, and Granby, Connecticut, have been very patient and helpful with my requests for material that no one has looked at for over two hundred years. Bill Nelson, proprietor of Bill Nelson Maps, is responsible for most of the maps in this book. To Richard D. Brown, Christopher Collier of the University of Connecticut, and Bruce Fraser of the Connecticut Humanities Council I owe thanks, to the first for getting me started on this backcountry road, and to the latter two for much undeserved encouragement.

Above all, I am fortunate to have six great kids, Adam, Amy, Ben, Taegan, Kaily, and Quincy, with an infectious sense of humor and unlimited willingness to listen to me carry on about people no one has ever heard about. And to my wife, Myck, who is ever tolerant of my quest to find meaning in the lives of the ordinary and the unknown, I can say this much in sum: without you there would not even have been a beginning, nor inspiration, nor endurance.

The Brittle Thread of Life

Prologue
Nothing for History to Say?

David Sherman Rowland did not have particularly comforting words to offer his people at Salmon Brook. "Your state and condition, O sinners! is infinitely hazardous, however insensible you may be of it," he warned; "there is but a step between you and the world of spirits, where they have no rest day nor night." That might have been enough to awaken his audience before he launched into the careful discussion of biblical text that was so often at the core of early New England preaching. But Rowland was not disposed to be careful, and instead he continued his commentary on the hazardous condition of his flock. "'Tis the brittle thread of life that sustains you," he lamented, "and prevents you from immediately sinking into endless despair and misery. Should God's patience be worn out, should he cut short the thread of life, into what a hopeless and miserable condition must you immediately plunge?" And he could go on: "What raging despair would you be fill'd with, to find your-self surrounded with insulting devils, those ghastly, those horrid fiends, whose rage and malice will add to your torment?"[1]

When Mr. Rowland first delivered this sermon, sometime in the 1740s at the Salmon Brook meetinghouse on the northern edge of Connecticut, he was not exceptional in the use of such frightening images. The so-called jeremiad had been around for some time, and in those days of the Great Awakening this type of sermon had found its way into more and more pulpits. If we were to visit a sampling of neighboring churches during the time that Rowland spoke these words, we would hear often about threads of worrisome weakness from which sinners were suspended above horrifying abysses. What we might find surprising, though, is that there was actually a large number of people at Salmon Brook who gladly—even insistently—chose to listen to Rowland's unhappy words, people who actually defied the local authorities that had ordered this parish, or ecclesiastical society, as it was called, to find another, less "enthusiastic" preacher. But the county association of ministers that deemed Rowland offensive, or too disturbing (or too empowering to ordinary folk), sat in Hartford, fifteen miles and a much greater cultural distance from the rugged world of hills, ledges, and ominous forests of Salmon Brook. The backcountry parishioners ignored the association, and Rowland continued to lecture the faithful of Salmon Brook on their impending doom.[2]

The inhabitants of Rowland's parish, and a similarly defiant group farther north in Huntstown, Massachusetts, are the subjects of this book. As in Salmon Brook, there were many in Huntstown who preferred to hear of the wrath of God in spite of the efforts of county magnates to establish a different sort of church. These two early American communities were home to some of the poorest, coarsest, and least influential people of their day—people who lived on hard land that was often situated on the grinding edges of empires often at war, and people whose faith naturally embraced the idea that life was a brittle thread that might snap at any moment. History has already paid considerable attention to the magistrates and clergymen who tried to guide these plain souls along orderly and godly paths. It has even found room for the rebels among the professional class, like Rowland, who sometimes turned early America into a firestorm of verbal divisions. The legacy of the eighteenth-century elite has been boxes—even buildings—full of pamphlets, letters, diaries, official records, essays, and sermons. But what of their backcountry constituents? The thoughts and words of those who listened to the likes of Rowland, and would not listen to county and colony officials, seldom appeared in print, or even in handwriting. This silence might tempt us to think of them as passive observers who had more mundane things on their minds than disputes over theology and authority. And yet, in Salmon Brook and Huntstown, such folk were adamant in their choices, and if we are to come to an understanding of them, it would behoove us to know why. These are the people whose story I wish to share.

For at least the first hundred years of its existence, Salmon Brook, or Granby, as it has been known since 1786, was a relatively isolated and poor community stretching back into the Berkshire foothills and fairly detached

New England, circa 1760. Huntstown (later Ashfield) in Massachusetts and Salmon Brook (later Granby) in Connecticut are outlined. (Sterling Memorial Library Map Room, Yale University)

from the mainstream of New England society. For most of the eighteenth century it was not even an independent township. Huntstown, not settled until the middle of the eighteenth century, was similarly remote in the midst of the Berkshires. In each case there were no major roads, meadows were scattered and few, access to water transportation or market towns was poor, there were no commercial or manufacturing establishments to speak of, and most of the people labored long and hard on miserly land broken by hills and ledges. In short, they were two of New England's less desirable places to make a living by farming, as most people did in those days. Yet, in spite of the obscurity that would reasonably seem to be the destiny of people who made such places their home, their experience is captivating.

One might reasonably wonder what could be interesting in the lives of such people. History, best-seller lists suggest, should be dramatic stories of great turning points, leaders, revolutions, new nations, and political systems. In fact, "the new social history," a movement some decades back dedicated to giving a voice to the ordinary people of our past, never did develop a popular following. Now, many scholars have turned back to writing about well-known events or biographies of heroes like Franklin, Adams, and Jefferson. Jefferson himself, for whom the "tillers of the soil" were the world's true heroes, still thought that they ought to remain exempt from history. "Wars and contentions, indeed, fill the pages of history with more matter," Jefferson once wrote. Then he went on to dream of a "more blessed" nation of farmers, "whose silent course of happiness furnishes nothing for history to say."[3]

He knew, of course, that this had not been the case in the past. His agrarian countrymen, from Georgia to New England, had endured brutal wars and contentions during the better part of his own lifetime. They may have wanted to pursue an anonymous silent course of happiness, but they had lived through a century of continental conflict that had played out, sometimes literally, at their doorsteps. Furthermore, as the new social history has revealed, when not fighting ugly guerrilla wars, or building palisades around their homes, they had still faced periodic social and economic upheavals as intense as any in our own so-called fast-paced world. The people of the backcountry were no exception, and in fact experienced the brunt of most of the turmoil. Many of their settlements were continuously exposed to attack, and constituted an "English front" during the long period of imperial warfare from the 1680s until 1763. As for internal disruption, it was actually that independence and interest in virtue that Jefferson hoped a quiet agrarian life

would secure for such people—what turned out to be, for backcountry inhabitants, a fierce independence and an unyielding sense of virtue—that was
at the root of much of the social turbulence they endured. At times the backcountry exploded in armed rebellion and threatened the stability of American society both before and after the Revolutionary War. Backcountry people
were, indeed, actors in some of the more exciting moments of our nation's
beginnings.[4]

As fighters, nonconformists, and rebels, they made their contributions
and furnished history with plenty to say. For me, though, there is another
way to approach their history. I have wanted to know the backcountry people as more than figures that show up in a crisis and then melt back into the
hills once the war is over or the jeremiad's echoes have faded away. Yet only
fragments of the rest of their existence come forward to us. So unimpressed
were they by the drama of their own lives (or so busy in the living of them)
that they kept very little record of their experiences. But I have found their
everyday stories etched into the ragged and disorderly pages of their town
meeting minutes, in the ax marks on their posts and beams, in the long,
straight courses of stone running through the woods that were once their
pastures and orchards, and in the hastily scribbled sermon notes their
preachers made when not trekking through the hills on visits. Tucked away
in land records between "warrant and defend" and "heirs and assigns forever" are tiny clues left by people for whom fields, dwellings, and house lots
were the core elements of their world and their very survival.[5]

As we make fleeting contact with them in the scattered records that they
have left, we may begin to imagine what they were like in their day-to-day existence. We can picture them with dirt on their hands and foreheads, a mixture
of mud and manure on their shoes, and hayseeds flecked across the backs of
their necks. Hard lines creased their faces, and taut muscles ranged along
slender bodies. As they squinted into the summer sun or a cover of fresh
snow, they considered not only the tasks of the day before them but also the
unseen predators and enemies very likely hiding in the woodlands across the
field. They stirred, brewed, and baked before open fires. Their arms ached often from scrubbing clothing across a large flat rock. Even so, those clothes,
except on rare occasions of modest festivity, carried a layer of grime. Calluses
outlined the palms of their hands. Surely they must have felt the powerful imagery as those cracked hands turned the pages of their only book and took in
the word of the God that the prophet Isaiah called a "hard Master."

Most of them lived in small, smoky one-, two-, or three-room houses that have long since fallen apart or been dismantled and reconfigured into the shops and outbuildings of the next century. Paint and siding were unacquainted. Dooryards were scenes of chaotic refuse, both organic and otherwise, upon which the passerby could gaze while serenaded by snorting pigs, honking geese, crowing roosters, and buzzing flies. Leaning against the sides of buildings were tools many times repaired. In contrast to this crowded exterior, there were few furnishings inside the dwellings—in some cases more firearms and ammunition than chairs to sit on. Space was instead reserved for the people themselves, who, although of one family, were numerous, and had no place else to hunker down during long winters.

These images of the work-filled, gritty, and often perilous everyday existence of the backcountry people form a backdrop for our story. Before it, in Salmon Brook and in Huntstown, action less noticeable yet no less important than wars and contentions played out in early America. As the people of these two settlements struggled each day with the challenges of backcountry living, they were also engaged in a protracted struggle for equity, independence, and respect. By the end of the eighteenth century they had largely triumphed, in spite of the inclinations of a social and political elite that was not ready to accept them as equals in the mainstream of New England life. In winning a place within rather than on the outskirts of New England, they helped to push a more democratic culture onto the region and the new nation. Occasionally, they engaged in disorderliness and armed rebellion. What is of greater significance to me, though, is that it was not those occasions so much as the steady, long-term application of what little leverage they had that led to success and profound change.

To understand this complex social and political struggle between two very different layers of colonial American society, we need to relive, from the perspective of the backcountry, the long-term evolution of that relationship. Only the close study of an individual community's story—or better yet, two communities' stories—can provide that kind of experience. In many ways Salmon Brook and Huntstown are very different. In fact, I have selected them precisely for their differences, and to show that, regardless of variations in the origins of the early settlers, land distribution decisions, social structure, religious disputes, institutional milieus, wartime experiences, and economic development, the circumstances of the backcountry in early

New England resulted in a distinct pattern of relations between its inhabitants and regional elites.

The two stories represent a single history that involves struggle and strife, but more fundamentally reveals how backcountry people, poor and lacking in influence though they were, shaped the dynamics and structure of their society. Settlers began to arrive in these places in the era between King Philip's War and the American Revolution when New England's leaders were trying to spread orderly, productive, and fortified communities north and west of the coastal and river towns established before 1675. They hoped to continue the model of godly communities that had guided the founding of towns in the early seventeenth century, and even develop a society in which they constituted an enlightened and benevolent gentry class. Yet recruiting settlers willing to endure the hardships and perils of life on the cusp of the English domain during nearly a century of continental war was difficult. It took decades and considerable expense for viable communities to develop at Salmon Brook and Huntstown. Eventually the promoters of these communities had to offer grants of free or cheap land to men of the social fringe— men who did not have the standing, resources, or family connections to receive grants in eastern Massachusetts or along the Connecticut River.

It was a disparate collection of former servants and slaves, religious dissidents, ethnic minorities, laborers, and others of low esteem or shaky reputation that became the rulers of Salmon Brook and Huntstown, and set these backcountry settlements off culturally from the towns along the coasts and river valleys. In the early years of the eighteenth century, leaders in both Massachusetts and Connecticut realized how much they depended on these people to serve in frontier garrisons during the French and Indian wars, to direct the development of their towns, to remain orderly in general, and to become productive. With this leverage, the inhabitants of these hill towns secured a place for themselves as freeholders, producers, and consumers in early American society.

They remained "outlanders" for some time, though, topography and bad roads being only the most obvious factors keeping them from becoming an integral part of New England. Hard living on rugged land in dangerous locations often generated religious preferences (such as Mr. Rowland's brand of preaching) and presumptions of rights to additional land and resources that did not sit well with the colonial elite, who nevertheless had to accommodate the concerns and needs of the backcountry settlers if they wanted an orderly and secure province. As a result, well before the American Revolution invited them to think about and fight for equality, the backcountry settlers grew accustomed to a degree of autonomy and begrudging respect from their "superiors." In the 1760s and 1770s the revolutionary ideology, stressing equality, independence, and property rights, resonated with these people, earning their devoted loyalty to the fight for independence from Britain.

Eventually, provincial officials, when incorporating Salmon Brook and Huntstown as townships, discarded those apparently primitive names in favor of a couple of English peers, Granby and Ashfield, but even so, they remained rough settlements until the last decade of the eighteenth century. During the era of the American Revolution, the people of both communities continued to agitate for a social vision in which they played a respectable, independent, and even prosperous role. When the Revolutionary War was over, many in Ashfield joined another armed rebellion that represented their disappointment with the new social and political order advocated by more conservative "Sons of Liberty." Connecticut authorities handled their backcountry constituents with greater accommodation, and Granby grew content and orderly. By the 1790s, both towns had finally merged into the mainstream of New England society. Yet they did so because, through their "negotiations" for land, respect, and independence, they had pushed that mainstream in a direction that made room for their ambitions, as well as a degree of continuing challenge to the status quo. They had determined that New England society was acceptable because they had had a hand in making it so.

This is what history should have to say for the people of the backcountry. It should speak of the wars and contentions they experienced, but on another level, it should recognize the quieter course (if not always a silent one) that they charted by themselves to achieve their goals—a course that made a great deal of difference for them, and in the long run, for us. In considering the origins of the American democracy, its economic system, and its huge middle class, readers may want to ponder the dynamics that have come to light here in viewing the nation's beginnings from the perspective of the backcountry. Even before the revolution, these were not medieval peasants resisting commercialization, as may well have inhabited other parts of "the countryside" in early America. Nor were they deferential members of the body politic willing to subscribe to the New England elite's vision of "ordered liberty." On the other hand, they were not exactly an oppressed and alienated underclass eager to reduce the social structure to rubble. They were not nascent socialists, commonwealthmen, primitive capitalists, or even democratic theorists, but at the same time they did not have to wait for the pamphleteers and essayists of the American Revolution to get them thinking about equality.[6]

Well before the American Revolution their collective statements of principle certainly had the ring of egalitarianism and self-determination. They were rough-hewn people who wanted land, access to other resources, autonomy, freedom to practice their faith, and respectability within the larger regional society. For the better part of the eighteenth century their lives were as "infinitely hazardous" as some preachers informed them was true of the state of their souls. Clinging to this world by a brittle thread and understanding the capriciousness of nature and the uncompromising rigor of their outland habitats, they had high expectations. Their leaders usually had little choice but to accommodate them and find room for their ambitions and their values. And so, it should not be surprising that those ambitions and values worked their way into the fabric of the American Revolution and America as a whole.

SALMON BROOK

On December 25, 1800, Samuel Hays II, a deacon in the Salmon Brook parish in northern Connecticut, died quietly at his home on the eastern slope of Bushy Hill. Placed precisely at the end of a century of tumult, and at the end of the story related here, his death is a milestone because of who he was and what he experienced during his lifetime. A brief look at this man can provide food for thought to shape our inquiry into the history of his backcountry neighbors and how they made a place for themselves in early American society.

Born in Salmon Brook in 1730, Hays witnessed the evolution of his community from a few small conclaves of frontier farmsteads to a New England town with a population of fifteen hundred. He was also a grandson of one of the first settlers, so he carried forward a legacy of the earliest years of frontier living in these parts. During his lifetime, he became quite prominent. We find in various public records that, prior to his appointment as church deacon, he was a successful yeoman farmer, cider manufacturer, and carpenter, father of eleven, militia company captain, and representative to the Connecticut General Assembly. When his parish joined with another to become the independent town of Granby in 1786, he was elected its first selectman. Clearly Hays had earned the respect of his neighbors, and it would be helpful to find out more about his visions and aspirations, as well as his involvement in the changing relations with Connecticut's leaders that are at the heart of the story here.

He lived through some of the most turbulent periods in American history: the Great Awakening, the last two wars with the French, the American Revolution, and the early years of the federal republic. No doubt he was among the principal leaders in the movement to separate Granby from Simsbury. And yet, Hays presents a bit of a mystery. He left us no papers—no speeches, writings, letters, reminiscences—no diary, not even an account book in his own hand. If ever there were any of these, Samuel Hays and his descendants probably thought they were not worth saving—just useless clutter. For writing, Samuel Hays, first among men of his town, had either no enduring concern, or simply no time. Perhaps the only written word he cared for was printed in the two books his executors listed in his estate inventory: "Bible, and a Testament," together valued at five shillings. What we know of him lies in the old standbys of genealogists and local historians: his name here and there in town and church records, land records, probate court records, and on a headstone, along with a precious few remarks made one summer day in 1875 by his grandson and recorded by a relative. In these documents are etched some fragments of the life and times of Samuel Hays II of Granby, Connecticut.[1]

Perhaps it is telling that he left no writings. Combine his near anonymity in script and print with his dual religious and civil leadership roles, his large family, and his participation in the span of a single decade in both the American Revolution and a local independence movement. Some historians might be tempted to see him as a classic example of a "traditional peasant mentality" that was making a last stand in the backcountry during the early years of the republic. Fiercely independent, religious, patriarchal, agrarian, and locally oriented, thousands of Americans may have actually been resisting the march of modernity. Was Hays? Well, maybe not—his inventory also lists "a right in the library." If only we could access his borrowing record!

Samuel Hays II House (1769) as it appeared in the late nineteenth century. The single door in the front was probably the left-hand half of an original double-hung door. (Photograph courtesy of the Salmon Brook Historical Society, Granby, Connecticut)

There is one piece of evidence to which Hays did put his hand. On a winding road that runs along the east edge of Bushy Hill in Granby stands the dwelling house he built in 1769. It features the center chimney characteristic of so many New England houses surviving from the colonial period, but it has an unusual shape. Unlike the familiar two-story rectangle capped by a single gable with the ridge pole running parallel to the street, this house is square. And it is not capped, but *crowned*, with a hipped roof rising steeply toward a massive chimney stack. The structure is an oddity in New England, reminiscent of the Dutch meetinghouses of neighboring New York colony, or perhaps even some of the mansions of the Virginia gentry.

Inside we are again confronted with the unexpected. In the classic center-chimney colonial we would normally find a first story consisting of two parlors in front of a large keeping room that is flanked by small utility rooms.

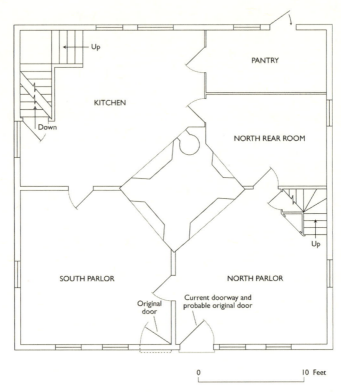

Floor plan for the first story of the Samuel Hays II House.

Between the two front rooms would be the chimney stack and a front entrance hall and stairway. This house, however, is different. The first story has four large rooms with fireplaces that face out toward the corners of the house, rather than toward the end and back walls. The chimney stack apparently twists forty-five degrees as it rises and finally exits the attic. Two small steep stairways are tucked into corners behind cupboards. Furthermore, nearly all of the interior walls are finished with planed wood panels rather than plaster.[2]

With this unusual dwelling Samuel Hays expressed himself publicly, and perhaps spoke of the visions and aspirations of his countrymen. Here we have distinct evidence of the builder's imagination. Rotating his stonework as he constructed his oddly angled fireboxes and flues, and working the complex cuts of his four ridges and fifty rafters of variable length, he left us clues to his character and to that of the people of his times. But what did he say?

For one thing, he seems to have said that his dwelling house was also a public building. In the front rooms the angle of the fireboxes, supposing a big enough fire were built in them, allowed the entirety of each room to be warmed, rather than a less encompassing arc directly in front. These rooms were created for a crowd even more numerous than his large family—a crowd that would apparently be ushered directly into either (or both) of the front rooms. No staircase was allowed to take up space that could be devoted to more people. The smooth panels on the walls were a luxury, their beveled edges projecting a sense of status and leadership. Even in the cellar Hays was not content with a simple, even-temperature storage space. There he constructed a huge open fireplace facing the outside hatchway. Perhaps there was some domestic application for this fireplace, but more likely the cellar was a gathering place for a rougher crowd than those whom he entertained in the front rooms above. According to his probate inventory, he owned a cider mill and kept a significant quantity of its output, in various potencies, stored in the cellar. No doubt his admiring militia company finished its training days here. This house was meant to invite, to set its owner apart, and to impress.

Students of early American material culture and architecture recognize a desire for "refinement" emerging among colonists during the eighteenth century. Americans, most of whom were landowners, were developing a taste for the aesthetic and following the lead of the English gentry. They furnished their homes with more carefully crafted furniture, served their meals on imported dishes, and generally became more decorative. The architecture of their homes also reflected this trend. Even in New England, despite much anxiety rooted in Puritan disdain for ostentation, people who could afford finer furnishings, clothing, and architectural detail seemed to aspire to a "simple respectability."[3] To an increasing extent even the "middling sort" began to believe that they should lead a genteel life.

Hays's building style surely reflects these aspirations toward respectability and even gentility, but it also raises important questions about how he, and his townspeople in general, had come to value respectability. His house was, after all, exceptional. Possibly only one other person in Granby built a house like this—Lieutenant Franceway Cossitt, second in command of Hays's militia company.[4] Aside from Cossitt's there is only one other extant house in Hartford County with such a design. So was Hays celebrating nonconformity? Did he see himself as a member of a postrevolutionary gentry class, or as a revolutionary mocking a gentry class? What about his constituents? How did they see him? In conferring all of his offices upon him, were his people deferring to him as their natural ruler, or applauding the rebel in him?

Perhaps it was both. If the architecture had the effect of distinguishing him, probably few who entered the house were much impressed by its furnishings. The keeping room was well-equipped with cooking utensils and tableware that would serve his family. The family slept in beds, some of which had feather mattresses and comfortable bedding. However, the main rooms of the house were furnished with only a few wooden chairs and tables, along with one writing desk and hardly any decorative items to speak of. His inventory lists a few pewter plates and utensils, and one brass clock valued at twelve pounds, perhaps a prize possession. Did Hays's reach exceed his grasp? After completing his house, did he not have the resources to furnish it appropriately? Perhaps he felt that a cultivated presentation had to be tempered by a nod to the plain people who partook of his hospitality. Hays is a microcosm of a puzzle, and the solution to it will open new vistas on the dynamics and evolving ideals of early American society.

What remains to us of Samuel Hays II seems contradictory. The lines of his prerevolutionary abode and the suggestions of intended public use in its interior design reveal a man who was conscious of fashion and sensitive to the trappings of status. On the other hand, his sparse furnishings and his dual role as a man of prominence in both the religious as well as the political sphere conform to a more familiar Puritan yeomanry that would reject imported design and anything smacking of vanity. A respectable man aspiring toward prominence, he seemed to draw the line not far beyond domestic utilitarianism. Where is the hole into which to fit this peg?

Unraveling the character of the people of this eighteenth-century backcountry town and their relations with the leaders of early America involves careful investigation of a complex historical context. That context is a tapestry into which Samuel Hays II and his contemporaries are stitched, but whose threads wind through a great tangle of lives and experiences. Fifty years before Hays was born, around 1680, the first English settlers of Granby—and some not-so-English—were putting together a community that dares us to find a category for it. By the time Hays rose to his positions of leadership, the stitching had become even more complex, with some threads of cultural continuity running throughout, and others newly added. It is difficult, without this historical context, to understand the seemingly contradictory aspirations symbolized by Samuel Hays's house. Nevertheless, once we look at all of the woven figures and the changing background on which they stand, and then step back to take in the whole, Samuel Hays II stands before us as a triumphant figure, the climax of a three-generation ascent into the mainstream of American society, and, at the same time, the climax of a long struggle to reshape that mainstream to accommodate him and his rough-hewn backcountry neighbors.

1. A Place Called Sammon Brooke

The first row of stones in the foundation beneath the sills of Samuel Hays's curious abode consisted of a struggle for existence on the often violent cusp of the English domain. That struggle defined the kind of people who would come to live in Salmon Brook in the northwest corner of Simsbury, Connecticut, and generated a complex set of social relations between the back-country people and the colony leaders who encouraged them to face the perils of the outlands.

Salmon Brook's roots lay in the early settlement patterns of the Connecticut River valley, in the various motives behind the colony's expansion, and in social and economic tensions that emerged in the course of the seventeenth century. These forces provided considerable momentum behind the creation of this frontier village. Yet, in contrast to the founding of communities in eastern Massachusetts and coastal Connecticut in the days of the Puritan Migration of the 1630s, it would take decades to establish a permanent and secure settlement at Salmon Brook, or even at Hopmeadow, the central village of the town of Simsbury. Promoters of the expansion of the English domain had to cast a broad net and reach deeply into their increasingly stratified society to find willing settlers. The result was not what they might have hoped.

Massaco, Simsbury, and Salmon Brook

The migration of English settlers to Salmon Brook in the late 1600s was part of a larger enterprise that occupied the colony of Connecticut at the time, namely the continuing search for open meadow and a variety of natural resources in order to accommodate a growing population, produce marketable commodities, and secure the colony's frontiers by displacing the Native Americans. One of the outcomes of that search was the founding of the town of Simsbury. To understand Salmon Brook's beginnings, one needs to have some sense of the urgency with which Connecticut leaders pursued these goals, and of what a long and halting process it was to launch the Simsbury township as a whole.[1]

The Connecticut River valley was lush and fertile, for the flooding river replenished the low-lying meadows with nutrients each spring. Yet it was a narrow valley, and the first families of migrants to river towns like Windsor and Hartford quickly took up all of the natural meadow there in the 1630s and 1640s. Ten miles up the winding Tunxis (later called Farmington) River from Windsor, on the other side of a long ridge, lay a great meadow, or *massa agu,* as its inhabitants, the Massacos, called it and themselves. The English at Windsor began calling it "Hopmeadow," and within a few miles of it there were a number of other meadows and small cleared areas nearly abandoned by the declining Algonkian population and not yet overgrown. This would become the site of the town of Simsbury.[2]

As early as 1642, residents of Windsor persuaded colony officials to "dispose of the ground Uppon that parte of the Tunxis River cauled Mossocowe, to Wyndsor inhabitants as they shall see cause." Not only did Massaco offer Windsor families a new, if limited supply of open arable land, but it was also well endowed with other resources for both subsistence and the market: pitch from pine stands for manufacturing tar and turpentine for the emerging shipping industry; hardwoods for barrel staves and planks, or, if burned, potash; and abundant fish and game. As early as 1646, John Griffin, a Welsh immigrant to Windsor, working in partnership with Michael Humphrey, a recently arrived merchant from England's West Country, began manufacturing tar and turpentine. A few years later one or two young Windsor men accepted grants of land along the Farmington River and began fencing in land for a grain crop.[3]

It was not until 1670, however, that Simsbury had enough residents to constitute a town. A number of factors had impeded progress. Immigration to Connecticut fell off in the 1640s, so pressure on land at Windsor did not become urgent until after 1660. Then there was the issue of the few remaining Massaco people, who were not eager to give up their claim to the land. Inconclusive negotiations ranged through the 1640s and 1650s. Even though disease seems to have depleted the Massaco people, they still had numerous

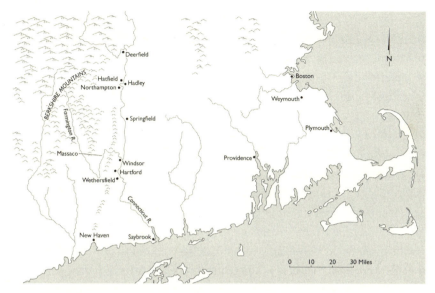

New England in the late seventeenth century, showing Massaco's location west of the ridge separating the Connecticut River valley and the upland plateau from western Connecticut.

relatives living in Poquonock and other villages north of Windsor who wanted to retain hunting and fishing rights. Connecticut's leaders were wary of pushing any of them too hard to allow English settlement, particularly after the discovery of Miantonomo's Narragansett "conspiracy" in 1643. Indeed, John Griffin and other local tar manufacturers had their kilns destroyed on more than one occasion by Massacos and others who apparently wanted to discourage the expansion of the English colony.[4]

One plain fact was that for mid-seventeenth-century inhabitants of Windsor, the meadowlands at Massaco were remote. Prospective settlers faced either a rough eight-mile trek through a forest and then a climb across an imposing ridge, or a canoe ride up miles of a river interspersed with treacherous rapids. Once across the ridge, they faced a hostile world. To their north the next Europeans they might encounter were the French in Montreal, and to the west there was the Dutch outpost of Fort Orange (later called Albany). Neither group was on very good terms with the English in Connecticut, and the inclinations of the Iroquois in between were uncertain. John Griffin and those other early migrants of the late 1640s and 1650s undoubtedly experienced a degree of nervous loneliness.

During the 1660s, Windsor's population grew quickly, and in return for some wampum, tools, and clothing, the local Algonkians appeared ready to accept the idea of English expansion. Furthermore, social tensions began to emerge within the town because of the origins of the new arrivals. The first English migrants to Windsor had been recruited in the West Country counties of Devon and Dorset in the 1620s and formed into a Puritan congregation under the leadership of John Warham even before embarking from Plymouth, England, in 1630. When this group could not find land to meet its expectations in Massachusetts Bay, it had migrated fairly intact to Connecticut in 1635. In the 1650s these settlers were joined by immigrants from London, some of whom were not even English but of Welsh, Belgian, or French Huguenot descent. Ethnic identity was still important to seventeenth-century English people, and differing customs, religious creeds, and even speaking accents were hard to mix in a close community like early Windsor.[5]

The increasing social tension soon found expression in connection with a well-known religious dispute. In 1663, merchant Michael Humphrey, a professed Anglican, and James Eno, a recent immigrant and son of a Belgian Huguenot, circulated a troublesome note on behalf of a number of other Windsor people. In essence, as members of the Church of England they demanded "privileges of church membership" even though they had not professed their faith and been admitted to Windsor's Puritan congregation. Reverend Warham wavered in response, provoking a major division in the town. Some of those alienated by the whole affair, including Eno and Humphrey, soon were looking to their west as a place where they might take refuge, not only from the religious controversy but also from the domination of town affairs by the West Country elite. Humphrey himself was already working with John Griffin in the tar and turpentine business. Colony leaders were interested in accommodating the dissidents if it would maintain harmony in Connecticut, or, as they put it, revive "a friendly correspondency." Since Charles II had returned to the throne, they could ill afford word getting out that they were persecuting members of the Church of England.[6]

Thus, the General Court became increasingly eager to annex Massaco to Windsor in the 1660s and repeatedly established committees to grant lands there to settlers from the town. Agreements placating the Indians, social dissonance, ecclesiastical discord, and the continuing pressure of population growth all contributed to a growing list of interested settlers. Still, it took fines and threats of forfeiture of their grants to get people to move across the ridge to live on and work their lands. By 1670 as many as forty families, some of West Country descent and others representing the newer Welsh and Anglican migrants, had moved west from Windsor to take up allotments. The Anglican and Welsh dissidents tended to congregate on the eastern side of the ridge, in an area later known as Scotland, while the West Country men got grants in the meadows on the west side. As the population grew, the General Court ordered the settlers to organize themselves as a town named for the West Country village of Symondsbury, the ancestral home of two of the more prominent early residents.[7]

It was a short-lived effort, however. Following the outbreak of King Philip's War, in 1676 the General Court of Connecticut looked to its newest and outermost settlement of Simsbury and ordered its families to abandon their homes and move back to Windsor. The order came none too soon. In August the Nipmucks and Agawams attacked outlying settlements on the western end of the Bay Colony. When ten families decided to return to Simsbury in the spring of 1677, they found their forty dwelling houses, as well as barns, outbuildings, fences, and fields, reduced to ashes. At this point, though, the desire for open meadow was becoming intense. At least fifty more families expressed interest in joining the original ten. Windsor's population had more than doubled since 1650, and cleared land was simply unavailable in any of the settled towns in Connecticut. In 1680 the General Court reported to the Committee for Trade and Foreign Plantations in England: "Most land that is fit for planting is taken up. What remains must be subdued, and gained out of the fire as it were by hard blows and for small recompense." Simsbury's meadows may have been the only easy land in sight for those not interested in dealing out a lot of "hard blows."[8]

Just the same, most people throughout New England were very hesitant about venturing into "the wilderness" to invest time and money that might, at a moment's notice, go up in smoke. The General Court was not able to persuade many of those who had expressed interest in Simsbury to move their families there. After two years, those who had moved became nervous, declaring that a greater "peopleing of the Towne" was necessary "so that the towne might be strengthened the better to with stand the assault of an enemy in time of danger [and] so that those lands might be made improvement of for helping to bear publique charges." In October 1679, a committee led by Major John Talcott, the colony's treasurer and a military hero during the war, initiated a campaign to enlist seventy families in all to

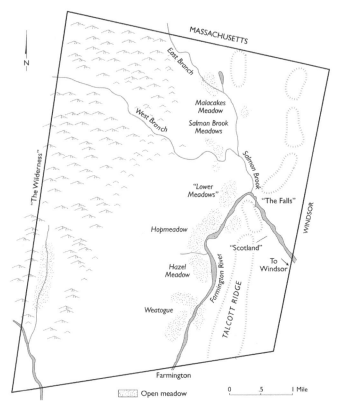

Map of Simsbury, formerly called Massaco, as surveyed in 1686, showing meadowlands that were already clear of trees before English settlement.

take up residence. They further stipulated that these families be granted meadow and house lots in different parts of the town. Fifteen of the families would have their homes at Hopmeadow, and seventeen more at Weatogue a mile south of Hopmeadow. Five would receive their allotments at Terry's Plain east of the river, and nine just east of the ridge. North of Hopmeadow eleven families would take up residence in the "Lower Meadows." Finally, thirteen would live at "a place called sammon brooke," two miles north of the Lower Meadows. The grantees had to be living on their allotments in a "mansion house" within six months or face a fine of forty shillings and the loss of their grant.[9]

The colony's leaders were indeed eager to get the town resettled. They understood well the necessity of providing good land to productive families. As it was, the river towns were crowded with landless young people who could not be assessed for taxes. Furthermore, they wanted to extend the colony's actual domain by occupation. They had negotiated with the Algonkians for Massaco for more than thirty years and achieved only marks on paper. Those marks would be meaningless unless there was a permanent English settlement west of the ridge. In Hartford as well as Windsor, Connecticut's colonists wanted a viable Simsbury. The question was how to make it happen.

A closer look at John Talcott's 1679 plan for the "peopleing" of the town reveals his answer to that question. First, the committee had obviously done a survey of the area and identified all of the cleared land within a few miles of Hopmeadow. Rather than concentrate the town's entire population at Hopmeadow, Talcott proposed to attract families by taking advantage of the several other parcels of meadowland nearby and offering a larger lot to each family. But there was another line of thinking evident in this scattering of families.

Talcott was a military man, and during King Philip's War he had learned the guerrilla tactics that would characterize warfare in North America for decades to come. As much as he considered the farming needs of his settlers, he was also acting on security concerns—just as the inhabitants themselves had requested more people to settle in the town for the same reasons. There was the risk in Talcott's plan of dividing the defensive force and thus weakening each part, but a greater risk would have been to have a single settlement in which all of the settlers could be taken by surprise at once. According to Talcott's designations there would be sufficient numbers in key places to sustain a defense long enough for neighboring settlements to mount a counterattack. In short, Talcott's distribution was not only an efficient use of available meadows but, even more important, an order of battle.

The main villages on the southern end of town at Weatogue and Hopmeadow were to have the greatest numbers of inhabitants: thirty-two families. They would function as the reserve. Only a few farmers would sit more securely on the east side of the Farmington River as conduits of information to the Connecticut River towns. Any attack would most likely come from the north or west, and the front lines of defense against it would be the eleven families at the Lower Meadows, and even more exposed, the thirteen at the place called Salmon Brook. Here the meadows were smaller and less fertile, so each family would get fewer acres and poorer land than those at Hopmeadow and Weatogue. But there was no way around it if there were to be enough people to present an effective temporary defense.[10]

Thus did Salmon Brook have its beginnings during the resettlement of Simsbury after King Philip's War. In fact, the planting of the thirteen families at Salmon Brook was the key to the success of the whole plan. It would be a strategic buffer—an early warning system. And in addition to their defensive function, these families would be the front line of English expansion. Who knows, perhaps even some veterans of the war could be lured to live there and make this front line all the stronger. There would have to be powerful incentive, of course, for the struggle to get people to move to Hopmeadow itself had already consumed nearly four decades. Even though officials had noted as early as 1667 that the meadows at Salmon Brook were "deemed to be as good" as those along the Farmington River, they had not been able to get anyone to do more out there before the war than some mowing for winter feed. Finding daring souls who would reside permanently on the town's most exposed flank would be far more difficult than anyone imagined.[11]

"Peopleing" Salmon Brook

Talcott's plan energized Simsbury inhabitants to create their buffer settlement at Salmon Brook. At a town meeting in January 1680, they outlined special "Articles or obligations" for those who would settle in that outland district. There were about 160 acres of meadowland there, and the grantees of these lands had to be settled "by their personal living upon their lands with their Familyes" by May 1680. Further, they were "to continue in possession there off by living on them Seven yeares and they are obliged to make improvement by Fenceing and breaking up of ye lands and personally live in them seven yeares before they shall have liberty to make alienation of any of ye Said lands: unless they may be taken off by some remarkable providence of God." There was to be a fine of five pounds assessed on any who left their lots before the seven years were up. To encourage people to move north under these conditions, the town also voted that the new residents at Salmon Brook would be free from paying town taxes for a year.[12]

Even before the town began making specific grants to the outland settlers, however, their evident determination to create a permanent settlement there, along with the ongoing mowing by those who had received grants before the war, must have provoked protests from the local Algonkians who still hunted and fished in the area. In March 1680, Major Talcott had to hammer out yet one more agreement with them regarding

Massaco lands if there was any chance of his plan succeeding. Most of the Massacos had left the area, but it was clear that quite a few Poquonocks simply did not yet accept the idea of English dwellings being built in the midst of their hunting grounds. Talcott invited more than a dozen leading Poquonock men and women for a parlay lasting several days. He fed them "meet and bread, beer and sider," and proceeded "to drive on the bargain" on behalf of the nervous proprietors of Simsbury. Several meals, coats, and bushels of corn later (and probably after some extra beer and cider), Talcott managed to establish in a signed deed that Massaco was now English, and, while hunting and fishing would still be permitted for the natives, they would not object to English houses and fences, nor would they mistake roaming livestock for game.[13] And so, ten years after the General Court had decided that Massaco was to become Simsbury, the local Indians gave begrudging assent.

A few days after he finished the agreement with the Algonkians, Talcott and his committee moved forward to the problem of finding people who would accept the "Articles or obligations" and the risk of bringing their families to live at Salmon Brook. They named just eleven men, rather than thirteen as planned. Some of these were already living in Simsbury, but most were Windsor residents, and some had just recently expressed interest in Simsbury lands. One of them, Nathaniel Holcomb, seems to have been living at Salmon Brook already.[14]

Talcott well knew the difficulties he faced enticing these people to move. A few years later, the town voted to give him three hundred acres anywhere he wanted in exchange for his efforts with the Indians. In his written reply, Talcott remarked that he could "find no one place, where anything considerable can be taken up: the most of that which some call meadow, is full of small Brush and Vines through which y^r is no passing; or full of Trees, small and great, which will be very cheargeable subduing." Even where there was good land, he continued, there was no way to get to it, "saveing onely [through] mighty Tall mountayens and Rockes," making it "dismally obscure and solatary to any that shall live upon it and very hard comeing at the Market, not onely because of ye remoteness, but badness of the passage and the Society or Neighborhood will be very thin, all which be discoraging."[15] In short, he himself did not find anything about Simsbury's outlying "meadows" that would attract a farmer, to say nothing of one who hoped to produce or extract surplus material to trade.

Even as early as the spring of 1680, when it came time to sort out the lots for the Salmon Brook families, he was probably not surprised when five men declined the offer of land there, and only two others stepped forward to replace them. This left eight families to get twenty acres each of Salmon Brook meadowland.[16] What was causing the drop in interest is not clear. Perhaps those seeking land in Simsbury had drawn lots, and many of those who drew Salmon Brook had been hoping either for a more southerly and less exposed house lot or for a different group of neighbors. Perhaps the three days between Talcott's "bargain" with the Algonkians and the surveying of lots was not enough time to convince the prospective settlers that the natives would respect English property rights. Most likely, many already understood Talcott's eventual assessment that living at Salmon Brook would be a "solatary" existence. Whatever the case, it is clear that adjustments had to be made if a settlement at Salmon Brook was going to become a reality.

In the summer the town recalled how eight men had agreed to bring their families to Salmon Brook, but "these failing except two persons," the town was not willing to execute the forfeiture and fine. They gave the others "three months further liberty." However, when none of them had moved by the autumn, the town met again "to agitate Concerning the breach of those articles." Again, the inhabitants relented and gave them until April 1681. If they were not in residence by then, they ordered, they "Shall forfeit and pay to the Towne for their use teen pounds." The doubling of the fine to what was for these people a harshly punitive figure indicates a fair amount of concern, even if the inhabitants were willing to grant extensions. The hesitancy of the settlers is understandable, of course. Regardless of the defeat of the Wampanoags and all of their allies, war-weary people, especially in a town that had been destroyed just four years earlier, were nervous about building dwellings in lands five miles north of Hopmeadow. It would be a challenge to raise a family while serving as a permanent perimeter guard. Furthermore, just recently the town had enacted a bounty of eight shillings per head on wolves.[17] If the predator population was becoming a problem due to the attraction of roaming livestock, and if relations with the Algonkians were uncertain, what sort of person would live permanently in the outlands?

Windsor's West Country elites had wanted to reserve all of the Simsbury meadows for their children. By 1681, they had succeeded in transplanting some of them to lots in Hopmeadow and Weatogue, but they could not generate much interest in Salmon Brook. At the same time, Talcott and other

Connecticut leaders surely hoped that the settlers at Salmon Brook would transplant the "New England Way" of piety, communalism, and "ordered liberty" to the outlands just as the founders of Windsor and Hartford had done when they moved from eastern Massachusetts in the 1630s.[18] Yet, as town and General Court records filled with notations of fines, forfeitures, and assignments and reassignments of lots, it became apparent to all of Simsbury's promoters that Salmon Brook was not attractive to the people they had envisioned as Connecticut's vanguard. That is, they had to settle for people to whom they would not normally grant free meadowland.

Consider, for example, Nathaniel Holcomb, Salmon Brook's first settler. Although his parents had come to Windsor in 1635 as part of Rev. John Warham's West Country congregation, he was an outsider in that river town from an early age. His father died when he was only nine, and his mother then married James Eno, the son of Belgian Huguenot refugees, a latecomer to Windsor and one of the 1663 petitioners claiming "privileges of church membership" in Warham's church even though they belonged to the Church of England. In addition to the Anglican upbringing, Holcomb probably learned the woodworker's trade from Thomas Barber, a Bedfordshire native who had come to Windsor in 1635 with the so-called Stiles group, which had threatened the Warham group's land claims. Barber had remained in Windsor even after the West Country elite had asserted themselves, but he was not among the woodworkers favored for town projects, nor was he an active participant in public affairs. Having inherited only a three-acre parcel from his father near the Indian village of Poquonock at the north end of Windsor, Nathaniel first moved to Springfield when he came of age. There he married and seems to have acquired some military training and experience during King Philip's War. When allies of Metacom (whom the English called King Philip) destroyed Springfield, he returned with his wife, Mary, and their three children to Connecticut, and apparently jumped at the opportunity to "take up" some meadowland at Salmon Brook even before it was being offered. The young family lived there on their own for some time.[19]

Then there were Josiah and Mary Osborn Owen, who moved to Salmon Brook from Windsor with their three children in the spring of 1680. Both Josiah's and Mary's parents were Welsh immigrants to Windsor in the 1650s and inclined more toward the Anglican form of worship. Josiah's father, who had some land in Windsor, though not enough to divide among his sons, had shown some interest in Simsbury in the 1660s, but had not returned after the war. Being Welsh apparently did not endear either father or sons to Windsor's leaders when it came to new grants of land along the Connecticut River. The Holcombs and the Owens were the "two people" referred to in the town records as the only ones to have taken up residence at Salmon Brook by the May 1680 deadline. The other six who had received conditional grants were young men and women of West Country parentage, and did not respond even to the more lenient April 1681 deadline. Thus, after numerous offers of land grants, the outlands had attracted a Welsh family and the stepson of an Anglican, people who would never get more than a few acres in Windsor, if that.[20]

Over the next several years Major Talcott and the leading Simsbury proprietors continued to be frustrated in their attempts to get the sons and daughters of the West Country or even East Anglian Puritans to settle in Salmon Brook's outlands. Lots changed hands frequently as designated grantees refused to actually make the move. It was not until May 1683 that the town and Talcott began to have more success by offering larger allotments to prospective settlers who, like the Holcombs and the Owens, would not have qualified for land grants anywhere else. A town meeting that month declared that there would be a row of house and pasture lots granted to those who would build and live on them within a year. The designated householders were all men who lived in Simsbury already, but had received relatively small grants. Some probably intended to keep up their old houses in more southerly locations as well as build new ones at Salmon Brook. There was, after all, no stipulation as to how long a family had to reside in the outer settlement each year, nor how big one's "mansion house" had to be.[21]

In defining "mansion house" loosely, in permitting seasonal occupation and extensions of deadlines, and in granting out larger portions of land to each family, the town and Talcott's committee were clearly working hard to encourage people to settle and work in the smaller meadows in Simsbury's northwest corner. Still, even after 1683, actual settlement proceeded haltingly. Town meeting minutes suggest that the townspeople became increasingly strict about adherence to deadlines and time commitments. At a meeting on December 31, 1685, the town declared that all lots had to be taken up within six months of the grant or be lost. During that meeting and over the course of the next two years the town assigned and reassigned lots numerous times, while close to two dozen prospective settlers tried their hands at making "improvements" and living on lands at Salmon Brook. A number of settlers decided either at the outset or after a few months to "resign up" their grants (or allow them to be forfeited). Some continued to make acceptable improvements on their meadowlands at Salmon Brook, but did not live among the house lots. The town also had to find other house lots for additional families who were ready to move to Salmon Brook by 1686. For example, John Matson, a single man of twenty-two and a newcomer to Simsbury, received a grant in that year. Nathaniel Holcomb, Nicholas Gossard, Josiah Owen, and John Slater wanted to reserve land for their oldest sons, who were not yet of age.[22]

The tangle of agreements, grants, enticements, forfeitures, and other evidence of changing of minds shows just how much trouble the town and the General Court's committee went through to settle that front line of the colony's defense at Salmon Brook. Even as the distance from King Philip's War grew, there were frequent alarms triggered by the sighting of unfamiliar Indians. New York had been in the hands of the English for twenty years, but in the 1680s competition for the fur trade north of Albany was becoming intense. The possibility of attacks on the English frontier from New France was very likely. These alarms periodically emptied the settlement, reminded its inhabitants of the need to maintain a backup dwelling in Hopmeadow or Weatogue to the south, and undoubtedly inspired considerable rethinking on the part of once enthusiastic grantees. By 1688, though, there was a group of settlers in residence in spite of fears of attack, the distant and isolated nature of the settlement, and the limited and scattered meadowland. Talcott and town leaders had finally succeeded in planting nine households.[23]

This was certainly a diverse group that the Talcott committee and town leaders had collected for their outermost householders. In places of origin, household composition, and economic status they seem to have had little in common. Some were already living in Simsbury when settlement at Salmon Brook began. Others moved into town just as the inhabitants decided to find willing settlers. Their places of origin ranged from Windsor and Hartford to eastern Massachusetts. There were bachelors, young couples with small children, and couples with teenagers as well as young children. Tax records for the 1690s show that there were some men of relatively little property, like Samuel Addams and John Matson, mixed in with Nathaniel Holcomb and Josiah Owen, whose estate was three or four times as great, yet still middling by Simsbury standards. In addition, the group encompassed diverse ethnic

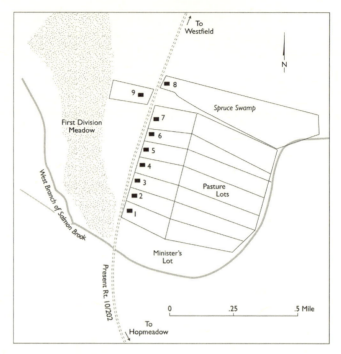

Salmon Brook house lots and households, 1688. The occupants of the lots were: *1.* Nathaniel Holcomb (age 40) and Mary Bliss Holcomb (37), and seven children (ages 15, 13, 10, 8, 6, 4, 1); *2.* Samuel Willcockson Jr. (22), bachelor; *3.* Samuel Addams (33) and Elizabeth Hill Addams (age unknown), and daughter (1); *4.* Nicholas Gossard (52) and Elizabeth Gillet Gossard (49), and three children (15, 11, 6); *5.* Richard Segar (36) and Abigail Griffin Segar (28), and two children (4, 2); *6.* Thomas Griffin (30), bachelor; *7.* Josiah Owen (37) and Mary Osborn Owen (33), and seven children (13, 10, 8, 7, 6, 4, 2); *8.* Joseph Owen (28) and Elizabeth Osborn Owen (unknown), and three children (5, 3, younger than 1); *9.* John Matson (24), bachelor.

backgrounds: a few had parents from England's West Country, but just as many had Welsh backgrounds, and Nicholas Gossard's parents had been Huguenot migrants to England.[24]

What all of these migrants to Connecticut's outer edge had in common was also true of the families of Nathaniel Holcomb and Josiah Owen: most did not come from Windsor's West Country Puritan families. Instead, Simsbury's recruiters had resigned themselves to granting twenty acres of meadow per household to a varied lot of Welsh, Huguenot, and Anglican men and women who, not being among the favored ethnic stock or religious persuasion, would have remained landless in their river towns. They would not have been considered for land even at Hopmeadow in Simsbury. As for the

few West Country settlers at Salmon Brook, they included Nathaniel Holcomb, whose older brother Joshua had had no trouble acquiring land at Hopmeadow while Nathaniel had the choice of living near his mother and
stepfather on poorer land in Scotland, east of the ridge, or braving the outlands at Salmon Brook. Two other West Country adults were women who
had married Windsor "outsiders." Finally, the only other person to qualify as
a mainstream Puritan of West Country ethnicity was Richard Segar, and his
claim to the privileges that background may have conferred on him was
shaky at best. Segar's father had, indeed, come from the West Country, but
his mother had been convicted of witchcraft. Although Governor John
Winthrop reversed her conviction, she later drowned under mysterious circumstances, an event that probably prompted the father's subsequent move
to Rhode Island in 1678. Thus, young Richard was probably not going to experience a warm welcome in either Windsor or Hartford society. Every one
of Salmon Brook's settlers came from the ranks of the landless, the uncon-
nected, the disrespected, or the disgraced. Twenty acres of meadowland would
have been a big attraction to them, and it appears that Talcott could not find
any others who considered this arrangement enticing.[25]

It is also probable that Talcott consciously sought veterans of King
Philip's War for outland residents. Many of those who ended up in the settlement appear in various records of troops paid for extended service, and because of this experience, men like Daniel Addams and Nathaniel Holcomb
soon found themselves called upon by town residents to lead Simsbury's
"train band."[26] Talcott and the West Country leaders of Windsor and Simsbury surely figured these people as naturals for Salmon Brook life. Hardened
by guerrilla warfare, unwelcome in settled Connecticut towns, and in some
cases scorned or disdained, they would probably be happy to find some-
where they could put a plow in ground they could call their own. And, having found that cherished ground, they would no doubt be as dedicated as
they were skilled to defend it.

By 1688, this group of bachelors and families of the fringe of Connecticut society had become well established at Salmon Brook. In fact, the
previous spring there had been enough householders at Salmon Brook for
the town to declare that the first division meadow, just west of the houses,
should be a common field with each lot owner taking care of his share of
fencing. In August 1687, Nathaniel Holcomb was designated a lister (tax as-
sessor) particularly "for Samon Brooke," and the following March the town

meeting set Salmon Brook up as a separate district with its own pound for keeping stray animals. The Salmon Brook settlers themselves met in January 1688 and drew up an agreement to fence in the meadow together.[27]

As the little band of householders planted itself more firmly, changing shelters into dwellings, bushy meadow into mowing and grain fields, and trees into fences, Simsbury town leaders grew more confident about granting small parcels of marshland and grassland to the north and west to town residents from lower Simsbury as well as to Salmon Brook residents, on condition they take up the land and "improve" it. Even town clerk John Slater asked for a house-lot grant, probably for his son, at the May 21, 1688, town meeting.[28] Simsbury and the Connecticut colony had found among their less respected residents highly suitable inhabitants for their exposed northwest flank.

A Season of War

In the St. Lawrence River valley, far to the north of Salmon Brook, French authorities had already set in motion forces that would quickly put an end to any optimism about Salmon Brook's future. There had, in fact, been some worry about the security of anyone's title to land in Connecticut when James II created the Dominion of New England in 1686. Even as that issue was subsiding with the arrest and deportation of the dominion's governor, Sir Edmund Andros, in 1689, escalating violence along the frontiers of the French and English empires made living on the colony's outskirts even more precarious. French emissaries had been busy since midcentury courting both Algonkians and the Iroquois of northern New York, forming fur-trading and military alliances and expanding their influence into the Great Lakes and Ohio Valley regions. While France and England were officially at peace in the 1680s, authorities in New France suspected that the English were behind Iroquois attacks on their Indian allies, and they wanted to prevent English expansion generally. Occasionally there were alarms as far south as Albany. With tension mounting, word spread throughout New England that outlying settlements could expect to be attacked.[29] Simsbury inhabitants, distant as they were from the New York frontier, had not forgotten the town's destruction during King Philip's War. And if their own imperial government was ready to take away their charter and all the liberties that went with it, who would protect them now that they would have to fight not just the weakened and disunited natives of New England, but powerful alliances of inland peoples, and perhaps French soldiers too?

In a moment of panic in February 1689, Edward Thompson, Simsbury's minister, negotiated an arrangement between Salmon Brook and Hopmeadow residents whereby the former would move south to live on lots belonging to the Hopmeadow farmers until the frontier quieted. But the frontier would not be quiet. In February 1690, as the War of the League of Augsburg commenced in Europe, Count Frontenac, the governor of New France, ordered a raid on Schenectady, New York. New Englanders under Sir William Phips countered in May with the capture of Port Royal at the mouth of the St. Lawrence River. Known as King William's War in North America, the conflict expanded from French and Indian raids on settlements in New Hampshire and Maine to an attempted invasion of Canada by Massachusetts forces in the fall of 1690. In Simsbury, the houses at Salmon Brook sat empty, and their former inhabitants joined with the train band at Hopmeadow to prepare for attack.[30]

Simsbury townspeople still wanted a front line of defense composed of households at Salmon Brook, so they began to offer mowing land near the old house lots to those who would return and reside there. There was increasing demand for livestock in Connecticut, if it could be brought to market, so grassland that could be exploited for winter fodder was attractive. During the 1690s, nearly all of the householders of Salmon Brook, and occasionally some who dwelt elsewhere in Simsbury, went before the town meeting promising to "make improvement" on various patches of open or semi-open land on the outer edge of Salmon Brook. Even as early as 1691 the town meeting thought there was enough work going on at Salmon Brook to justify ordering, once again, a "common field [for the first division meadows] and every man to fence the Breadth of his Lott: and Each End to be fenct in a common way."[31]

It is unlikely, though, that many of the lot owners remained in residence year-round. In fact, there is no record of any response to the town's order. Neither a revived settlement nor even a common fence appeared at Salmon Brook for some time. The Canadian expedition of 1690 had been a disaster, and the war promised to drag on for years. Joseph Owen, one of the early Salmon Brook settlers, could not be persuaded to remain even in Simsbury, and pleaded to be given "liberty" to sell his allotments to some other Simsbury inhabitant before he left town. In April 1692, a town meeting granted John Matson ten acres on "Crooked Brook," a mile northwest of the village, on the condition that he return to Salmon Brook within two years and improve two acres. Matson raised "cattle, swine, horses, corn, flax, and tobacco," so additional grassland would have been helpful. Although he must have planned to abide by the condition, he did not move back until 1697 when his grant was "renewed." He may have been holding out until the town agreed to support his wife's mother, who had been ordered out of town when she found herself widowed in 1695.[32]

Toward the end of the war, a few Salmon Brook people did move back to their outland houses. In the spring of 1697, the town offered some of them new house lots and fields on the wooded upland just north of the original row of houses, providing the claimants could work together to clear and fence in the area. How efficiently men could do that carrying guns and sacrificing manpower to patrols is questionable. Town leaders might have considered abating taxes to induce more people to resettle at Salmon Brook. As John Matson's mother-in-law well knew, though, they could hardly afford that incentive. Simsbury was in general so poor that the inhabitants could barely defend their crops from their own livestock, and it was a constant challenge to collect funds for something so basic as compensation for a settled minister. Tucked away in the town records, a 1696 report of persons owing half or more of their tax bill is practically a census of the town.[33]

For those who were trying to build a farm at Salmon Brook, it was doubly challenging, as the plight of the Segar family shows. Richard and Abigail Segar and their three children, ages twelve, ten, and two, seemed to be having a hard enough time in 1696 when Richard had to beg off from appointment as collector of the minister's rate because of some hardship—perhaps long-term illness. Then disaster struck. Richard died on March 19, 1698, with Abigail eight months pregnant. She died in childbirth on April 28, leaving four children without parents. The inventory of their estate reveals a desperate situation. Household items included some tallow and bees wax for making candles, earthen dishes and bowls, one cup and two spoons, two glass bottles, a meal sieve, an "old iron pot," an iron kettle, and a frying pan. Together the ironware alone was valued at more than Richard's clothing.

For furniture, there was but one bed, a chest and a box, and one blanket and a quilt—no chairs or table. Richard must have had to borrow a plow, for he had none. He had no ax, no hoe, nor a saw. He did have four "old barrels," a pail, two tubs, two "old siths and sith tackling," "arms and ammunition," and a hammer. The family's livestock was limited to an ox, "one old horse," a three-year-old heifer, "one swin," and one calf with its mother. For real estate, the children would inherit the six-acre house and pasture lot, twenty acres of meadow spread out around Salmon Brook, and ten acres of marsh and swamp land. The "mansion house" Richard was supposed to have built at Salmon Brook did not even rate a line in the inventory. In terms of capital, the Segars owned two pairs of "Lumes" with pertinent equipment, and associated with that were some "sheeps wools" (worth four shillings—not as much as a wolf's head), some "swinged flax," "two skeins of twine [and] one skein of woolen yearn." In exchange for the use of tools they did not have, and purchase of what little they did, the Segars must have woven cloth and linen. Lest one think they were among the poorer inhabitants of the settlement, the tax rate they were charged for 1696 was exactly average for those who owned house lots at Salmon Brook.[34] The possibility of attack does not seem to have completely discouraged poor people like the Segars and the Matsons from trying to establish their households on Connecticut's frontier, but it is hard to imagine how they managed.

Even after the Treaty of Ryswick officially ended the war in 1697, the outlands remained unsafe, and willing settlers continued to be hard to find. As people throughout Simsbury raised more livestock to pull in some extra cash or credit for essentials they could not produce on their own, and as they grew more corn to keep those animals fattened during the winter months, they created more attractions for wolves and crows. The town had doubled the bounty on wolves to sixteen shillings in 1693, when it added blackbirds (two pence) and crows (four pence) to the list of condemned species. Of course, for the more resourceful of the outland settlers, the bounties could mean income without raising surplus grain or livestock. Nathaniel Holcomb's two eldest sons did quite well with their "Wolfe Pits," and even brought in a mountain lion at one point.[35]

The convenience of being close to one's wolf pits, however, was not incentive enough to reconstitute Salmon Brook. By 1701 only four of the nine men who had agreed to create a common field on the upland above the Salmon Brook houses had actually done any work on the common fence within the time allowed. In that year they created a bonded agreement among themselves to restore a fence that had been burned the previous spring, causing them to "suffer the loss of our winter corne." As for the rest, their names appeared among yet another series of forfeitures and replacements. Those replacement grantees included some young men who had grown up in Salmon Brook families. Others had recently married into some of the families that had persisted, so that the community began to resemble a single extended family or clan, rather than a group of independent households.[36]

As hard as town and colony leaders worked to attract settlers, Salmon Brook was still attractive only to people on the colony's social fringe. Outside the clan composed of a few of the 1680s settlers and their children and in-laws, only three new families settled there in the decade after the Treaty of Ryswick. Peter and Mary Rice originally lived in Concord, Massachusetts, where land was virtually unavailable. George Hays was a Scot who arrived in Windsor in 1680 as an indentured servant. The town meeting in Simsbury did not even offer him a free grant. But there was no future for him in Windsor, so he scraped together enough cash or credit in 1698 to buy a cheap parcel at Salmon Brook. Benjamin Dibble had lived in Wethersfield before he came to Salmon Brook with creditors on his heels. In 1698 he purchased, apparently on bad credit, meadow land at Salmon Brook. He had such difficulty making ends meet that at one point he abandoned his wife and children, hoping the town would support them.

As suitable as Dibble may have been for settling at Salmon Brook, he was, indeed, a problem. His Wethersfield creditors issued "cautions," and in 1702 one of them attached some of Dibble's land at Salmon Brook. Anxious about having such land in the hands of absentee landowners, the town declared in January 1703 "that Benjamin Dibble and John Adams who also now lives at Samon Brook are *not* inhabitants of the town." Still, Dibble did dwell in town, at least until he got himself arrested in Suffield for trespassing on land then contested between Simsbury and Suffield and for trying to cart off some barrels of turpentine. He died penniless in 1712, his property mortgaged to creditors from Hartford to Westfield, Massachusetts. That the town looked the other way while he really was an inhabitant (and that the church even admitted him to full membership) is testimony to the desperate need for settlers at Salmon Brook.[37]

Dibble may have been one of those people the town had in mind when it passed an act in 1701 "against leting in of Strangers." The inhabitants complained of "being greatly damnified by persons thrusting themselves into our town . . . greatly to the Damage of the Towne," and ordered that "for the Future no Persons shall croud and thrust themselves into our Towne to reside there above one moneth without liberty first obtained from the said Town." Admitting people as "inhabitants" carried with it the obligation to offer grants of land. In addition, it meant that if that person was to become unable to work, the town would provide public support—something it had not been willing to do in the case of John Matson's mother-in-law. In other words, the townspeople were not going to admit just anyone, unless of course they would reside, well armed, at Salmon Brook.

There must have been, in general, an emerging understanding that the Salmon Brook people—some of them "strangers"—were playing an important role as sentries, or guardians of the frontier. The town's leaders well knew that the peace was temporary. Scouts in the hills between Westfield and the New York border continued to send reports of what appeared to be Indian reconnaissance activity, and as late as 1701 the town was adding more timber to the minister's house so that it could serve better as a place of refuge. At the same time, town leaders worked all the harder to build a stable, orderly, and permanent settlement at Salmon Brook, a place that "by reason of troubles . . . has lyen to the Commons a while and now comes to be peopled again." They appointed John Matson and Nathaniel Holcomb Jr. to oversee the construction and maintenance of the long-awaited five-rail fence for the first division meadows. George Hays, having apparently risen from the rank of "stranger," became the hayward in charge of rounding up the stray animals to be committed to a pound under the charge of Matson.[38] Surely the town's residents recognized their dependence on the few people they could persuade to live on their northwest flank.

In turn, as poor and ostracized as they were, Salmon Brook inhabitants must have experienced a measure of pride that they had achieved some social standing in facing the perils of the outlands. Not only had the town been willing to grant them land and freeman status, but they also benefited from rights to resources on common lands. This was not simply a matter of grazing and mowing land for marketable livestock. Salmon Brook sat squarely between two large stands of pitch pine, and tar and turpentine had become so valuable that barrels of it now served as a form of currency in Simsbury and surrounding towns. The town had tried to limit "the cuting any turpentine tree within the Town comon . . . until they can agree upon some way of equality" (which meant "every man shall have his proportion of pin trees according to his lyst," and pay twelve shillings per hundred trees). But people took what they wanted anyway—and, as we know, Benjamin Dibble was not above poaching from Suffield's pine stands.[39]

All of these incentives were powerful, but their attraction to people of the fringe of Connecticut society continued to be tested in the new century.

It took only the death of an heirless king in Spain to ignite a new round of clashes in both Europe and North America. England's King William died in 1702, the year the war opened, passing the crown to his sister-in-law, the last Stuart, Queen Anne, after whom the ensuing struggle for empire in America was named. In New England, Abenaki raids hit settlements in Maine in 1703. Then, for inhabitants of Simsbury, the situation they had feared during the years of quiet since 1697 was upon them: in the winter of 1704, a French and Indian force attacked Deerfield, Massachusetts, just forty miles to the north, killing or carrying off nearly all of the inhabitants.

At this point the Connecticut General Court took strong action. In case anyone at Salmon Brook had thoughts of repeating the retreats of 1676 and 1689, the court declared that anyone deserting any of the "frontier towns," such as Simsbury, would forfeit his land grants. The legislature further authorized a permanent garrison of ten men to protect Simsbury, and called for four hundred volunteers, including local Algonkians, to fight a campaign against the French. In the winter of 1707, the government further ordered "a sufficient number" of houses to be fortified, and a group of scouts to ride into the northern territories to look for enemy raiding parties. For four years Simsbury's militia trained, its scouts rode on patrols, and its paid garrison stood watch while fearful inhabitants did their best to manage their farms.[40]

In the fall of 1708 a dramatic event reminded Salmon Brook inhabitants of their role as Connecticut's front line. George Hays's twenty-two-year-old son Daniel set out one morning in search of a horse that had broken loose. Barely two hundred yards into the meadows across from the little group of houses, in broad daylight and in full view of his horrified neighbors, a group of Indians set upon him. One put a hand to his throat, while another held a tomahawk over his head. Others bound him with the bridle he had brought along for his horse, and they dragged him into the forest. The attackers knew where to wait, the story goes, because they had been "lurking about" outside a husking bee the night before and had heard Daniel announce his intention to find his horse at daybreak. A few years earlier, by some versions of the story, Daniel had managed to alienate an apparently friendly Indian. A group of local natives had been observing Hays and his neighbors frame a house. During a rough-and-tumble break from the work, Daniel managed to sever the tail of one of the Indians' dogs with an ax. The dog's master was so enraged that no amount of apology would appease him. There were some present then who felt that the Indian appeared resentful enough to carry a grudge for some time, and that what happened in the meadows in the fall of 1708 was an act of vengeance. More likely it was a co-incidental wartime maneuver designed to discourage Connecticut from send-ing its soldiers to aid Massachusetts. The colony responded quickly with a rescue party, but the troops could not catch up to the captors. Daniel Hays was gone and presumed dead.

We have this story mostly by way of family tradition retold in genealo-gies and local histories. Official records corroborate Daniel's capture during the war, but not much more of the details.[41] Taken as a folk tale, though, the story represents Salmon Brook's early years quite well. Native Americans and whites mingled together eyeing each other uneasily, the whites never sure whether they were looking at friends or enemies, the Indians uncertain how best to cope with the strangers in their land. Moments of relaxation were spent wielding an ax recklessly. And finally, there was always the need to be armed and with friends when out of doors—even in the settlement's thirty-second year!

Daniel's capture marked the beginning of four even more fearful years for both Salmon Brook and Simsbury in general. With funds appropriated by the General Court, the town built and manned two forts, one on the plain be-low the Salmon Brook houses, and one a little north of the settlement. The colony also attempted to go on the offensive and strike deeply into Canadian territory. An attempted invasion in 1711, however, failed miserably after nearly half the troops died of disease before the expeditionary force left Mass-achusetts. Salmon Brook men made up half of Simsbury's quota during this war, no doubt lured by the willingness of the colony's government to pay cash for military service. While Simsbury became a fortified town and head-quarters for scouting expeditions, predators raged out of control. Crows and blackbirds caused "great damages in our corn," and, as farmers conserved their ammunition for the greater danger, wolves hunted the livestock.[42]

In spite of renewed security concerns, Salmon Brook in 1709 was a much more permanent community than the one that had been there in 1688. As the General Court and Simsbury's leaders had hoped, most of the fami-lies clung to their freeholds with determination. The continued election of a fenceviewer, a hayward, and a poundkeeper specifically for Salmon Brook is a clear indication that these families were not going to give up on what they had built, and that they saw their local garrisons as adequate security. They also had their own schooling, Goodwife Rice having responded to a 1704 town meeting declaration that money would be expended for a "school Dame" at Salmon Brook. She was paid forty shillings each year (enough to get her thirteen bushels of corn at current rates). Young men coming of age continued to ask for house lots near the first row of houses, and the town opened a new road and bridge running east toward the area known as "the Falls." After more than three decades of trying to get a buffer settlement going, Simsbury had its front line of houses.[43]

Perhaps the Salmon Brook settlers had no choice but to stay the course where they were. After all they had built, the General Court had threatened to take it away if they ran for their lives in the face of probable attack. In the process, they had struggled against the challenges of converting an Algonkian hunting ground into a domain of English goodwives, husbandmen, sheep, pigs, cattle, and those who preyed on all of them. Their homes were still small, crowded, and sparsely furnished, and their lands still had plenty of stumps and rocks to be cleared, but they were there to stay. With halting progress over four decades, they had put together their common fence, hunted down the wolves, helped one another through childbirth, cared for orphans, drained sap from trees, put up barns for livestock, spun wool and flax, and begun to teach the children to read and write so that they could do more than put their "mark" to deeds as most of their fathers had. Continuing all that depended on maintaining their residences in the outlands. Considered the "meaner sort" of their society, their only chance for a sizable estate lay in this dangerous land.

And that is where the colony's leaders were happy to have them living. The arrangement is noteworthy. The leadership was giving status and independence—a place in Connecticut—to people from whom they might normally withhold it, and the town was giving them extended deadlines on taxes, a garrison for protection, additional freehold land when they asked for it, and an opportunity to make money by hunting predators. In return, town and colony leaders saw their own position become more secure. As the colony expanded and prospered, so did the status of the leaders. What difference did it make if these "outlanders" took in a few of the black sheep who had not found a place for themselves in other towns? What if it did cost a few pounds to help them build solid fortifications and to pay some of them to serve in the garrisons? The fact was that, aside from the Hays kidnapping, and another similar incident in Waterbury in 1710, the colony had not been attacked in either King William's War or Queen Anne's War, and the Algonkians who remained within the domain had been friendly and had led quiet lives at increasing distances from the settlements. The policy of encouraging the fringe of society to develop frontier towns such as Danbury, Waterbury, and Simsbury, with its little collection of houses at Salmon Brook, had been a wise one—a policy that was to be repeated in colonies all along the Atlantic seaboard for years to come, in fact, by orders from the ministry in London.[44]

All of this wise policy, however, revolved around the willingness of these families to take on the rigors of the "wilderness" in return for land, livestock, and turpentine. But, in the early years of the eighteenth century, the town had begun to resist certain people "thrusting" themselves into its midst. It had also tried to restrict the exploitation of its pine trees. Some of those at Salmon Brook may have wondered if, when the war wound down to another settlement, those who had risked everything would be pushed aside in favor of those whom they had protected.

2. On Penalty of Loosing Our Freeholds

Among Simsbury's land records there is a survey of a land grant that encapsulates what happened at Salmon Brook as Queen Anne's War came to an end and its residents continued to stake out a place for themselves in Connecticut society. The document, at first glance, appears unremarkable, yet with some imagination we might be able to breathe some life into it. It is April 28, 1720, and town surveyor John Humphries is perambulating "Land in Simsbury belonging to Nathaniell Holcomb: junr: being the third nathaniell." Humphries is standing about a mile "west ward of Samon Brook houses . . . between the branches of Samon Brook," a little north of a small tributary he calls Crooked Brook. He names as his beginning point the "northeast corner," and without so much as a surveyor's chain or even a compass, he begins to pace out Holcomb's lot: "run south and by west down the Brook thirty two Rods to a white ock Stump." Back to the first corner: "thence by Lamsons lyne run west twenty Rods." He piles up a heap of stones. Then with doubtful precision he turns "the square and run south and by west thirty two Rods." More stones—presumably twenty rods west of the white oak stump. "This piece contaynes four acres," he notes. Then in like fashion he paces off another two acres south of the first, marking a maple tree on one corner, piling up more stones at other corners, "So that both pieces contayne Six accres according to his grant which was granted to him at a Town metting of the Inhabitants of Simsbery: Januarey the nine teenth—1719/20 See

44

3rd Book of Town acts fol: 15th—Sd land is bounded north on Ebenezar Lamsons lott the other Sids on the Commons."[1]

John Humphries was doing what he and hundreds of other surveyors in colonial America had been doing for decades, and would continue to do for some time: marking free grants of land for young men ready to begin independent lives. Year after year New England towns parceled out pieces of their "commons" as their youth came of age. There is not much in the region's history that is more ordinary.

As we stand with Humphries, though, and look around, we soon encounter more of interest. For one thing, he does not seem to be pacing off his lines in the midst of a forest. Quite the contrary, some of his landmarks for this and other nearby plats are stumps, the species of which he can identify—someone has taken down the trees. And not only do we see that the lot is already partially cleared, but we are astonished to find that young Holcomb, "being the third nathaniell," has already built a substantial house on this land! The record of the January town meeting to which Humphries refers specified that Nathaniel Holcomb was to get his lot "where he hath built a house." Nathaniel and his wife, Thankful, accompanied by a toddler and an infant, are probably watching Humphries mark out these boundaries from the house they built last summer. And the same is true for four other families in the immediate vicinity. Simsbury seems to be allowing its young people to pick a spot for their homestead, "improve" it, and by that act alone, get title to the land.[2]

In fact, the story by which Holcomb presumed to become a freeholder of this six-acre piece of ground is anything but ordinary. For Nathaniel III, and some other young people of Salmon Brook, the 1720 house-lot grants on Crooked Brook represented a moment of victory in their pursuit of standing as freeholders and independent yeomen. For over forty years Nathaniel's parents and grandparents had paid dearly in uncertainty, fear, and backbreaking labor for parcels of land granted by a town that would offer them little more than the small and scattered meadows of Salmon Brook for their trouble.

In the later years of Queen Anne's War and the early years of the uneasy peace that followed the negotiations at Utrecht in 1713, Salmon Brook's outlanders, who were now freeholders, began to think about their children who were soon to come of age. Would the town and the colony continue to be stingy about giving out land? Would they enact more restrictions on the use of the common land? Once the frontier was more secure and Salmon Brook was not such a terrifying place to live, would they allot anything at all to the next generation of outlanders? Tension between the inhabitants of Salmon Brook and the leaders of Connecticut society continued into the 1720s and 1730s, as young people in need of land came of age and as the community there asserted its independence. Although colony leaders were less appreciative of outlanders as a frontier buffer, they still wanted an orderly province, if only to avoid interference from England. Just the same, it would require continued hard work, angry words, assertiveness, and even defiance for Salmon Brook people to get the respect, the land, and the independence they thought they deserved.

Becoming Freemen

Nathaniel Holcomb Sr., grandfather of the "third Nathaniel," had already earned a good deal of respect in the town by the early 1700s. He and his family had lived virtually alone for a decade before King William's War. Although he had withdrawn to his house in the Lower Meadows during that war, people throughout Simsbury still held him in high esteem. They entrusted him with the duties of militia sergeant, selectman, representative to the lower house of the colony's legislature, church deacon, and supervisor of the town's grist mill. To be sure, his success was exceptional. But his ambition was typical of those who continued to reside at Salmon Brook in order to secure their freeholds. During Queen Anne's War the settlement did not grow much beyond the stalwart few who had taken up residence by 1701, and, as Daniel Hays discovered, it remained dangerously exposed to attack. Nevertheless, besides holding on to their land grants by occupancy, there were benefits that encouraged them to stay. Eventually, Nathaniel Sr.'s sons and their Salmon Brook neighbors, while not rising to his level of prominence, were able to take advantage of some limited opportunities to raise their standard of living.

One of those opportunities had to do with the colony's war needs. Connecticut troops participated a good deal more in Queen Anne's War than they had in the previous conflict. At least three of Salmon Brook's young men had happily accepted their pay for service in one campaign, even if a camp epidemic prevented them from cashing in on the bounties for scalps. At home, every family recognized the possibilities of profiting from the demand for provisions. Simsbury inhabitants, including those at Salmon Brook, had raised surplus livestock for a number of years. New acquisitions of mowing land during the war confirm that both demand and the accessibility of markets were improving considerably.

Salmon Brook's settlers were also able to add to their land holdings, and they worked hard at fencing in marshland and other parcels that could be converted easily to fields of corn and hay to fatten profit-bearing livestock. In turn, the town was eager to help the growing prosperity of these outlanders, for their well-being meant a permanent buffer, to say nothing of increased revenues for town coffers. When John Matson, Nathan Gossard, Daniel Hays, and William Rice went before the town meeting in 1706 to ask for some remote land northwest of the Salmon Brook houses, the town readily granted them eight acres each as long as they agreed to "break up said land within the space of one year . . . and to pay rates for the land."[3] The following winter, the town passed an act allowing "that any Inhabitant of s^d towne shall have liberty to make use of any of the out lands . . . Either by plowing or mowing and at the end of two years he or they shall have confirmation of s^d Land." There soon developed a growing demand for land in Simsbury's outskirts. By 1713 the town pushed the occupancy requirement to eight years and, to encourage new residents, limited new grants to home lots. Meanwhile, Salmon Brook inhabitants began trading land with one another, consolidating larger parcels in one place for more convenient access.[4]

In a number of ways, in fact, Salmon Brook's farmers appear to have been eagerly engaged in commercial activity during and after the war. Even though Simsbury had begun to restrict the "boxing" (draining of sap) and cutting of pine trees before the war, the lumber, tar, and turpentine that the outlanders could bring to market sold for good prices. Other "merchantable commodities" included tobacco, cider, and grains such as wheat, rye, and corn, which the town declared could be used to pay taxes at set rates. Still, the poor quality of roads and the prevalence of predators made it difficult for anyone at Salmon Brook to market much more of these commodities than what would pay for glazing a few windows or purchasing some tools and hardware.[5]

Slow growth in these enterprises may explain the enthusiasm with which the town as a whole greeted the news in the fall of 1705 "of either sillvar or copor mine or Mines all found within the Lymetts of the township of Simsbury." The pursuit of copper during and after Queen Anne's War is a good example of the strong desire of people in Simsbury, including those at Salmon Brook, to take advantage of commercial opportunities to complement their subsistence farming.[6] The controversy that emerged as they leaped into the enterprise also reveals a growing rift between the outlanders and a colonial elite that was reluctant to accommodate their aspirations unless it was forced to do so.

From the start, the majority at town meetings assumed that since the copper veins were on town commons, they belonged collectively to the inhabitants of the town, as did all land in practice. But this assumption raised a sticky issue that had its roots as far back as 1686. In that year James II decided to bring Puritan New England under tighter control by sending Edmund Andros to demand the return of colonial charters and to establish the Dominion of New England. When Andros reached Boston he collected the Massachusetts charter and declared it revoked. Then he moved on to Connecticut. Worried that the legislature's incorporation of towns would be disallowed and that the keystone of self-government, the town meeting, would lose its authority, Connecticut's General Court had already begun issuing patents to groups of proprietors for lands of towns that had already been incorporated. Simsbury's was voted on in May 1685 and issued the following March to "the proprietors inhabitants" of Simsbury, led by John Talcott, who was, actually, not an inhabitant. The patent, therefore, was a defensive measure against what was viewed as an impending attack on the right of town inhabitants to control their land and, for that matter, to organize themselves to secure their future prosperity.[7]

When Andros came to Hartford, Connecticut's General Court was less than cooperative, and someone even had the gall to spirit off the charter to a hollow in an oak tree, legend has it, until he left. Fortunately, the crisis dissolved when James abdicated in the Glorious Revolution of 1688, and a rebellion in New York resulted in the jailing and deportation of Andros. At that point, Connecticut revived its charter government and the new monarchs, William and Mary, chose not to interfere. Simsbury's patent was still in place, however. Technically, it was now the proprietors, not the town meeting, who had control over the allocation of town lands. Nevertheless, since most of the admitted inhabitants of 1690 were proprietors, no one raised serious questions during that decade or the next as the town meeting continued to make grants of land.

Thus did the town meeting presume to grant shares of the prospective mine, located on a ridge some three miles east of the Salmon Brook settlement, to all the inhabitants who wanted them. Salmon Brook residents John Matson, Benjamin Dibble, William Rice, and George Hays, though not patent proprietors, subscribed to the shareholding agreement in this way. This created a good deal of discontent among proprietors and their heirs, who claimed that the more recently admitted inhabitants had no right to the mine, or, for that matter, to any grants of common land! Regardless of rights, however, it was apparent that no one had the skills to create a profitable mining and refining operation anyway. Actual excavation did not begin until 1714 under the auspices of absentee speculators.[8]

All of these various entries into the market economy, while not producing boundless wealth, did have the effect of improving the quality of life for the people of Salmon Brook in the early years of the eighteenth century. Even poor Benjamin Dibble's estate inventory of 1712 confirms this. Though deep in debt, in arrears on his taxes, and embarrassed by one episode after another, Dibble did at least own a broad ax, a saw, a hoe, a sickle, a horse, a gun, a Bible, "one of Mr. Williams books," a decent cloth coat, two blankets, and an inkhorn and pen.[9] If someone was putting a roof over his head he was living a little better than Richard Segar, the average farmer of 1698.

Samuel Willcockson Jr., who died in 1713, is representative of the lifestyle of the more established residents of Salmon Brook. He and his family worked his lands at Salmon Brook with rakes, chains, pitchforks, axes, an ox sled, and, astonishingly, a plow. There were seven animals in his barnyard, including three horses. He had stored quantities of tobacco, cider, flax, peas, deerskins, Indian corn, twenty pounds of wool, and twenty-eight "runn of lining yarn," although the appraisers would not put the wool and yarn in the inventory "because the family hath very great and presant nesesity for cloathing and probably would bin made use of on that account if siknis had not prevented the family having bin much exersised for the space of a whole year or more."

Willcockson was also a literate man, with a personal collection of five books, including a Bible, a sermon book, a psalm book, "another book," and a "phisickbook." He was appropriately armed with three guns and two pistols. Apparently he owed at least some of his wealth (and possessions) to his skill with his "gunstocking tools," and to his wife's use of her wool cards and spinning wheel. Their house was relatively well furnished: five "old chairs," four beds, four chests, trays, "knot dishes," tubs, fourteen "trenchers," and assorted pots, basins, and kettles. Willcockson was Richard Segar's brother-in-law, and he had done well for himself, leaving an estate valued at £326, including over 150 acres of choice pieces of land, to his wife and six children.[10] But then we might expect a gunsmith to make a good living at Salmon Brook, where houses needed to double as fortifications.

As for the "siknis" that afflicted his family and killed him at the age of forty-seven, that was unusual. Although the nearest physician lived in Windsor, life on the frontier in Simsbury was apparently more accurately distinguished by good health, longevity, and low infant mortality. Occasionally, smallpox epidemics appeared in the port towns, but outlying areas often missed them. Of the nine adults living at Salmon Brook in 1709 whose birth and death dates are known, the average life span was seventy; of the sixty-six children in those families, only four are known to have died in childhood.[11]

Along with being robust and well-nourished individuals, they developed, even while living in a war zone, a healthy independence as a community. Their four principal men, George Hays, John Matson, and the Holcomb brothers, Nathaniel Jr. and Jonathan, took charge of enforcing agreements on the "common field and particular field" fencing, and collecting and keeping those stray animals that had broken through fences and destroyed crops. They mandated the mending of fences by a certain date each spring, so that swine could forage freely in nearby woods without "yokes or rings" and not put the crops at risk. They could send their children to school, take up new parcels of marsh or even woodland and improve them, and join the rest of the town in paying a respected minister.[12]

Of those four leaders, John Matson presents the most interesting success story, and a good illustration of the opportunities Salmon Brook offered to enterprising individuals. Born in Boston to a family of gunsmiths in 1664, he had come to Simsbury as a relatively young bachelor with his business partner James Miles. They settled first in the area called Scotland, and then in 1686 he ventured to Salmon Brook where he acquired a grant of meadowland. By 1692 he was married, but still near the bottom of the economic scale in Simsbury. Although the town would not help him to support his wife's mother after her husband died, it did grant him numerous parcels of land in recognition of his apparent value as an inhabitant of Salmon Brook. Perhaps people saw him as a good soldier. Perhaps he brought his family's gunsmith trade with him, or he simply impressed them with how hard he worked his land and how enthusiastically he would defend it. Over the years, he gradually added to his land holdings, receiving grants totaling well over two hundred acres within a few miles of his house. Raising an extra steer or hog here and there, spinning yarn for the neighbors, and assisted by their children as they grew in the early 1700s, the couple gradually added to their estate so that by 1728, when John died, his inventory amounted to £382. In a society that still tried to pay attention to "estate and dignity," the Matsons are an example of the reality of opportunity, even for the poorest, as long as they agreed to live on the empire's front lines.[13]

Led by people like the Matsons, the community of Salmon Brook had survived the worst of times by 1713 when diplomats in Europe signed the Peace of Utrecht. Scouting patrols continued in Connecticut, for few trusted that the peace would last, and there were occasional alarms during the next decade. But in 1713, the people at Salmon Brook celebrated what was, for them, a true sign of good times to come. One day in the autumn of that year, Daniel Hays walked into the settlement, alive and well, full of tales of running the Indian gauntlet, being sold to a French trader, and working for his freedom. The colony legislature granted him seven pounds for his troubles in October, and the town followed with a renewal of his home-lot grant at Salmon Brook.[14]

Even in 1713, Salmon Brook was only a tiny community. Institutionally, however, it encompassed nearly every dimension of a recognized township except the town meeting and a gathered congregation. Furthermore, its residents had found ways to increase their well-being. They had done more than simply survive a war. They had embraced the opportunities their community afforded them to make a place for themselves in Connecticut society. None of them had become rich, but they had a new road and new grants of land among large stands of pine, and all that meant at least a little more income to purchase what they could not produce on their own. Their willingness to stand guard on the town's outskirts had earned some of them a bit of stature, and in Nathaniel Holcomb Sr. they had a strong voice in town, militia, and church governance. Given these accomplishments, it is not hard to understand their sense of entitlement to the copper mine when it was discovered. The response of the proprietors and proprietors' heirs might have worried some of them, but we can well imagine that they would not easily give up their perceived rights to free grants of commons.

In a Town Way

As it turned out, Salmon Brook's settlers did have reason to worry about how much longer they could expect the sort of accommodation they had enjoyed during the war. An intense struggle for what they perceived to be their rights to additional grants from the common lands consumed more than a decade after the Peace of Utrecht, and constituted a major test of their hard-won status as freeholders. Those who could claim to be "proprietors" of Simsbury had been unhappy with the outcome of the copper mine issue, and they were determined to prevent further inroads into what they considered to be their proprietary privileges.

No sooner had the war ended than the original proprietors and their heirs set to work to establish their claim to control over Simsbury's lands. In 1713, they managed to limit grants in the northeast, or Turkey Hills, section of town to themselves. Other inhabitants countered by holding a town meeting in 1715 that, among other actions, granted a series of ten-acre parcels to John Matson, Daniel Hays, and others on the East Branch of Salmon Brook. In addition, at the request of Salmon Brook settlers, the town allowed inhabitants one last run at the pine trees on the commons and then "forever after this be prohibited from cutting any boxes for Turpintine . . . anywhere . . . in the Town comons." These measures provoked a protest from Samuel Higley, who wrote the town clerk on August 31, 1716, that, as a "Proper Proprietor," he intended to "utterly forbid disalow and protest against any act or Acts Votes or Vote that shall be made Taken or Recorded in any Town Meeting in Simsbury concerning or Relating to Rights or Title of land or Lands."[15] Higley was a lawyer (among other professions), and based on the 1686 patent, he felt that he had a case.

The non-proprietor inhabitants, on the other hand, could make an argument based on precedent, the very basis of English common law. As people began to move into new areas outside the three river towns in the 1640s, the General Court had given the selectmen, who were chosen by each town's inhabitants, the power to decide how common lands were used, divided, and improved. Thus, prior to the 1686 patents, it had become traditional for the town meeting to be the ultimate source of both political and proprietary, or economic, status. Higley might still have argued that the 1686 patents had changed all that, but everyone in Connecticut knew they were intended to change nothing. The term "proprietors inhabitants" had been carefully chosen terminology to ensure that the *practice* of corporate government within the towns would continue. These patents named some names, but the accepted interpretation at the time was to include all the admitted town inhabitants among the town's proprietors. Throughout the 1680s and 1690s the Simsbury town meeting clearly assumed the power to grant lands, and further, granted lands (and even shares to the copper mine) to newcomers willing to risk their families' lives in the outlands.[16]

As in-migration picked up after the Peace of Utrecht, however, those who claimed proprietary rights from the patent began to feel differently. There were disputes in town about who could be considered an "admitted" inhabitant. George Hays, in fact, was admitted all over again, just to make sure; but at other meetings, some residents were denied inhabitant status, lest they begin to act as proprietors. Samuel Higley, who may have secretly discovered another vein of copper on common land, was determined to put a stop to the trend of acquisition of economic status through the town meeting.[17]

The conflict became increasingly intense because of regional economic changes after the war. Demand for products that Simsbury's settlers could produce, such as lumber, tar, turpentine, potash, flour, and livestock, continued to be strong. On top of the needs of the Royal Navy and merchant ships, Connecticut's rapidly growing population required vast quantities of wood for tools, carts, fences, barns, and houses, as well as fuel for home fires, forges, and kilns. In addition, New England ships carried goods to the West Indies. With cash or credit from the sale of their surpluses, even outlanders could purchase imported salt and spices, textile goods, and tools to become even more productive.[18]

The twin keys to success were access to markets and access to land. There was certainly a growing cadre of merchants who were becoming quite wealthy collecting products from farmers and financing their purchases of tools, imported goods, and land at 10 percent interest. Timothy Thrall of Windsor, who died in 1724 with an estate that included £411 in store goods, land valued at £1,145, and £2,923 in mortgages, bonds, and notes, is a good example of the era's nouveau riche. He had grown increasingly wealthy as farmers in the outlands borrowed against their expectations for future surplus to buy themselves a bit of productivity and comfort in the present. But

access to land was another matter. Simsbury was beginning to restrict burning, lumbering, and turpentine extraction on the commons at the same time
that both land and store goods were becoming more expensive and prices for
farm and forest products were beginning to decline.[19] A widening gap between the prosperous and the ordinary would soon suggest to the ordinary
that their hopes for the future did not necessarily lie in the well-being of the
already prosperous.

For a few years after the Peace of Utrecht, Salmon Brook settlers looking to produce some surplus for trade were able to satisfy their lust for land.
The Simsbury land records from 1713 to 1721 are a good indication that outlanders throughout the town were doing all they could to exploit the resources
in their immediate surroundings. Meadowland was relatively expensive at one
to two pounds per acre, but land that needed work could be had free under the
current regulation that granted land to any inhabitant who cleared and fenced
it (and clearing could be done by burning, which produced marketable
potash). John Matson and George Hays began buying up land that river-town
creditors were eager to unload, assembling considerable estates to divide
among their heirs by the late 1720s. Hays seems to have built a sawmill at this
time on the East Branch just north of the village. Other longtime Salmon
Brook residents and some new to the settlement began purchasing parcels
here and there, even as far as three miles north of their houses. And as they
cleared more land and raised more livestock (with the help of a town collection of bulls, provided at public expense), they continued to collect hefty
bounties on wolves. The town even obliged these farmers by surveying a road
north of the original Salmon Brook house lots to a group of meadows they
had not yet cultivated, and from there on to the Massachusetts line.[20]

By 1719, though, the appetite for land was getting out of hand. On February 28, the clerk noted that "it is found by Experanc that maney men who
have had Lands Granted to them in our out Lands and do by their Exesive
Surveys or falce bound claim mutch more Land then was Granted them con-
treary to the Intent." The result was "mutch UnEquality in Such Exesive Surveys." In order "to prevent futer Trouble and to Regulat the Sam" the town
meeting chose a committee "to Inspect and also to Demaund a Regulatin of
all sutch Exesive Surveys of aney parson or parsons So incrotching Town
Lands into his or their hands." This resolution may have been in response to
concerns of men like Samuel Higley who saw ambitious outlanders grazing,
lumbering, and boxing unbridled. Or it may simply have arisen from a

general perception that, unless the town stepped in, everyone would be at each other's throats. At any rate, there was apparently "mutch dispute" about the use of the common lands, and the town appointed a committee of three, led by Rev. Timothy Woodbridge, to draw up a plan that would "make us Sitt Easie in respect of our comon and undevided lands." It was also at this time that various men came forward to secure their status as inhabitants, in order to be included in future land distributions. Among these were George Hays, Joseph Segar, Josiah Alvord, Josiah Alvord Jr., and William Rice of Salmon Brook.[21]

The Woodbridge committee came back on April 28 with four recommendations, the first of which suggested that the solution to the whole uneasiness was for the town to get the colony government to grant several thousand acres to the town from colony land on the western boundary. Second, the committee equivocated on the inhabitant-proprietor dispute, saying that the right to dispose of common lands should be vested in *both* present and future inhabitants or their heirs *and* proprietors or the proprietors' heirs. Third, it recommended that land "sutable and suffcent for comonage . . . may be sequestred for Ever." And finally, they declared that land should be divided "as a major part shall alow of said major part to be acounted not by number of parsons but by a Trew List of their Ratable Estate."[22]

The committee report must be understood in the context not only of a local conflict between the Samuel Higleys on one hand and the John Matsons and George Hayses on the other, but also of a frontier town attempting to avoid interference by provincial leaders in local affairs. Woodbridge and his colleagues did want to see if they could satisfy everyone, resident proprietor, non-resident proprietor, and non-proprietor resident alike, both by providing plenty of division land and by reserving a perpetual commons. But, in the last recommendation, an underlying concern is evident. By insisting that more weight be given to the preferences of those who had a larger "estate," they were appealing to the conservative instincts of the provincial leadership, hoping that this concession to a more traditional notion of decision making would dissuade the lawyers in the colony's government from declaring flatly for the proprietors, and, in the process, igniting a rebellion in Simsbury. They were clearly close to chaos. Land was everything.

Apparently persons from the proprietor class, possibly even those of Simsbury's proprietors (other towns were also having these sorts of disputes), had already approached the General Court at the October 1718 session about the problem. At that time the government had asked the towns to show their "state and condition" regarding common lands. Probably government officials knew very well that they were going to have to tread carefully to avoid alienating frontier farmers, while responding to demands of some very influential people whose continued loyalty was needed if the colony itself was to maintain its independence from royal authority. But Samuel Higley was not letting them off the hook. Not satisfied with the Woodbridge committee report, he and others petitioned the General Court on May 14, 1719, demanding lawmakers take action on the issue. In fact, he complained that the town had not yet laid its report before the assembly, even though he and the other proprietors had already prepared an answer.[23]

Meanwhile, west of the ridge, town meetings were getting hotter. A growing majority was bent on spiting the proprietors and demonstrating openly the rebelliousness Timothy Woodbridge had wanted to keep hidden from the legislature. At a town meeting on January 5, 1720, the town voted to ask the General Court to confirm all past grants and actions taken regarding land by the town. Furthermore, in an intermediate victory for outlanders, it made new grants to young men who had already been hard at work building houses and fencing land on the commons. This was when Nathaniel Holcomb III staked his claim for a house lot northwest of the Salmon Brook houses. George Hays's sons were among the new grantees. Undoubtedly these men joined the confrontational majority to select the senior Nathaniel Holcomb, a respected elder statesman who could well understand the concerns of the outlanders, as their representative to the May session of the General Assembly, and as their new town clerk.[24]

In May, Holcomb arrived in Hartford with a portfolio of papers, including copies of town acts of the 1680s reversing the original proprietor grants of the 1670s and setting conditions for land-holding in the outlands. He also brought the report of the Woodbridge committee, and was ready to answer Samuel Higley's arguments with a litany of anecdotes about the risks of living on the front lines of Connecticut's domain, and the expectations to which such risk takers had a right to hold their government. The lower house committee that heard these arguments tried to stall, no doubt hoping that the controversy would fizzle, but neither side would give an inch. By December, the conflict was so intense that a town meeting adjourned without action, only to meet again in January, and adjourn again. One can imagine the growing anger of Salmon Brook inhabitants as they trudged through the snow to these fruitless confrontations—and so it went for another year! Meanwhile, the town meeting did make small grants, but the young men of Salmon Brook were not going to be content for long with four-acre grants when thousands of acres of hardwoods, turpentine trees, and grazing lands were lying unused and under "Regulatin."[25]

Time, as a matter of fact, was running out. While the outlanders could claim victory in dispensing the 1720 grants, they were under a lot of pressure from another direction. The economic expansion of the early eighteenth century was coming to an end, leaving those who had overextended themselves in a desperate situation. Once benefiting from the inflationary forces unleashed by the wartime paper money issues, and having borrowed heavily to build houses and buy land, tools, and breeding stock, outland farmers throughout Connecticut were now beginning to feel the pinch of interest payments, growing families, and declining produce prices (not only from increased production, but also as a result of a constricted money supply and a new war between England and Spain that made the Caribbean a treacherous marketplace). Barnard Bartlett, for example, had borrowed to buy land at Salmon Brook in 1715, and was forced to sell some of it in 1719 to keep the rest. At one point Alexander Allyn, a Windsor merchant, summoned him to pay a three-pound debt. Bartlett assaulted him before Justice of the Peace Samuel Mather, only to incur a jail sentence with bail set at twenty pounds. He could not post the bond, but escaped from jail, piling up more fines and court costs. He tried to sue John Howard of Simsbury for one pound without result, and then disappeared for a few years until the court gave up on him. Others, such as Abigail Segar and Samuel Slater, were selling out to land speculators. Actually, nearly all of Salmon Brook's leading men made appearances for debt in the county court around 1720. As Jonah Westover and other friends of Samuel Higley bought land at Salmon Brook, it appeared to Simsbury's debtor class that packs of wolves were closing in.[26]

A principal plaintiff in many actions against these men was William Thrall of Windsor, who had inherited his father Timothy's merchant trade. In the 1720s he was snatching up deeds to land grants as fast as Salmon Brook farmers could be granted land. Nathaniel Holcomb Jr. owed him as much as forty-one pounds at one point. Thrall had him confined to the county jail when he could not pay, but Holcomb "from thence breaking the gaol made his escape, and has since gone at large," requiring Thrall to petition the legislature to order the sheriff to pursue Holcomb "with horse and foot, and to remand said prisoner back again to the gaol, there to remain until he satisfy said execution and be by law released."[27] The larger grants of land the out-landers sought were becoming more important for yesterday's expenses than for tomorrow's prosperity.

As the economy soured and the conflict over the commons dragged on without resolution, class-based resentments became more apparent. A peti-tion in 1723 for an addition to the town noted that, not only had Simsbury taken the lead in promoting copper works and in developing tar and turpen-tine operations important for the empire's navy, but also, in being a frontier town for forty years, it had suffered "a double part in the expense and fa-tigues of war, being fastened down by an act of this assembly [the 1704 law outlawing abandonment of homesteads in frontier towns] on penalty of loosing our Freeholds, which however just it might be for the present, yet challenges a consideration when the Assembly have the wherewith and leizure to do it."[28] In other words, the outlanders had given a great deal to people who laid claim to a considerable amount of power over them.

The proprietor class in Simsbury increasingly faced the deep-seated frustrations of the other inhabitants of town, and debates went well beyond questions of legal precedent and statutory privilege. Those in the middle, like Reverend Woodbridge, who hoped to maintain order and some degree of harmony, found themselves unable to get everyone to "sitt Easy," and were pushed aside in the growing confrontation. The leaders certainly made every effort to appease the outlanders. John Matson Sr. was finally allowed forty shillings out of public money "towards keeping his mother Miles," the same woman who had nearly been expelled for her poverty from his house and the town in 1696. At one point, the town meeting voted that a surplus in revenue be paid to Jonathan Holcomb to give instruction "in reading and in wright-ing" to the children of Salmon Brook. In an ironic action, they contracted with Daniel Hays to take up loose stallions in the woods west of town. Yet nothing would do. Nothing would satisfy the majority of residents yearning for release from the town's stranglehold on thousands of acres of land.[29]

The majority's moment came on December 31, 1722, when a town meeting convened to address the issue head on. The arguing and protests carried on all day, only to resume at dawn for another full day. Finally, a res-olution passed: "they would dispose of the undevided Lands in a Town way by granting out the same." Then followed another day of bickering, and near sundown the majority agreed to follow the original recommendations of the Woodbridge committee to grant land in proportion to estate. They also stipulated that grants would be "sized" for quality of land; that wood, stone, and clay in the remaining undivided land in each part of town would be for the common use of that district; and that every effort would be made to lay out an individual's lots in close proximity. Then, at Andrew Robe's house, on into the evening and toward daybreak it went, arguing and disputing over each person's proportion. One hundred seventy-two individuals, including some widowed women, received grants ranging from Thomas Gleason's nine acres to Captain Thomas Holcomb's three hundred.[30]

In the midst of it all a number of proprietors leveled their objection in writing and had it entered in the town records. Twenty of them signed their names and planned to launch further protests with the legislature. The majority ignored them, and sent a committee once again to the colony legislature with a petition asking for more land, reminding the legislature that for forty years Simsbury had been a frontier town, its inhabitants "fastened down" to their exposed location on pain of "loosing our Freehold"—that which they held so dear. Furthermore, they declared that the assigned acreage was just the beginning, and that future grants would continue to be made in the same proportions. This was the meaning, apparently, of "in a town way." The whole town commons would be divided up, eventually, not by the proprietors or with any regard to what the General Court might say, but by the authority of the town meeting itself, where all admitted inhabitants had a voice.[31]

Immediately after the meeting, the inhabitants drew lots and the town leaders distributed land in the various districts, or "squadrons," of the town. The Salmon Brook men got their first grants in a long tier northeast of their settlement. Some who already had grants west of the village received greatly expanded lots around their new homesteads. Samuel Higley appealed to the General Court in May, detailing the long history of land grants up to the patent, and arguing that the inhabitants had never had any right to grant to "strangers" lands belonging to proprietors. Now after "much Disturbance," he went on, the General Assembly should "disanull" all of the grants made in the winter town meeting. He brought forth witnesses who described the great meeting in detail, revealing that four Salmon Brook residents, apparently not even admitted inhabitants, had "acted and voted" at the meeting. How could this be anything but a mockery of legality?

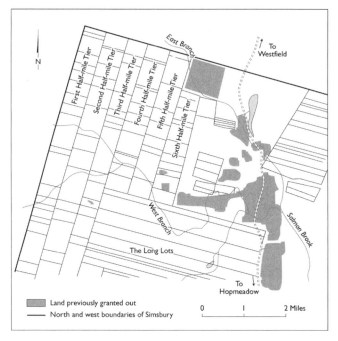

Map of lots granted in the Salmon Brook section of Simsbury, 1723–40. Nearly all of these lots were granted to Salmon Brook inhabitants.

The legislature proposed a compromise whereby former town grants would stand, but proprietors would be in charge of land distribution from this point on. Again, the majority in Simsbury ignored proprietor and colonial magistrate alike. The surveying of lots continued throughout the decade and into the early 1730s, when the committee had huge tiers of lots marked out on the west end of town. Even as late as 1747 grantees or their heirs were choosing miscellaneous lots in prime spots to "make up their proportion." To all of this, Samuel Higley and his fellow proprietors protested in vain.[32]

The legislature could hardly do otherwise than accommodate the outlanders. During the summer of 1723 the General Court was advised by authorities in Albany of the breakdown of treaty arrangements with Canadian Algonkians and the possibility of attack. "Symsbury and Litchfield," declared the court, "are the frontier towns of this Colony, westward of Connecticut River, which are most exposed to danger by those parties of Indians." The court then ordered scouting parties of Englishmen to the Housatonic Valley. Sergeant Jonathan Holcomb headed up one of these, and young Nathaniel III

went with him. Rumors of an enemy force of two hundred headed for Connecticut kept Simsbury's scouts and garrisons busy during the next two summers. All of this delayed the building of farmsteads at Salmon Brook. The
legislature did pay the scouts three to four shillings a day, but a 1725 petition,
arguing that they had not been paid on the Sabbath when they were out risking their lives as much as on any other day, suggests that they were in need of
every penny of their pay.[33] No, it would not have been wise to decide at this
time that the town commons belonged only to the proprietors.

The lawyer had made his case before the provincial government, a
forum where he might well have expected the sympathetic support of prosperous conservatives alarmed at the presumptuous behavior of Simsbury's
outlanders. But in Simsbury all this had accomplished was the igniting of
smoldering resentments among an increasingly debt-ridden group of people
who saw themselves as defenders of the commonwealth. There was so much
land—filled with timber, grass for livestock, and minerals. The outlanders
felt they deserved it by their residency in this forbidding wilderness. They
had been wanting in material needs for too long, and they were beginning to
look upon proprietors, creditors (whom they would pay off with their land
grants), and colony magistrates with the same affection they had once reserved for Algonkians, wolves, and mountain lions. The legislature was not
about to sit on this powder keg, no matter how devoted it was to civil order.
Samuel Higley and his allies would have to accept their grants "in a town
way" along with everyone else.

Pleas and Allegations, Orders and Disorders

The controversy over the commons was not the only time that the outlanders asserted themselves or that both town leaders and colony officials felt
the need to tread carefully. Another issue that had been simmering in the
background of the dispute between proprietors and inhabitants was what the
town clerk on February 20, 1716, referred to as "the great affair of providing
a comfortable and decent house for the publick worship of God and differ-
ances arising amongst us which we desire may be healed." Obviously, the
"great affair" had been on the agenda for some time. Now the selectmen put
the question forward whether the meetinghouse should be repaired or re-
built, and if the latter, where.[34] In addressing these questions over the next
twenty years, Salmon Brook residents demonstrated not only their sense of

entitlement to their rights as inhabitants, but also, collectively, an emerging desire for autonomy as a community.

In the good times after the war many inhabitants could conceive of paying higher taxes, so public expenditures, even for a new meetinghouse that could accommodate a growing population, were not out of the question. There may have been a number of people who habitually balked at taxes, but the really big issue in all of this was location. Simsbury had a central village, at Hopmeadow, but as was the case with many New England towns, the great majority of the population did not live in that central village. In fact, by 1736, only 8 percent of Simsbury's population lived at Hopmeadow.[35] Thus, with centers of population in Weatogue, at the Falls, along the east side of the river between Terry's Plain and East Weatogue, on the east side of the ridge at Scotland, at Salmon Brook, and at Turkey Hills, there was bound to be a lot of argument over where to place a new meetinghouse.

It was not just the convenience of getting to town meetings that was at issue. Church services, which people attended sometimes twice a week, were held in the town's meetinghouse. In the early 1700s Connecticut's established Puritan church had become more centrally controlled and more coercive. According to a series of resolutions known as the Saybrook Platform that were enacted into law in 1708, each county's ministers comprised an "association" to oversee a county divided into "ecclesiastical societies," delineating, as did English parishes, the boundaries of each church's jurisdiction. Everyone within a society's bounds, except "sober dissenters," had to attend services with the Puritan church of that society and pay taxes for church expenses, particularly the minister's salary. Society boundaries were generally the same as town boundaries at first, so everyone in town was interested in the location of the town's meetinghouse. In the summer, when the roads were in repair and dry, most families did not mind what was for many a five-mile trek to meeting. It was a major social event, after all, and often the town's militia trained on Sundays after services. But everyone thought about the advantages of a meetinghouse closer to home in the winter when roads were impassable and few had sleighs, or in the spring before the surveyors of highways had turned out their districts to make repairs on what had become pothole-strewn muddy gutters. Salmon Brook inhabitants surely found the trip to Hopmeadow, where the meetinghouse had been located since the 1670s, an arduous journey. Those who had to cross the Farmington River or trudge over the ridge were even more unhappy.

In view of the importance of this issue, the town meeting of February 20, 1716, sent a committee to meet with colony magistrates to get their advice on what ought to be done. In March the committee returned with the recommendation that the present meetinghouse should be repaired and enlarged, and the town did put fifty pounds into alterations and repairs. Beset by the controversy over dividing the common land, the town did not take up the matter again for ten years. During that time, the town's population grew considerably, and that forced the issue once the land dispute subsided. A town meeting of October 7, 1725, seemed to be moving toward building a new meetinghouse, but could not agree on a location. Soon after, the inhabitants agreed to obtain some impartial advice from the legislature, but when no one accepted that advice "in a Christian and peaceable manner becoming such a work," the inhabitants spent a year deciding to divide into two ecclesiastical societies, north and south. This prompted petitions to the General Court, visits from committees of magistrates, and even more angry meetings.[36]

In 1727, the people of Salmon Brook, who now numbered twenty-one families, met and began to sort out where they stood on the matter. The plan to divide the town north and south would have put them together with the people of Turkey Hills, and they were not happy with that. In a petition to the legislature they argued that they had never wanted to be a separate society, and they did not think the northern society could support a minister without their having to pay more taxes than they already did. More importantly, they were opposed to building a new meetinghouse for the proposed northern society, particularly at the site the legislature had chosen, "Wee Being so far distant one from the other and a Rocky wods where sd Stake is set that it is easer for us to Joyne with the whole Town then Come their the Land being so infertile."[37]

It can be inferred from this petition that the pressure for two societies was coming largely from Turkey Hills residents. The population of that section of town was growing rapidly, up from two families in 1709 to thirty-five in 1727. In fact, Turkey Hills was the section of town that was growing the fastest, not only from the natural increase, but also from migration from Windsor on the part of formerly absentee proprietors of Simsbury, many being the same men who had opposed grants of land to Salmon Brook's non-proprietor inhabitants. The petition's wording "so far distant one from the other" could, perhaps, be read to express a kind of political and cultural "distance" that the Salmon Brook inhabitants felt toward the people of Turkey

Hills, people like Samuel Higley, whom they had fought bitterly (and continued to fight) in the common land conflict.[38]

More town meetings, memorials, and petitions followed, and the legislature sent another committee in October 1728 to investigate all of the "pleas and allegations," to "finally determine" whether there should be two societies or the town should "continue undivided," and to make an "Utter End of Controversy." In the meantime, the south society, as originally proposed, had begun to have meetings to organize itself. Feelings were becoming so intense that tax collectors were beginning to have trouble collecting the old society's rate, which was supposed to fund Timothy Woodbridge's salary, and the building committee was becoming weary of carting the timber for the new meetinghouse from one "finally determined" location to another.[39]

After another failed effort by a colony committee in the fall of 1728, the town leaders made an effort to settle things at the local level, and perhaps salvage the town's sagging reputation. On December 26, inhabitants opened their annual town meeting of election by passing "orders and Constitutions to prevent disorders in Town Meetings for y[e] future." Enforced by stiff fines, these set more restrictive procedures for choosing a moderator, giving the moderator absolute control over who could "argue and dispute," and granting the majority the power to adjourn the meeting. In April 1729, in accordance with these new regulations, a very orderly town meeting, one assumes, voted again to divide the town into two societies, north and south.[40]

The controversy raged on nonetheless. The Turkey Hills people tried to hire their own minister, provoking a petition that accused Samuel Higley and his neighbors of developing a "design . . . to weaken [the southern part of town] and so to obtain the meetinghouse on the East side [of the river] and to be so set as to be attended with much greater difficulties than ever."[41] A General Court committee tried to "persuade the people of said town to surcease their contentions," and at a July town meeting, with Governor Joseph Talcott in attendance, majorities voted against dividing the town. Then they voted against building a new meetinghouse at the same place as the old one, against building a meetinghouse on the east side of the river, and in favor of remaining united and building a new meetinghouse at a place that they had rejected five years earlier. The legislature quickly approved all this at its October session, but it seems as though that was reason enough for the inhabitants to change their minds. The December election meeting was the scene of great arguing, two adjournments, and finally a decision to let each section of town go its own way as long at it would "maintain ye gospel amongst themselves either whole or separate."[42]

At this point Reverend Woodbridge complained to the county association, probably concerned that he would be traveling all over the countryside day and night doing services, and getting paid no more than before, if at all! The association agreed with him, saying the church at Simsbury was so destitute "of a good and christian frame of spirit, as to be unfit for communion at the Lord's table," and said he ought not to feel obligated to continue his ministry in Simsbury. To this the next year's town meeting answered that it would not pay him for 1731 "for sundry Reasons which to us seems sufficient," principally because "he not being obliged to us we cannot be obliged to him." This collective insolence continued into the following year, when town officials attempted without success to raise money to cover his salary since 1729. Again the legislature stepped in, noting that no measures had "had the desired success of quieting the minds of the people and settling them in peace," and that the colonial government itself would have to enforce the collection of the minister's rate.[43]

While all this may sound like a silly argument among stubborn and petulant farmers, the dispute carried many of the class-based undertones of the conflict over dividing the common land. Obviously the Turkey Hills people were one strong interest group who felt that their rapidly growing numbers and estates should exempt them from arduous travel every meeting day. Generally more wealthy than the average Simsbury resident, they carried more influence in the legislature. The General Court, in turn, was reluctant to alienate the outlanders at Salmon Brook, itself a growing settlement, whose inhabitants were probably feeling increasingly estranged from anyone of higher economic or social standing, including not only proprietors and creditors, in this case, but also the association of ministers who seemed to give no good reason for supporting Woodbridge over ministers they might have preferred. As the most contentious became more practiced at the art of obstructing solutions that were in the least bit inconvenient to them, it is not surprising that the "contentions" lasted so long.[44]

Until 1733, the Salmon Brook people seem to have been non-aligned, on one hand, eager to have a meetinghouse a little closer for the sake of their aging parents and more and more numerous children, and on the other hand suspicious of uniting with the inhabitants of Turkey Hills, who were "so far distant" from them. By that spring, their position was hardening as thirty-six men submitted a petition to the town meeting asking that "the place Called Salmon brok . . . shall have Liberty to be a distinct ministeriall Society by themselves." They further stated that they were giving up on the town's finding a place for the meetinghouse with which everyone would be happy. As the legislature stalled, they became impatient and hired a Mr. Roberts, "a young candidate" for the ministry, and held meetings at Daniel Hays's house. Claiming that their estates were growing considerably, they argued that they could support this man as their settled minister.[45]

Petitions, complaints, and memorials continued to roll in from each section of town. Samuel Higley of Turkey Hills submitted a masterful map to the legislature, exaggerating the distance between the northern half of Simsbury and the meetinghouse, and showing great mountain ranges and other natural barriers sealing people off from one another. Finally, at the October session in 1736 the legislature's committee came forth with a plan for division of the town that was very close to what Salmon Brook had wanted all along. According to this plan, there would be four societies: in Salmon Brook (the "Northwest Society"), Turkey Hills, Wintonbury (an intertown society), and "First Society"—the rest of Simsbury south of Salmon Brook. Some of the more prosperous families that Salmon Brook hoped to include on its tax list went to Turkey Hills and First Society, but otherwise, the legislature had granted Salmon Brook its independence.[46]

All the while the controversy was going on, more and more people were moving to Salmon Brook, including Philip Loomis, whose estate ranked the highest on the 1736 list, and Nathaniel Higley, who had moved into young Nathaniel Holcomb's house at Bushy Hill. These two men, in particular, had holdings in the other societies, but would, no doubt, sell them to increase their holdings at Salmon Brook, which they would improve. Thus, the future looked bright. They would have their own meetinghouse, select their own minister, both of which they were increasingly able to afford, and, in turn, more and more people would be interested in moving to Salmon Brook, thus driving up the value of their division land.[47] Taking on their own "minister's rate" now would be more of an investment than a sacrifice.

In less than three years the people of Salmon Brook voted to build a meetinghouse for themselves, and a hopeful legislative committee arrived in the summer of 1739 to pitch a stake at the north end of the village. By the next spring the frame was up. Measuring thirty by forty-five feet, and twenty feet in height with no steeple, it was not the most impressive of meetinghouses.

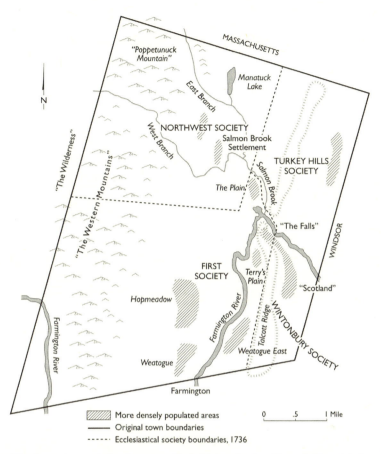

Map of Simsbury, circa 1736, showing areas with the highest density of households and the boundary lines of the four ecclesiastical societies established in that year.

One visitor commented that he had seen many of God's houses, but this was the first time he had been in one of His barns. As for their "young candidate," he appears to have moved elsewhere, for in 1739 the society actually paid Timothy Woodbridge to preach to them.[48]

It was a humble beginning to be sure, but it is hard not to remark on how far Salmon Brook had come in three decades. The community was now spreading north toward the colony line, and west toward the "wilderness." It was equipped with a sawmill, a storekeeper, and a grist mill; and as of 1740, it had a meetinghouse. Forty families—over two hundred people—supported these establishments. Some were newcomers, but most were the growing families of the second generation—the children and grandchildren of the nine families living there during Queen Anne's War. Nathaniel Holcomb III was chosen a selectman in 1736, in a new, more complex town order that called for five selectmen, one from each of the major "squadrons" of the town. He was also elected captain of Salmon Brook's own militia company in 1739.[49]

The view from Hartford was probably a satisfying one. Colony leaders would have been delighted to observe a stable congregation operating under the watchful eyes of the county association, and a new community of hard-pressed debtors and people formerly on the fringe of society becoming "ordered." Indeed, in spite of all the controversy and the anger expressed in some of the petitions, there had been no "tumults" that would weaken the colony's front lines, nor arouse authorities in England to challenge Connecticut's chartered independence. The people at Salmon Brook, however, had exacted a price for their relatively civil participation in town decision making: they had taken their wolf bounties and soldiers' and teachers' pay, added acre after acre to their freeholds, laid claim to enough land to give each of their many children a hundred-acre farm within walking distance, and had secured the privilege of managing their own ecclesiastical affairs. Two generations had held off proprietors, creditors, crows, wolves, mountain lions, and colonial magistrates. While those magistrates might well have balked at continuing to accommodate the outlanders' needs after a quarter century of peace with New France, the second generation of settlers at Salmon Brook seems to have become convinced of their entitlement to their freeholders' status and their autonomy, and equally skilled at arguing their case. This history of contention and assertiveness would create habits that soon presented difficulties for the cohesiveness of Salmon Brook as a community. For the moment, though, letting them have what they wanted had "had the desired success of quieting the minds of the people and settling them in peace."

3. Zeal for the Support of the Darling Liberty

Sunday morning, September 15, 1776: Captain Samuel Hays and his company of twenty-one Salmon Brook men lie uncomfortably in a one-foot-deep trench on the eastern side of Manhattan Island. Their position, such as it is, overlooks a small inlet known as Kip's Bay. Facing into the rising sun they can see the silhouettes of four British warships just outside the inlet. Several other troop transports are moving up the East River. Hays and his company, accompanied by their minister Rev. Joseph Strong, have been in New York for three weeks, but as yet have not fired a shot. Instead, the Eighteenth Regiment of Connecticut Militia, under the command of Colonel Jonathan Pettibone of the south end of Simsbury, has battled dysentery. There have already been several fatal casualties. Hays has sent four of his men home, including his second in command. It is a weakened regiment that faces crack British troops flush with recent victories on Long Island.

The bombardment begins at seven o'clock and lasts about a half hour—enough time to throw the Eighteenth Regiment's entire brigade into a state of disarray. The cannonballs kick up so much dirt that many of the men are buried in the ditch. When the British troops come ashore, the militiamen run in all directions. Some flee west across the island. Others retreat northward in such a state of panic that they run through the rear of British lines that are advancing on Harlem Heights. On hearing of the panic, General Washington rides to the scene and tries to rally "the disgraceful and dastardly" troops, but nearly gets captured himself. Most of those who are not captured, killed, or confined to a hospital bed, from wounds or sickness, desert, or are quickly discharged before the month is out. Among those captured are Jesse and Roger Cossitt, two brothers from the northern part of Salmon Brook. They will die in a British prison ship in New York harbor.[1]

The wonder is that the Simsbury militiamen are there at all. They are hopelessly ill-prepared. Their few experienced soldiers have trained them to fight in the backwoods of North America, or at best to lay siege to or defend frontier fortifications. Hays's company joined in the siege of Boston but saw no action. None of their officers have any experience fighting pitched battles in an open field. And what is the fight all about, anyway? For years the campaign against British colonial policy has been waged in the port towns. Farmers like Samuel Hays and the families of Salmon Brook took no part in the resistance to Parliament until the spring of 1774. What brought them to Boston in 1775, and now to New York the following year?

Besides addressing the issue of the origins of the new nation, the answer to that question reveals much about the continuing evolution of relationships between the backcountry and the leadership of early America. Backcountry militiamen marched to Boston and New York in droves, carrying with them a rich legacy of resistance to authority. That legacy was rooted deeply in their first generation's determination to become freeholders and the second generation's strong devotion to autonomy. Then, between 1740 and 1776, an onslaught of turmoil and change threatened the place that those first two generations had made for themselves in Connecticut society. Once again, Salmon Brook's residents demonstrated their desire to maintain their status as independent freeholders with control over their community affairs. And once again, facing the ongoing threat of invasion from the north, as well as a general need for order amid turmoil and change, Connecticut's leadership allowed the backcountry parish the autonomy and respect to which its inhabitants had become accustomed. After the French and Indian War, Salmon Brook's third and fourth generations gradually became convinced that their best hope for continued respect and autonomy involved taking up arms with those who opposed Parliament's new imperial policies. When the Salmon Brook militiamen marched to New York in the summer of 1776, they were engaged in one of a number of campaigns to sustain the equal station they and their parents and grandparents had become convinced was their birthright.

O, Sinners!

As the inhabitants of Salmon Brook, or the "Northwest Society," shingled the roof on their modest meetinghouse in the fall of 1740, the relative quiet they had recently settled into was about to be disturbed. England had gone to war with Spain the year before, and that conflict would eventually escalate into another round of imperial struggle for North America that would involve Salmon Brook. Events closer to home, however, would have a more immediately unsettling impact. That fall the "Great Itinerant" George Whitefield made his triumphal tour of Connecticut.

Revivals were not new to New Englanders. Puritan ministers had employed the "fire and brimstone" jeremiad throughout the seventeenth and early eighteenth centuries whenever they thought religious devotion was on the wane. New Englanders were used to hearing that calamities such as epidemics, fires, war, untimely deaths, and earthquakes were evidence of God's continuing quarrel with His people and of their need to pay more attention to the state of their souls. Most ministers recognized the need to speak to both the mind and the heart. As Simsbury's Rev. Edward Thompson had once preached, conversion was a "soul satisfying Enjoyment" of heavenly things in which "our heads will be so full of knowledge and our hearts with joy, that we shall say Lord we have enough!" When Whitefield first arrived in New England, the Hartford North Association of ministers welcomed his ability to stir large crowds of people into heartfelt conversions.[2]

Whitefield, however, did not reciprocate with collegial affection. He lambasted the clergy in general for their inability to awaken faith among the people and blamed the ministers' own lack of conversion for a protracted decline in godliness. "The reason why congregations have been dead," he wrote in his journal, "is because they have dead men preaching to them." Obviously this attitude was destined to offend some. The leading Connecticut clergymen, in particular, thought that by founding Yale College and enacting the presbyterian order of the Saybrook Platform they were ensuring a more able clergy and thus more godly congregations. As unlicensed itinerant ministers began traveling the region imitating Whitefield's style and making similar charges, the established clergymen changed their minds about evangelical preaching. In 1741 the Hartford North Association, which had jurisdiction over Simsbury's Northwest Society, declared that, "Besides Reading, hearing, meditation and Prayer, [the people] should seek to their own stated pastors as their Local guides, and to neglect them and ordinarily betake themselves to Lay persons is irregular and unsafe."[3]

It is not clear where the people of Salmon Brook stood in 1740 on the issue of revivals. The "contentions" that had resulted in the birth of their society had involved, at least on the surface, the location of a meetinghouse and whether or not they could afford to build their own and pay for their own preacher. Timothy Woodbridge of Simsbury was not an evangelical minister to be sure, and it was he whom the Northwest Society asked to preach to them when they began to hold their meetings at Salmon Brook in 1739. And when their "Prudential Committee" went looking for a permanent minister in 1740, they found Eli Colton, also a fairly conservative preacher.[4] Nevertheless, it would soon become apparent that underneath Salmon Brook's concerns over the location of the meetinghouse and the division of Simsbury lay an ever-growing desire for autonomy, which would mix explosively with a history of hard living and the so-called Great Awakening.

When the Awakening arrived at Salmon Brook in 1741, the leaders of the congregation and society were hoping to settle Eli Colton as their permanent minister. They had even sent a committee to the Hartford North Association to ask its advice on what to arrange with Colton, and in June the association had agreed that settling him in the Northwest Society was the right thing.[5]

Then the trouble began, although the records do not say how. Perhaps the association thought the society should pay Colton more than already planned; perhaps some of the society had heard Whitefield or other evangelical, "New Light" preachers. In July, Jonathan Edwards had preached his famous sermon "Sinners in the Hands of an Angry God" in Enfield, just ten miles away, and itinerant revivalist preachers were becoming more and more a part of the landscape. Whatever the case, sometime during the fall of 1741 a movement to reverse the decision to settle Colton developed. After arguing throughout the winter, the inhabitants of the society put the question in May 1742, "whether Wee should setel Mr. Colton on our former Trety with him or on the advice of the association or conclude anything Else concerning him." With Captain Nathaniel Holcomb III in the moderator's chair, they voted against settling Colton on any terms and dissolved the meeting. Colton continued to preach without a permanent settlement.[6]

After a month the leaders managed to pull people together and extract a vote to send a committee to the association to seek advice "under our presente Difocoltys with Respect to Seteling a Minister." In the meantime, the association had made its declaration against "irregular and unsafe" preaching, and its "Old Light" members had convinced the legislature to pass a law against revivals conducted by ministers who were not licensed by an association. In Salmon Brook, this inspired renewed efforts by the Old Lights to keep Colton, but also a vote "to open a doer for preaching agreeable to our Late Law."[7] Colton responded guardedly to the new developments, but the movement to send him packing was growing stronger.

The squabbling continued through September, along with desperate efforts to reach a compromise. On September 13, the society voted to invite "some neighboring *ordained* ministers of the North association," along with some others from Massachusetts, to see if any could appeal to the congregation as a whole. The emphasis on the word *ordained* is significant here, for it suggests that many were listening to unlicensed preachers and agitating for an evangelical minister. The New Lights of Salmon Brook apparently were not interested in compromise and created such an uproar at a meeting the next week that the moderator had to "divide the Meeting House" (stand the yeas on one side and the nays on the other) in order to get an accurate vote count. And even then there was contention over who was qualified to vote. Colton gave up and left without having been paid more than a quarter of his past salary due. The association ordered that the society accept a committee of area ministers to arbitrate what they owed Colton, but no one in Salmon Brook seemed to pay attention.[8]

On and on the bickering went. The Old Light leaders, such as Captain Nathaniel Holcomb and Daniel Hays, barely holding their seats on the Prudential Committee, tried to install an "orthodox" or "regularly ordained" minister. At the same time, a large contingent of the society wished to bring the Awakening permanently to Salmon Brook, even against the wishes of the colony's ecclesiastical hierarchy. In December another angry meeting squeaked through a vote to give "the call" to a "regularly ordained" minister whose character must be known to a major part of the society, and to disqualify "any that are not free from any Censor of being Disorderly in there Ministry or Eronous in there Doctrine or Scandelous in their lives." During 1743 the association proposed four different ministers, but none of them met with the approval of the majority.[9]

Some in the society left the church at Salmon Brook and joined a new Anglican congregation in Scotland, south of the Falls. The earliest settlers of the Scotland area, principally persons of Welsh and Huguenot extraction, had expressed their preference for the Church of England when Simsbury was first trying to settle a minister in the 1680s. It was nearly impossible to organize an Anglican church in Connecticut in the seventeenth century, but in adopting the Saybrook Platform in 1708, the legislature had passed a law allowing people "who soberly differ or dissent from the united churches [to] worship and discipline in their own way according to their consciences." In the 1720s the legislature went further, freeing Baptists and Quakers from paying for establishment ministers' salaries and allowing Anglicans a proportion of the local society taxes equal to their part of the society's population. The people in the Scotland section of Simsbury gathered an informal society during the 1730s when there was so much turmoil over the dividing of Simsbury into separate ecclesiastical societies. During the Awakening, they began to attract people who were dissatisfied with the disorderliness that seemed to be infecting the established churches in the area. This was the case with the people who left Salmon Brook, and some of those were quite prominent individuals. As the Anglican congregation grew, London's Society for the Propagation of the Gospel dispatched William Gibbs, an ordained minister, to establish St. Andrew's Church in 1744.[10]

Meanwhile, at Salmon Brook, there were fewer people of stature who supported Old Light preaching. That, combined with resentment over the loss of tax revenues that would support a minister, if they could agree upon one, deepened the bitterness that people felt toward ecclesiastical authorities. While revival activity in Connecticut had waned, and even Whitefield found most pulpits closed to him upon his return to the colony in 1744, Salmon Brook remained inclined to be "disorderly." In the winter of 1744–45, with new, more radical leaders on the Prudential Committee, the New Lights invited a young man named David Sherman Rowland to come to preach to the Northwest Society.[11]

Rowland had graduated from Yale in 1743, and was ordained by the Fairfield Association the following year. In spite of these credentials that might otherwise have endeared him to the Hartford North Association, he did not take long to display his New Light colors. First, he invited George Whitefield to preach at Salmon Brook. Furthermore, he was quite capable of awakening his congregation with the same themes found in Whitefield's sermons. In the prologue to this book, we heard him warning the sinners of his audience (by which he meant everyone) of their "infinitely hazardous" condition.

He promised "no rest day nor night" for their souls. "Should God's patience be worn out, should he cut short the thread of life," they would be cast into the grip of a legion of "insulting devils, those ghastly, those horrid fiends."[12]

Rowland did speak to the hearts of a majority of the Northwest Society. The idea of a wrathful God, who could nonetheless bestow infinite mercy for reasons no one could understand, probably made good sense to people whose lives had often wobbled on the edge of destruction. For those in the society who were the New Lights, life was as hard as the granite they carried annually from their fields to their boundary lines. Such work was an act of heartfelt faith that their stone walls would stand by them and mark out the freeholds that kept them alive. They saw their faith in God in those terms. It was a sort of faith that was not to be explained or understood through reasoned discourse, or through respect for duly constituted authority. It could only be experienced through a true spiritual awakening, they believed. Such an awakening could occur only when people realized their "infinitely hazardous" condition. Rich or poor, high or low, all were miserable sinners under only one true Authority.

The reaction of the Old Light Hartford North Association to Rowland's preaching was predictable. In October 1745, these clergymen wrote the society "that under the present circumstances of things, they do not advise to his settlement in the work of the ministry there." When it became apparent that the majority was not listening, they called forth Rowland, demanded to know if he would be loyal to the Saybrook Platform, and, more important, if he would refuse to "countenance and Encourage Mr. Whitefield by inviting him to preach or attending his administrations or any other Itinerant preachers or any other of the errors, Separations or disorders prevailing in the country." Rowland refused to comply, and, consequently, the association proceeded to advise once more against his settlement in Salmon Brook.[13]

The parish was in an uproar. The new leaders, including Samuel Hayes Sr., father of the future militia captain, had inspired collective action that now turned to open defiance. The society voted to keep Rowland, and to "be Setold a Congregational Church," separate from the centralized power structure of Connecticut's churches. Their only rules for "Church Government and Disapline," they declared, would come from "yᵉ Scriptures of yᵉ old and New testament." They openly rejected the Saybrook Platform, announcing that they knew of no "human Compoasiour yᵗ come nearour to yᵉ Scriptuor than Cambrig platform in yᵉ Substance of it so we chuse yᵗ yᵉ Church in this

Society Shall take it in ye Substance of it." According to the Cambridge Platform of 1649, each church or congregation was expected to order its own affairs and make its own choice of its minister. The society also welcomed
members of neighboring congregations to join them at Salmon Brook "as the
opportunity may present."[14]

Fortunately for Rowland and his assertive congregation, the beginning
of his illicit ministry coincided with news of war between England and France.
Provincial authorities, including Old Light associations, were trying to find
ways to reconcile differences, particularly as more and more new ministers
were coming forth from Yale inclined toward New Light ideas. In general,
clergymen everywhere returned to old themes, such as the supremacy of the
Bible and New England's holy mission, which had always held the region together in hard times. The outlands of Simsbury still marked the northwest
frontier of Connecticut, so the Hartford North Association basically ignored
Simsbury's Northwest Society in return for its residents' loyalty. Rowland
continued to preach there until early 1749.[15]

Eventually, less radical voices returned to leadership positions at
Salmon Brook. Captain Nathaniel Holcomb and others never did give up trying to cooperate with the association. They watched and waited until a meeting when attendance was low and quietly voted to "invite some proper person
who is a candidate for the ministry." Rowland sensed their growing influence
and resigned. Then followed a period of maneuvering. The Old Lights brought
in the elderly Isaac Burr from Windsor. New Lights brought in Evander
Morison, an itinerant from Pennsylvania. Burr left, probably horrified, and
the Old Lights tried to get the association to throw its weight against Morison.
The New Lights threatened again to be openly defiant and keep Morison no
matter what; the Old Lights publicly protested; the whole society fasted and
asked God's direction; Morison left for the new parish beginning in West
Simsbury; the New Lights tried to bring in Ebenezer Booge, a recent Yale
graduate, to assuage the Old Lights; the Old Lights countered by inviting
Aaron Brown, whom the association had licensed. Finally, in 1752, the congregation found its minister.[16]

His name was fitting: Joseph Strong. He must have been a remarkable
man to pull together this contentious, god-fearing, painfully independent, and
determined group of farmers in Connecticut's northern hills. Only twenty-
three years old, he came, spoke, formed a church, laid down doctrine, and
converted the lambs in droves by "profession of faith." How? Not with fire

and brimstone. Not with tomes on obedience and accepted truth. Although he did devote some attention to "church discipline," he worked primarily through simple, straightforward plain talk that brought joy to a people weary of quarreling. "That wisdom which is from above, or true religion, is first pure, then peaceable, gentle, and easy to be intreated," he told them; and they all breathed a collective sigh of relief. Perhaps with France and England briefly at peace and more people moving into Salmon Brook, many were ready for a gentler message.[17]

Still, he carefully walked the middle road. He allowed his newly formed church to object collectively to certain parts of the Saybrook Platform (actually practically all of its most important features), as long as it declared acceptance of it "in principle." He introduced singing, a practice independent-minded congregations had often rejected when Old Light ministers had tried it in the early part of the century. Eventually, he created a subscription library, "to promote useful knowledge, piety and virtue." He argued quietly, yet firmly and logically, that individual ministers (not congregations) could legitimately differ with association doctrine. And while he called forth professing communicants with one hand, he baptized infants and admitted people under the Halfway Covenant with the other. In December 1752, his relieved congregation gave him house, land, salary, and a covenant of his own dictation; they brought in ministers from across the region to ordain him, and they celebrated at a banquet for which the society footed the bill for fifty-three meals, six quarts of wine, and three quarts of rum.[18]

Ecclesiastical peace at last reigned in the Northwest Society of Simsbury in 1752. Most of the moderates, who were bulwarks of the community, were reunited with the radicals. After a dozen years of searching, an independent and contentious group had entered into a covenant to love and watch out for each other. Some might see in this some deft leadership and the inevitable triumph of the "middle way," but that would be missing a lot that had happened in those twelve years of bickering and division.

First of all, the whole experience must have been a wrenching one. Most of the parishioners were children of the first settlers, born and raised in Salmon Brook, and no doubt united by a bond of frontier living. There had been a great deal of intermarriage among children of these first families, and within these webs of intermarriage there were strong voices on both sides of the dispute. In spite of numerous reconciliations within these families, there were still some who did not return to the church. Obviously, resentments over that lingered on. In 1754 the Anglican Reverend Gibbs was beaten and thrown over a horse to be transported to the Hartford jail for not paying ecclesiastical taxes. He never did recover from the experience. Some radicals like John Gossard and Isaac Dewey, who would not compromise their New Light views, eventually separated from the church and held Baptist meetings in the 1760s. All this depleted funds for Strong's salary and other expenses, and the society had to seek permission from the legislature to tax absentee landholders on unimproved lands.[19]

Even more important than these lingering bad feelings was the heritage of independence and rebellion passed on to the next generation as a result of the struggles between the ecclesiastical hierarchy of Hartford County and the rank-and-file of the society, who obviously preferred the hard message and emotional style of the evangelical preachers. Local leaders like Captain Nathaniel Holcomb, Daniel Hays, and Joseph Willcockson appear to have been unable to do much to mitigate the hostility being expressed by either side. Probably they themselves sympathized with their neighbors, if only on the issue of the right of the society to choose whatever minister and abide by whichever platform it wanted. After all, they were veterans of the conflicts of the 1720s and 1730s where autonomy was a bread-and-butter issue. The society did, technically, acquiesce in the end and settle a minister acceptable to the association; but it was only Strong's firm parrying of a deep-seated impulse to be an island unto themselves that quieted, for a time, expressions of anger and disrespect for anyone who made claims to authority over a community and a congregation which had always wanted to rule itself. In time, the lessons these residents had learned about resistance to interfering authorities would assist in the dissolution of an empire, and the founding of a town. For the moment, they had simply learned to live uneasily together.

Extended Families, Extended Freeholds

Beginning in 1744 a new season of war between France and England, and their colonists and Indian allies in North America, shaped the environment in which Salmon Brook people not only took advantage of more lax ecclesiastical supervision, but also moved with resolve to secure their own freeholds as well as new farms for their numerous offspring. Their determination in this regard is strikingly evident in the lichen-covered rows of rock that stretch back into the hills of West Granby today as monuments to the standing and independence to which their builders aspired. Much of that part of town is now the McLean Game Refuge, and even though the forest has returned, the walls tell us that there were once open fields, orchards, and farms here, even in these ledge-encrusted hills. "This is where I became a historian," I say to my students. They stare curiously into the stands of oak and beech. Here and there a piece of barbed wire protrudes from the middle of a tree. What does he see in it, they wonder?

It is, in fact, the wondering. A stone-lined pit opens before us. Who were these people who carried on their lives within the now disintegrated walls that once rose above that cellar? Who would persist at farming in this rugged terrain, with its steep slopes and thin soil filled with glacial debris? Who would even dig a cellar here? Even the Indians knew this ground was most suitable for a game preserve. Why would people who were industrious enough to pile up mile after mile of walls, and skilled enough to build them so straight, have any interest in living here?

Those piles of granite are a historian's gold mine. No one has had any interest in moving them since farmers began to work in these hills in the 1750s. This becomes apparent when one uses the surveyors' records to mark out the lots and western tiers on twentieth-century aerial surveys and finds that nearly all of the stone fence lines photographed from the air fall under those lot lines. The surveyors of the 1730s paced through forests, across ledges and gorges, with little equipment besides a compass and a chain, and still they got it right. And when the farmers arrived, they marked their surveyed boundaries with these walls, straight and true, not giving an inch. Perhaps "not giving an inch" is a good way to characterize those who came up here to make their homes—and to characterize the community that they helped to shape as it grew and spread out in the years before the American Revolution.

Between 1723 and 1740 many Salmon Brook inhabitants had used at least some of their tier lots in the west half of the parish to extract themselves from debt or to raise cash to buy more attractive and convenient land near their homesteads. Land speculators from Windsor, Hartford, Simsbury itself, and even as far away as Boston, had leaped in to provide the cash, and by the mid-1730s, a number of the lots in these tiers were in the hands of absentee owners poised to take profits, or to extend credit and take even more profits in the long run. So intense was the regional land speculation frenzy at that time that the legislature began organizing towns like Hartland and

Barkhamsted west of Salmon Brook and auctioning them as proprietorships
to raise revenue. To the north of Salmon Brook, wealthy Massachusetts investors John Hunt, Robert Breck, and Charles Apthorp prepared for a sell-
off by dividing up their holdings in an area called "the Wedge," between the
Simsbury town line and the newly surveyed Massachusetts boundary.[20]

Since most Salmon Brook residents of the 1730s were interested in
consolidating their farmsteads near the original village, those who actually
took up lands in the outer hills at that time and through the 1740s were largely
newcomers. Like the original settlers of Salmon Brook, they were looking
for more land or better opportunities than what was available to them in the
settled towns of the Connecticut River valley. They came from a variety of
places and backgrounds, and tax lists indicate a wide range of individual
wealth. Some did quite well for themselves. Rene Cossitt, born of French
nobility but captured and held prisoner in Connecticut during Queen Anne's
War, had made the colony his home by the 1720s. As lots were being surveyed in Simsbury in the 1730s, he established his residency and obtained
grants north of Salmon Brook village that he turned into a large and prosperous farm by the 1740s.[21]

Others eager for cheap outlands were not so fortunate. Five Halladay
brothers of Suffield paid £120 for a two-hundred-acre lot in the hills west of
Bushy Hill in 1738. The attraction of this particular lot was the gorge where
the West Branch flowed "out of the mountain," and into the flatter land northwest of Barn Door Hills. No one lived in those flatlands yet, but the Halladays
saw "grist mill" written all over this beautiful piece of rock and waterfall, and
moved their families there in 1741. Unfortunately, farmers needing a convenient place to bring their grain did not arrive for another decade, and the Halladays themselves had to build a road east to the houses on the other side of
Bushy Hill to encourage business. In the meantime, they struggled with their
debts.[22]

The ever present creditors and the outbreak of King George's War in
1744 helped to acculturate the newcomers who took up lots in the western
and northern reaches of the parish. That is, they soon shared the common
experience of perilous and debt-ridden frontier living with the families who
had been at Salmon Brook for the past four decades. Aside from discouraging the older residents from sending their young people too quickly to take
up land in the hills, though, the war had minimal impact on Salmon Brook.
New England, in fact, took the war to the Canadians with a successful attack

on the fortress at Louisbourg at the mouth of the St. Lawrence in 1745. Samuel Pettibone of Simsbury recruited a group of men from Simsbury to join in this attack, but that was the extent of the town's exposure to the war. In fact, with prices for provisions rising, Salmon Brook's farmers began thinking about "improving" what tier lots they had saved, or could now purchase from speculators.[23]

At this point, after King George's War and before the outbreak of the French and Indian War, a number of the families near the original village began to move their young people who were coming of age to farms in the outer hills. The standard of success for Salmon Brook inhabitants had evolved from keeping creditors at bay and maintaining one's freehold to setting up one's children with sizable farms—a considerable task considering that each family had from six to as many as fourteen children. One common strategy was for young people to move in groups of relatives. The efforts by Samuel Hayes Sr. and David Holcomb to find homesteads for their third-generation children illustrate these new land settlement patterns. In 1751, David Holcomb, who lived in the old Salmon Brook settlement, acquired the last lot of the Sixth Half-mile tier. He held on to this until 1757 when he gave it to his son Reuben as a share of his estate. Reuben had already purchased the Fifth tier lot to the west of this land to make a total of 180 acres. By 1762, he had bought even more land contiguous to his new farm and moved into a house on the west side of Bushy Hill.[24]

Not far from Reuben's house, Reuben's father-in-law, Samuel Hayes Sr., also invested in some land for two of his five sons on the west side of Bushy Hill. He began by purchasing a relatively new farm in 1750 for his eighteen-year-old son Asahel (who had just married Reuben Holcomb's sister Martha). A few years later he bought land from Solomon Halladay, who was in the process of giving up on Salmon Brook and returning to Suffield, and saved it for his son Andrew. When Asahel, Andrew, and their brother-in-law Reuben Holcomb used £135 of the late Samuel Hayes Sr.'s estate in 1762 to pay speculator John Roberts of Windsor for a large lot nearby, this collection of brothers and sisters had pretty much laid claim to that little valley at the foot of the Halladays' gorge. At this point town officials surveyed a road south from "the road to Halladay's" toward Hopmeadow. The survey confirms what the Halladays were relieved to know: the farmers had come at last.[25]

Other young couples were also venturing across Bushy Hill into the town's western tier lots at this time, beginning the long, slow process of carving farms out of the heavily wooded hillsides near Halladay's mill. In 1755, George Hayes Jr.'s son Elisha purchased a fifty-six-acre lot on a mountain above the gorge. This lot had already been through three speculators in the preceding five years and had nearly doubled in price. His brother Benjamin also moved to the same neighborhood, and Serajah and Eunice Stratton brought their family from Hopmeadow to build a trip-hammer shop, a sawmill, and yet another grist mill above the gorge. Numerous family heads, in fact, were filling the western hills with their newly married children.[26]

Even though they scattered their farms widely about the land, they moved as groups of in-laws, forming neighborhoods that amounted to a few extended families. These networks helped with the hard work of dealing with the rougher, uncleared terrain that former meadow-seekers had dreaded. They had to take down the timber (or burn it), plant apple trees, build fences for sheep, cattle, and hogs, and trade around their lots until they had a good balance of land for vegetables, orchards, pasture, grass, and grain. To buy tools, hardware, glass, paint, and other imported products on which they relied to build their farms, they exported lumber, cider, beeswax, candles, honey, wool, and some woolen clothing (mittens, stockings, caps) that they could make at home. There in the hills, the walls they built still stand, testimony to their ambition, toil, and, in some cases, frustrations. The walls marked boundaries, served as foundations for rail fences to keep animals out of grain fields, and simply provided a nearby spot to dump the abundant stone that they were constantly harvesting as the frost pushed up glacial debris each spring. It is not difficult to imagine how devoted each family was to the freehold those walls enclosed.[27]

While the sprouting of farmsteads in the outlying hills was an indication of some confidence in the future, the continuing hostility between England and France did keep many people from venturing too far to the north and west. The final round in the conflict began in 1754, and by the time peace was established in 1763, one out of three New England men able to bear arms had enlisted at some point. Virtually every family in the region had at least one soldier. Salmon Brook men enlisted immediately, first in a Suffield Company, and then in greater numbers in a company formed by Jonathan Pettibone of Simsbury that fought in the Lake George area in the fall of 1755. The next year Connecticut dispatched soldiers to Crown Point and Lake Champlain to block what seemed to be imminent invasion, but not many Salmon Brook men participated in this campaign.[28]

Then, in August 1757, came the news that Fort William Henry, at the south end of Lake George, had surrendered to a besieging force of French regulars and Hurons; and as the British soldiers, militiamen, and their families were leaving the fort, the Hurons had killed them all. To people living on the outskirts of Connecticut and Massachusetts the implications were clear: only Fort Edward just east of Lake George protected them from a cruel fate. It was at this point that many of the families hoping to take up land in the tier lots put their plans on hold. Jonathan Pettibone raised a large company from Simsbury to reinforce Fort Edward, including fourteen men listed separately as "Samon Brook Companey." Again the next spring, scouts sent warnings that Connecticut could be attacked. This time Captain Nathaniel Holcomb put together a much larger company of Salmon Brook men.[29]

The 1758 and 1759 campaigns marked the turning point of the war. Louisbourg and Quebec fell, and in 1760, so did Montreal. A disastrous effort to capture Cuba in 1762 ended the war for New England on a sour note, even though the French ceded Canada to the English the next year. Casualties were light for Salmon Brook in the various Canadian campaigns, and enlistments continued strong. In the Cuba expedition, however, twelve of the fourteen Salmon Brook men who went with the Simsbury company died of malaria.[30]

All the fighting between 1744 and 1760 had slowed, but not halted the steady expansion of Salmon Brook. Daring souls like the Halladays and Strattons, the young Hayses and Holcombs, desperate for land and opportunity, continued to work on farms in the western tier lots throughout the period. After the fall of Montreal in 1760 families surged into the hills. Simsbury's population had grown considerably since the days when surveyors were first marking out those lots, and over the next two decades it would double again. All of these people needed land. When settlers first cleared land in the hills, the soil, fortified by centuries of leaf mold, was not as bad as some had thought it might be. Prices for acreage rose, and more newcomers moved in. Salmon Brook itself was becoming a more complex community, with competition among mill owners, numerous new road surveys, and an expansion of regulatory officers and ordinances. Growing numbers of farm families eager to sell their timber and other surplus produce encouraged traders to set up shop. Ozias Pettibone, for example, moved north from Weatogue to establish a store near the Salmon Brook meetinghouse and soon became the wealthiest man in the parish. With merchants like Pettibone willing to take just about anything in exchange for credit, other young people began looking to the brooks as a source of water power for such trades as tanning and the manufacturing of cider and cloth. Some of this business may have challenged Parliamentary regulations against colonists producing manufactured goods, but no one seemed to care.[31]

By 1763 Salmon Brook had changed and grown dramatically since its three dozen families had convinced the General Court to set them off as a separate ecclesiastical society in 1736. A few families had moved closer to the upper meadows or cleared farms within a half-hour walk of the original settlement before 1740. In 1763 the majority of residents were now spread out three to four miles from the meetinghouse. New people had come from three or four towns away to settle, tradesmen had begun to specialize in manufacturing, and each year town committees traveled northwest to survey new roads through the hills. There was at least one constant, though. The Northwest Society's newly arrived or newly married inhabitants had risked much and labored long in building farms and mills in forests among ledges and boulders. As it was for the first two generations at Salmon Brook, subsisting or even acquiring a small freehold had cost them dearly. They would be reluctant to part with what little control they had over their lives, or what little cash or credit they could obtain from the production of surplus, unless they could see a direct benefit. Like the walls they built, they would not give any ground when it came to their land and their communal right to manage their own affairs.

The Liberty Pole

In 1753 Samuel Hays II took his place as a freeman of the town of Simsbury. At almost the same time, he and his wife Rosanna professed their faith and were admitted as members of Joseph Strong's church in the Northwest Society. During the next decade Rosanna gave birth to five of their ten children, and Samuel acquired over 150 acres of land and held a number of minor town offices. When he was elected to the Prudential Committee for the ecclesiastical society in 1765, he had clearly become one of the more prominent men of his part of town. In the 1740s his father had sat on this committee and asserted Salmon Brook's independence from the county association. Now it was young Samuel's turn to maintain that legacy of autonomy.[32]

One way to understand how Salmon Brook responded to the revolutionary crisis of the 1760s and 1770s is to look at events from Hays's perspective—a perspective that worshipped autonomy. We might be inclined to view him and his neighbors as "reluctant revolutionaries" if we considered only the relatively late entry of Simsbury into the ranks of the resistance to Parliament. But Salmon Brook had a long history of resistance in the name of independence. Hays's generation had grown up in an environment marked by dissent and defiance. While that spirit did not turn immediately toward the controversy over Parliamentary taxation in the 1760s, it was very much active throughout that decade in a heated debate over taxation and representation. Samuel Hays II stepped into the center of that debate when he was elected as one of the selectmen of Simsbury in December 1768.

Salmon Brook had always had spokesmen among the town selectmen, since each geographical "squadron" of the town had its own selectman. For some time though, this had seemed hardly important. After the turmoil of the 1720s and 1730s, which had been resolved by land grants and division into separate ecclesiastical societies, there were few issues dividing Simsbury's different settlements. Each ecclesiastical society collected the bulk of the taxes people in that society paid and spent the money on local schooling, the minister's salary, and upkeep of the meetinghouse. The town rate was relatively modest and most men worked off their highway tax on their own roads each spring.

Yet, in 1768, civil relationships were deteriorating between the people of First Society of Simsbury and the inhabitants of the northwestern parish over the issue of taxes. Growth was catching up with the town. A large number of people were living in what used to be its frontier regions. The town meeting responded to growing pressure for land by granting the last of its commons scattered about the town, but these grants were made only to heirs of inhabitants of the 1720s. Increasing numbers put a strain not only on the natural resources, but also on the availability of credit, space in meetinghouses, and the ability of local government to keep up with emerging problems such as the need for schools, regulation of stray animals, the building and upkeep of roads and bridges, and the care of a growing number of paupers. Town government continued to become more complex. To the usual list of offices (listers, surveyors of highways, fenceviewers, and howards) were added leathersealers, packers of beef, packers of pork, packers of "tabacca," and branders of horses, creating a bureaucracy that must have taken hours to elect on an annual basis.[33]

In particular, more people were calling on the government for improvements in roads and bridges. The residents in the outlands were anxious that the town survey new roads in their districts where they would more willingly work off their yearly highway tax. When it came to bridges, though, those same outlanders were opposed to public expenditures on facilities that could be maintained by tolls. Until the 1760s private firms or individuals had taken care of ferries and bridges across the Farmington River. Between 1767 and 1770 merchants in the south part of town, who seem to have enjoyed some influence in the legislature, battled unsuccessfully against a coalition of people from other parts of town to raise taxes for the building of free bridges over the Farmington River. Numerous adjournments indicate how heated the debate became. The outlanders also tried to have the site of the town meeting changed on a number of occasions, no doubt to make it more convenient for them to collect majorities to fight increased taxes.[34]

Many of the town's rank and file, particularly at Salmon Brook, were probably experiencing some financial duress at the time. Settlement of the western hills still continued apace, but surely that was stretching the budgets of the young people who had little to their name but the rocks and trees and the lots those rocks and trees marked off. No matter how much they were involved in the world of commerce as producers of surplus, they were not eager to pay extra taxes for bridges ten miles from their farms. In 1765, for example, John Halladay had to sell a majority of the interest in his mill place to Simeon Baxter, a wealthy land speculator. Probably everyone was affected by the tremendous hailstorm in the summer of 1768, which ruined fruit trees, gardens, animals, and whole fields of grain. To top it off, the damaged glass in the houses could not be easily replaced, since glass was one of the products port-town merchants had been boycotting. In general, the Townshend Duty boycotts must have driven prices up on manufactured goods before the repeal by Parliament in 1770.[35]

Samuel Hays was not exactly suffering during this time. It was in 1769 that he built a new house that was more suitable for an up-and-coming community leader. No doubt being a manufacturer of cider and cider brandy during a tea boycott helped some. His perhaps liberal dispensing of those products at his new and impressive house, along with his leadership of the opposition to bridges, had its effect. In the local militia he rose to the rank of lieutenant in 1770, and captain in 1773. In church affairs he continued to be a leading figure, serving regularly on the Prudential Committee and, after

1770, on the committee to deal with the issue of whether to repair the society's meetinghouse or rebuild it at a new location.[36]

It was not an easy time to be a church leader in Salmon Brook, however. As comfortable as he and some of the sons of early families were, he was not rich. Most people of his community, in fact, continued to struggle through hard times in the early 1770s. They fought against renewed efforts to build bridges in the south end of town and bridled at increased taxes to support growing numbers of "indigents and debtors." A serious cankerworm infestation in 1771 and 1772 ruined their orchards and further complicated their problems.[37] Building a new meetinghouse would be an expensive proposition, particularly if it was to accommodate a fast-growing population. Then there was the question of where to put it, since the center of population had shifted north and west with the settlement of the western hills. And finally, would the meetinghouse be "seated"? That is, would its congregants sell pews at different prices as a fund-raising technique, relying on the sense of social distinction that might not sit well with some, to solve their financial problems?

These issues were touchy subjects for Salmon Brook farmers, and yet, through all the arguing and bickering for the next five years, Hays held on to his seat on the Prudential Committee. What is more, this was a good time for the church itself. Reverend Strong's continued support of singing and the abandonment of segregated seating by gender met with approval. Where there had been only nine professions of faith between 1761 and 1769, there were that many admitted every year over the next six years. Even some former radicals like Nathaniel Higley rejoined the church at this time. Essentially what was happening in Salmon Brook was that the church was becoming a truly popular institution, even at a most stressful moment. Hays, while in the background of much of this change, was surely influential. It was he, after all, who brought members of the County Court to Salmon Brook in the spring of 1775 and kept them at his house until they, at last, pitched a stake for the new meetinghouse at a spot the majority could accept.[38] He had become central to his community, perhaps understanding as well as anyone its continuing need for autonomy.

It is not surprising, then, at a time when people were thinking about preventing their tax money from being spent on projects several miles to the south, that they would begin to consider turning their ecclesiastical society into a separate town. A petition from a group of people north of the Simsbury town line in "the Wedge" provided the impetus for a separation movement. The Wedge was a somewhat undefined area that had been the subject of some dispute between Massachusetts and Connecticut because of a mistake in surveying the boundary between the two colonies in the seventeenth century. By 1713 a corrected line had been established that included this area within Connecticut, but not as part of any town. In 1768 there were over forty families living in this "colony land" who had found "by experience that the said Tracts of land when cleared from the heavy timber &c are good and profitable Tillage and pasture &c and may well answer the Expectation of the Farmers and Husbandmen" who would come to populate the area and need schools and a church. They, therefore, asked to be incorporated as a town. When the legislature balked at the idea because the proposed community was too small, leaders from Salmon Brook jumped in with their own proposal to make a town out of the Northwest Society and the Wedge combined. "The Wedge," they asserted, "is presently in great measure without Law and order where (there being no Town nor civil Officers) anyone may avoid distbusting [sacrificing] anything for the defraying of publick Charges and with impunity do what is right in his own Eyes; and the public worship is quite utterly neglected and the Place is become infamous as a Nest for spurious Births." And since many people of the Northwest Society could not "without great labor and Difficulty attend the public meetings of the Town and Freemen in said Simsbury," it made sense to create a new town of about 160 households. The description of the householders to the north of the Simsbury boundary was certainly not very flattering. A number of people there were part of a newly formed Anglican congregation led by Rev. Roger Viets, so their morality was probably dubious to the Salmon Brook Congregationalists. It is hard to say how convinced the petitioners were of the truth of their assertions, though, since the arguments were obviously put forth to convince the legislature of the need for a town government.[39]

After summoning the selectmen of Simsbury to answer, the legislature ignored the matter again. In Connecticut, the freemen of every town were allowed two representatives in the assembly, and the legislature was a little hesitant to allow these additional votes unless the area represented was roughly equivalent in population to other towns in the colony. Three years passed and the same group put forth basically the same argument, but this time asked that the Wedge be annexed to the town of Simsbury, adding that the children of the families in the Wedge were growing up without an education.

Some in the south part of Simsbury who opposed the Northwest Society becoming a separate town were suspicious that this was the first step toward detaching Salmon Brook from Simsbury. They called the whole effort "only a scheme of Judah Holcomb Esq. and some of his neighbors at Salmon Brook who live Northward of the center of s^d Society in order to bring the meeting house which they are about to build nearer to them." Although the annexation of the Wedge in 1775 did result in the placement of the new meetinghouse closer to Judah Holcomb's house, the primary motive of the Salmon Brook petitioners was, indeed, to enlarge the ecclesiastical society to the point where it could be considered of sufficient numbers and wealth to qualify as a town.[40]

The next step after annexation of the Wedge to Salmon Brook would have been to petition for separation, but matters of larger scope became distracting. In the spring of 1774 news arrived that Lord North's ministry had pushed through a series of measures devoted to punishing Boston for the "tea party" of the previous December. Among these strictures was an act closing the port there until the East India Company was paid for the destroyed tea, and another putting an end to town meetings in Massachusetts that did anything other than elect officers. This brought cries of indignation from all over the Atlantic seaboard.[41]

Until this point, Simsbury had largely ignored, officially at least, the conflict with Parliament while worrying about its own problems building bridges and roads, taking care of its debtors and paupers, and maintaining its churches. But in the summer of 1774, a special town meeting responded forcefully: "This meeting taking into consideration the unhappy Difference and Contention arisen Between the British Ministry and the Province of Massachusetts Bay especially the Arbitrary Proceedings against the Town of Boston by the Act called the Boston Port Bill and . . . blocking up their Harbour Stopping their trade etc and consedering our near connections with said Province and how much our Trade and interest is affected thereby Do Judge ourselves loudly called upon to make the following Declarations and Resolves." The constituents noted that, in spite of their loyalty and willingness to contribute constitutionally to the welfare of the empire, the Parliament was violating their charter and the rights of Englishmen in general, passing taxes illegally without the consent of those being taxed, and placing the people of Boston "under the cruel hand of oppression and arbitrary government." In response they determined to contribute to the relief of Boston, and to support the Continental Association established by the Continental Congress to boycott British goods. They then set up a Committee of Correspondence to keep the flames of rebellion burning bright and to collect donations to be sent to Boston.[42]

Salmon Brook people, of course, were no strangers to resisting authority and claiming independence. "We hear from Simsbury," read a report in the *Connecticut Courant*, "that a number of the most respectable inhabitants of Salmon-Brook society, being deeply affected with the present melancholy state of affairs, on account of the unconstitutional proceedings of the British Parliament with regard to American Liberty—Met together, as well to display their loyalty to the King, as their united zeal for the Support of the darling Liberty, which is the birth right of every American, as well as Englishman; and after having erected a stately pole as an ensign of Liberty; they formed themselves into a circle round the tree, and having a table well furnish'd with liquors of various kinds, a number of loyal toasts were drank;—after which everyone repair'd to his usual employ, the whole was conducted with the greatest decency and good order."[43] What was probably most newsworthy about this gathering in the eyes of many in Hartford was that the inhabitants of Salmon Brook, having consumed sufficient quantities of alcohol, were still capable of "decency and good order." Perhaps the outlanders there were trying to make a good impression. Whatever the case, the Coercive Acts, the network of correspondence committees, and a town resolution had struck a chord with people in Salmon Brook who surely felt that a protest against the Parliament was consistent with their own desire for communal independence.

By the end of 1774 these respectable inhabitants had returned to the business of asserting their local autonomy. In December, the annual town meeting was the scene of considerable bickering over both expenditures and representation on the board of selectmen. After an angry "discourse" on the town debts, Captain Hays did get elected as one of the usual five selectmen. Then, two adjournments and much discussion later, the town added two more selectmen, one of whom lived in the western part of Salmon Brook Society (the parish's new name, now that the Wedge had been added). That may have been a compromise aimed at putting off the matter of Salmon Brook's separation as a town.[44]

In early 1775 more news of "intolerable acts" filled the papers, and protests and pamphlets became more incendiary. That Salmon Brook inhabitants read these reports and arguments is a certainty, for the print media were becoming thoroughly established in Connecticut. People from Salmon Brook even advertised in both the *Connecticut Courant* and the *American Mercury,* and one advertisement in the *Courant* showed Jonathan Humphrey, Simsbury's representative to the General Assembly in 1774, offering political pamphlets for sale. In addition, if Joseph Strong was anything like the vast majority of Congregational ministers across Connecticut, Salmon Brook people heard on a weekly or twice-weekly basis about the direct relationship between the British Parliament and the Anti-Christ who was planning the destruction of God's people of the Word. Shortly after the argument over representation among the selectmen at the 1774 annual election meeting, the town meeting set up a Committee of Inspection to enforce the boycotts rigidly.[45] But in April 1775, before spring planting and before the Continental Congress had reconvened to assess the situation, war erupted in Massachusetts. In a matter of days towns all over New England dispatched militia units to the aid of the farmers in the Boston area who were soon laying siege to the city.

In spite of the growing conflict (or, perhaps, inspired by it), there continued to be agitation for division of the town. At the December annual town meeting, the number of Simsbury's selectmen returned to five, Samuel Hays among them, but those assembled then voted that the "selectmen shall warn a town meeting before the 1st of May to consider dividing the town." War or no war, the people of Salmon Brook wanted to spend their tax money in Salmon Brook, take care of their own bridges and paupers, have their own leaders, and have town meetings closer to home. Before the appointed day for discussion on dividing the town, however, it was clear that these concerns would have to wait. In April 1776, considering "the present situation of Public Affairs," referring both to the war and to a smallpox epidemic then raging in Simsbury and throughout Connecticut, the town voted to defer doing anything about separation. The matter was not taken up again until after the war. In place of debating this issue, the town petitioned the legislature to help with the building of roads in the recently annexed Wedge.[46]

In the meantime, three companies of Simsbury militia had waited out the British and watched them depart from Boston. Then, in the summer of 1776, the call came to join the Continental Army in defense of New York. Captain Hays selected his men and marched them south to take part in what became known as "the panic of Kip's Bay." They had good reason to think the New York campaign would not be like Boston—that the British would arrive in force ready to redress their embarrassment in Boston. But they went anyway.

Until 1774 there really was no indication that anyone in Simsbury would consider the differences with Parliament a fighting matter. They had been too concerned with bridges and the location of town meetings, too worried about their crops and their mortgages. In 1774, though, the arm of imperial power reached inland. Lord North's ministry was threatening to take away their town meetings, to send their representatives home from Hartford, and to bar the export of items residents hoped to sell to their merchants. And what is more, this authority would not be dissuaded when people who had fought the French and had helped the empire grow prosperous raised objections or looked as though they might cause a stir. Reverend Strong might have brought up the matter of an American bishop or other evidence that Britain would interfere even with their churches.

The ambitions of the backcountry people of Salmon Brook to maintain the gospel in their own way, to secure their freeholds, and to set up their children on farms of their own had merged with the Whig pamphleteers' "zeal for the support of the darling liberty." To their long list of enemies and pests—wolves, creditors, French soldiers, French Indians, crows, proprietors, the ecclesiastical hierarchy, and First Society—people of Salmon Brook would now add the British ministry. It had become all one fight for the land and for autonomy. They had chosen Captain Hays, their champion in the debate over taxes, heir to the New Light legacy of heartfelt faith and congregationalism, and builder of a fine house with a cellar full of cider, to put forth their views forcefully in selectmen's meetings and in presenting petitions to the legislature. And now they chose him to lead them into battle. It is noteworthy that, having spent decades "quieting the minds" of these backcountry people, Connecticut's leaders were now happy to have them challenge authority, fight for equality and self-rule, and be suspicious that every government measure was an attack on the freeholds of a godly people. Connecticut's leadership had earned the loyalty of the backcountry by celebrating ideals that the backcountry people had been living for three generations.

4. In Our Corporate Capacity

On October 10, 1803, the selectmen of the town Granby, Connecticut (formerly the Salmon Brook and Turkey Hills ecclesiastical societies), convened a special town meeting to consider the act of the legislature that had lopped off a piece of their town and ceded it to Massachusetts to settle a boundary dispute. Since the state government had not consulted Granby in the matter and had ignored the objections of its leaders, the town meeting passed a series of fuming resolutions. Even though they recognized "the Duty of all good citizens to yield a ready and Cherfull support" to their government, they nevertheless believed that the act represented "a serious injury to the town in its Corporate Capacity & more especially to the Eclesiastical Society which by the opperation of said act is severd & perhaps broken up." They begged to "inquire wheather the ordinary Legislature of the State are vested with Constitutional powers to ceed a part of the Territory of this State so as to Place the Citizens living within the limits of the Ceded Tract under any Foreign Jurisdiction by subjecting them to Laws and Customs to them unknown and without their consent." What was the great "Publick Emergency," they asked, that should require "the Inhabitance of this Town as such or as members of the Eclesiastical Society to sacrifice so Great a partition of our substantial comfort and conveneance as the proposed measure of the Legislature if carried into Effect will inevitably Deprive us of?"[1]

Underneath the rhetoric, the fuss was all about some prime taxable property around the Congamond Ponds. Even so, the rhetoric itself is full of meaning. Granby people considered Massachusetts a "foreign jurisdiction." They condemned the "ordinary legislature" for its high-handed disregard of

the fundamental ideal of "consent." They also claimed to be champions of ecclesiastical unity. Of course, petitioners to a legislature are usually more interested in appealing to the sentiments of the legislators than in representing
their own. Connecticut's leadership consisted of a conservative Congregational
"Standing Order" that subscribed to notions of communal harmony dating to
the early Puritan settlements. Yale's president Timothy Dwight captured these
notions in his poem "Greenfield Hill," where he celebrated the ideal New England village, in which "smil'd / The heav'n-inviting church, and every town
/ A world within itself, with order, peace, / And harmony, adjusted all its
weal."[2] And so, in their "corporate capacity," the people of the town of Granby
tactfully complained that the legislature was ignoring their desire to create
their "world within itself." Many in town may have actually believed in this
vision.

Granby had not, however, reached a state of covenanted grace. Nor
was it a land of "order, peace and harmony," for, as their ancestors before
them, its residents themselves could not avoid challenging the authority
of the ordinary legislature. Between 1776 and the town's incorporation in
1786, the backcountry people fought hard in what they considered not just a
war for a new nation and political order, but more fundamentally a struggle
for their own independence and property rights. The town's incorporation
and a subsequent surge of economic growth might suggest that Salmon
Brook people had achieved their century-old goals. Growth and change,
however, led to even more internal turmoil, and the new town's leaders had
to work hard to establish order. All along, it seems, Salmon Brook people
had hoped to be part of the order, and not the turmoil, but the latter remained an indelible part of their political culture.

Winning Independence in "a Mellancole Time"

The community had known disorder and controversy, but for the people of
Salmon Brook the scale of it was far greater after 1776 than ever before. The
war did not come to Simsbury in the form of marching redcoats as it did to
some towns near Long Island Sound. It came, as for most rural New England
towns, in the form of shortages, requisitions for supplies, calls for soldiers to
fill the ranks of the Continental Army, a smallpox epidemic, rampant inflation, and constant interruptions in the ability of the workforce to make a living. Simsbury town records are filled with references to these problems.

Town committees sought beef cattle, grain, and clothing, and paid precious little in return. The most acute shortage was in salt, a necessity in a world without refrigerators. The School Committee was responsible for doling out what little salt was allotted to the town by the new State of Connecticut. At first it was proportioned equally per person, but a quantity was kept in reserve and used in 1778 to give extra to widows and the families of soldiers in the Continental service. As for smallpox inoculations, the town could afford to pay only for those administered to the town poor. Everyone else had to purchase his own, or risk infection. Alcohol abuse raged. In a town that was *still* paying bounties on dead wolves, conditions were deteriorating fast.[3]

"It is a mellancole Time," wrote Ensign Jonathan Pettibone's young wife, Hannah. Both her husband and their hired hand had gone off to New York in the summer of 1776, leaving her to care for their three children (including a newborn) and Jonathan's seriously ill father, who was supposed to be the regimental commander. "I feel very much troubled about you," she continued, "but I hope God will preserve you in all your dagers. I shall send you a pare of Stockings as quick as I can. . . . I can Hire Tom Tary but his prise is three pound a month and I cannot hire anybody els. Martha and Hannah send there love to their dady." "Father Pettibone" soon recovered and, before departing himself for New York, wrote additional testimony to his son regarding the stress and worry on the home front: "I take this oppertunity to Let you know your biseness goes on your Harves is got in all but your first crop of hay your hilling dun flax pulled your plowing som lys behind we do as well as we can but . . . what to do I know not."[4] Jonathan Sr. later became sick again while in New York, and he died in Rye as Jonathan Jr. was trying to bring him home. Considering that this was a fairly prosperous family living on good land in Weatogue, we can imagine what life was like for families at Salmon Brook who had men fighting in New York.

In Connecticut prices skyrocketed, even though few had money to pay for anything. Inflation between 1776 and 1779 was as much as 2,400 percent on some commodities. Apparently Rev. Joseph Strong, who had gone with the militia to New York and who continued to pull converts in dozens to the church, was not being paid, or was being paid in worthless currency. In February 1779, the society voted to set up "a committy to treat with the Revd Joseph Strong Respecting the unesiness that subsits between him and his people." Samuel Hays was on this committee, and served as moderator of the meetings that followed to try to devise some way to keep their minister of a quarter century. Yet Strong left the Salmon Brook Society, even though it offered to increase his salary, an increase apparently as worthless as the paper it was printed on.[5]

Raising troops for the Continental Army presented one of the more serious problems of the time. There were three classifications of soldiers in this war after 1776: those in the Continental Army under Washington and engaged in full-time service; "state troops," raised for specific regional campaigns by inducements from the state government; and local militia units, which had always existed. The militia units were based on the towns from which they came, were designed primarily for local protection, and elected their own officers. Before 1776 the Continental Army had been composed largely of militia units. This worked for bottling up a few regiments of British regulars in Boston, but when it came to pitched battle in an open field, the farmers and their elected officers were no match for trained troops disciplined to heed the orders of officers who never had to ask twice.

It is understandable, after the experience of the panic at Kip's Bay, that the town would have considerable difficulty filling its quota of recruits for the Continental line. The militia regiments responded on occasion to calls for units for particular campaigns, as did the Eighteenth in the spring of 1777 when Danbury was raided and burned. Simsbury men also furnished units at Saratoga, and in other campaigns in New York in 1778. At Saratoga, at least, they had played a pivotal role, for it was numbers and not so much fighting ability that had convinced General John Burgoyne to surrender.[6]

In general, it was very difficult to get men to serve when they were commanded by people they did not know. In March 1777, the town meeting informed the governor and the Committee of Safety of the State "that under the present Circumstances of the Inhabitants of this town that it appears very difficult to Raise ye soldiers in this Town to furnish our Quota for so long a term as 3 years or during the continuance of the present war." They asked, therefore, for permission "for the soldiers in this town to Inlist themselves to the number aforementioned for our Quota and to be formed into suitable Captains, Companies and they to have Liberty to chuse their own officers in a Regiment they shall chuse and to be holden in said service only for the term of Nine months."[7]

The governor and the committee were not sympathetic, and in September the town meeting was busily figuring out ways to entice individuals to serve in the army. It offered a salary of four pounds per month in addition to whatever Congress decided to pay (which would also be four pounds, the meeting hoped, and offered to make up the difference if it wasn't). The town was divided into a number of "classes," and each class was supposed to provide a soldier. How each came up with its soldier was up to its members. A solution for Ranna Cossitt and Ezra Holcomb of the north end of Salmon Brook was to go to Litchfield and purchase Philip, "a Negro . . . from Andrew Adams . . . and freed him for his agreeing to serve as a soldier in the Continental Army." This seemed to be an innovation at the time, since the selectmen had to ponder a bit before deciding that "he may answer for Continental Service." Philip, it should be noted, had the presence of mind to have the agreement registered in the Simsbury record books so that there would be no question when the war was over about his status.[8] Cossitt and Holcomb's "class" was lucky to be able to come up with the money. A number of other classes, particularly in Salmon Brook, remained delinquent throughout the war, unable to pay a recruit and unwilling to lose a farmhand.

When hostilities ceased in 1781, economic problems actually intensified. Inflation continued unabated as the state tried to pay its soldiers with worthless money or worthless land. Creditors, furthermore, would not accept paper money, no matter how much farmers complained in the state legislatures. Finally, the end of the war opened up land in western New York, Vermont, and even across the Appalachians for settlement by young ambitious people declaring their own independence from their families. Productivity on the New England farms correspondingly fell off as some farm families lost their prime labor force. Nathaniel Higley's children were among the earliest to set out for these new lands. Captain Samuel Hays incurred a significant debt to purchase Higley's and another sizable farm to encourage his two oldest sons to stay in Salmon Brook.[9]

When the town meeting returned to issues of internal improvements, the farmers of Salmon Brook were in no mood to consider them, and relations between Salmon Brook and First Society again became hostile. During the war, the town had built a bridge in its southwest corner that had yet to be funded, and had made an aborted attempt at a lottery for another bridge across the Farmington River. In an angry meeting in July 1781, Salmon Brook men won a vote to petition the legislature to divide the town, but a meeting the next year rescinded that vote. At that point the Salmon Brook people took matters into their own hands. On May 2, 1782, three selectmen of Simsbury (no doubt Samuel Hays, Timothy Cossitt, and Elisha Graham, all of whom favored separation) ordered a town meeting to be held at the meetinghouse in Salmon Brook Society. There was a good crowd of nearly a hundred voters there to begin with, and a narrow majority chose as moderator Asahel Holcomb, a justice of the peace from the Turkey Hills Society. As more people arrived at the meetinghouse, the minority began to agitate that the meeting was improper. Following a close vote to carry on "accordin to the said warning," the meeting selected two Salmon Brook men and Asahel Holcomb to petition the legislature to divide the town. In addition, they discussed "whether this meeting will proceed to Doom those Military Classes who have been Negligent in procurring a Continental Soldier ye year past." The outcome was a close negative vote (95 to 87). By then the meetinghouse was packed and debate had become quite lively. The next vote was to annul a 1767 resolution to hold meetings only in Hopmeadow, and to hold the next meeting in Turkey Hills. "The moderator says" that the next meeting will be in December, grumbled the clerk, who may have been forced to come to the meeting.[10]

The refusal to "doom" those classes who had not procured their Continental soldier is interesting, particularly in light of the issue's apparent relationship to dividing the town. The two northern ecclesiastical societies had allied themselves for the moment, and the alliance seems to have been based upon a determined resistance to outside interference in their affairs. They wanted to separate from Simsbury (and its expensive bridges), they thought it wrong that the state had forced them to procure soldiers for army units commanded by people they did not know, and they hoped to have at least some town meetings in their own areas in order to get the votes to continue to win on those issues.

At the December meeting, the rest of Simsbury must have pulled together a majority that would venture out to Turkey Hills, for they managed to repeal all of the measures passed in May. The 1783 annual town meeting was again the scene of quarreling, this time over the issue of bonus payments to Continental officers. The United States Congress had recently passed a bill to give the officers five years full pay in place of a pension. People in every state were in an uproar about this special bonus. Together with the emergence of the Society of the Cincinnati, the bonus suggested that a cabal of professional soldiers was trying to create a national aristocracy. In Simsbury, where most of the soldiers had served in the militia and would not be eligible for this benefit, the town meeting resolved to oppose the plan and to send delegates to a statewide protest convention in Middletown. The protest probably emerged from Salmon Brook initially, for none of its residents were Continental Army officers. The next year the town even considered refusing to pay state taxes because of this issue. Samuel Hays got himself elected collector of state taxes for the town that year—perhaps to keep anyone else from actually collecting them.[11]

Again in January 1785, Salmon Brook inhabitants brought the separation issue before the town and lost a close but well-attended vote (172 to 149). The following year they tried again, and won. In the October session the legislature divided the town north and south, with Turkey Hills and Salmon Brook joining to form the new town of Granby. A good part of the Turkey Hills Society actually did not want to become part of the new town. In the 1730s they had outnumbered the residents of Salmon Brook and had petitioned for one northern ecclesiastical society. But now the Salmon Brook Society had grown to be nearly twice as populous as that of Turkey Hills, even though the Turkey Hills farmers had much more valuable property. This group did not look forward to being taxed to pay for the many roads, bridges, and paupers of the Salmon Brook Society. In fact, in December 1786, the first Granby town meeting elected Judah Holcomb as clerk, and Captain Samuel Hays, Lieutenant Pliny Hillyer, and Asahel Holcomb as selectmen. All but the last were inhabitants of Salmon Brook Society.[12]

Thus, after a bitter fight in melancholy times, two ecclesiastical societies separated themselves from Simsbury and joined, uneasily, as the town of Granby. The majority in this town consisted of people who had a long history of resistance to outside authority and a devotion to autonomy. It was hardly surprising that their delegate to the 1788 convention to consider Connecticut's ratification of the Constitution of the United States voted "no." Even if Hezekiah Holcomb personally had liked the new national government, he knew his constituents and how habitually suspicious they were of distant authorities, including the state government fifteen miles away in Hartford and the Simsbury government in Hopmeadow. In fact, they had been incensed when the state allowed them but one delegate to that convention and one representative in the legislature. Each town normally got two, but there were so many new towns hiving off in the 1780s that the state's leadership was unwilling to begin filling the House of Representatives with men elected from towns like Granby.

As Asahel Holcomb thumped the gavel at the first "town meeting of the inhabitens of Granby" in December 1786, rebellion raged just to

the north in western Massachusetts. The sentiments of "Regulators" like
Daniel Shays were not unlike those felt by the majority of the militiamen
in Granby. Farmers were hard pressed to pay their taxes and other debts,
good money was scarce, and aristocrats seemed bent on taking over the
government and abandoning the ideals of the revolution. And the hard
times continued. Samuel Hays, newly elected deacon of the Congregational Church, was engaged in a difficult search for a minister, and he may
even have personally paid for and remodeled a house to attract one.[13] Yet
his militiamen were now gathering at their own meetinghouse to determine their own town's affairs. At their next freeman's meeting they would
elect their own representative who would carry a petition to Hartford and
agitate successfully for a second representative. No one had come to fine
those who had not paid for their Continental soldier. Indeed, they had secured a lot of what they wanted, thanks to the willingness of those in Hartford to let them go their own way. So they did not march on Hartford as
the Shaysites laid siege to the Springfield armory. After decades of resistance to every authority imaginable, their minds were quiet and settled in
peace.

Prosperity

After the town's incorporation in 1786, there was yet more reason to be content. Granby's economy experienced a dramatic turn for the better, owing
largely to accelerated population growth. Between 1770 and 1790 the two ecclesiastical societies that became the town more than doubled in size, to
nearly twenty-six hundred people, making Granby as populous as any rural
town in Hartford County, and not all that far behind Hartford itself. Both
natural increase and in-migration contributed to this growth. Underneath
the expansion in numbers was even more dramatic change in the composition of the population. In fact, a close look at the lists of family heads in 1790
and 1800 shows that there was an astonishing level of in- and out-migration,
which the slight increase of 140 people between 1790 and 1800 disguises. More
than half of the heads of families in the 1800 census were not listed in the
1790 census, and similarly more than half of those listed in 1790 were no
longer listed in 1800. While some of this was due to mortality and coming of
age, it is clear that the face of Granby changed considerably in the last two
decades of the eighteenth century.[14]

As Granby's population changed in the years after its separation from Simsbury, its economy boomed. It is impossible to develop the sort of statistics we have today on overall production of goods and services and business income and profits, but surviving town records and business accounts contain considerable testimony on the extent and nature of economic growth at the time. The town was alive with enterprise and prosperity. Craftsmen opened new businesses, lumbermen were busier than ever, farmers trooped into the county court to acquire tavernkeepers' licenses, people began clustering together in small village centers of trade and manufacturing, and those who made early profits began to look for even larger and more ambitious investment opportunities.[15]

An example of one of these entrepreneurs is the charismatic James Huggins, who settled in the newly coalesced village of West Granby in 1783. A war veteran from New Haven, recently married to a woman from Wallingford, he came to West Granby a man of regional contacts and great ambition. He and a business partner from Southwick, Massachusetts, bought controlling interest in the Strattons' mill business above the gorge. Huggins saw a bright future in the west village of Granby. He moved in and began operating the grist mill and at least three different shops—a distillery, a triphammer shop, and a wire shop (for carding machine wire). There in the 1780s he and his wife went about the business of launching their family into prosperity—no easy task in what was still a thinly settled, rock-strewn world of hills and forest. By 1790, they were a success—enough to hire three laborers for the mills and to build a new house.[16]

Quite a few other people from the outside found Granby and its fast-running brooks attractive. As of 1790, in addition to the Hayes, Holcomb, and Halladay families, who had been building their farms around the gorge since before the revolution, there were now Joab Griffin, originally of Turkey Hills, Giles Hickock, Lemuel Kilbourn, Sadoce Wilcox, Philo Kilbourn, Elnathan Strong, and Asher Frank, an African-American Revolutionary War veteran. Lemuel Kilbourn had been in the clothier business and Sadoce Wilcox was a blacksmith. Other tradesmen, including a shoemaker, a hatter, and operators of a bark mill (for tanning) and a sawmill, soon followed. During the 1790s the population of West Granby was growing so rapidly that a group of investors sank fifteen hundred dollars into the construction of a new mill at the old Halladay mill site. This firm was something new for this area, for none of its proprietors actually lived in West Granby. The grist mill must have been a success in this period of growth in West Granby, for the value of the property grew by 67 percent in the first four years of its operation.[17]

Along with new farmers, millers, and craftsmen, the village also housed a growing industry: manufactured clothing. Surviving land records do not include the deed by which clothier Alpheus Hayes acquired an advantageous location on the bank of Salmon Brook, but the Granby town records provide a valuable clue to the dramatic change that was taking place in West Granby in the 1790s. In 1794, the town meeting approved "the Doings of the Select men in Laying out a Road from Joab Griffens to Mr. Nahum Holcombs." There already was a north—south road from Joab Griffin's land to Nahum Holcomb's. However, that road, surveyed back in 1769, ran among farmers' fields. The new road ran along the brook. From land records of the early 1800s, we learn the reason for this change. Alpheus Hayes had erected a new dam just below the sawmill dam, and was using water power to drive a fulling mill (for making felt), a dressing shop and dye works, and a clothing shop. He probably purchased wool carded in Huggins's or some other shop and spun and woven by neighboring farm families, dressed and dyed it, softened some of it into felt, and created clothing from the finished cloth. The survey-ing of a new route for the road along the brook and between his shops and his new house signifies that this was a major operation, at least as ambitious in scope as the new grist mill had been.[18]

As the area around the old "Halladay Mill Place" changed from a col-lection of farms into a recognizable village, more families set up homesteads among the surrounding hills. Surely they profited initially from the timber they struggled to remove from their lands, as had the generation before them when people first began living in this part of town before the revolution. With more building than ever going on throughout the town, they had a ready mar-ket for lumber without the need to deal with river-town merchants. Some dips among the hills actually contained arable land when cleared. Where the to-pography proved too rugged, craggy, or rock-strewn for the plow, farmers learned to specialize: the carding and the clothing shops down on the brook were as eager for their wool as the grist mills were for their grain, so they raised sheep in abundance. Without fail, probate inventories from the period generally list a small collection of anywhere from five to twenty-five sheep in every farmer's holdings. In addition, settlers here found that boulders held heat well, and although late spring frosts might ruin a potential crop of apples for their lowland-dwelling neighbors, their hilltop blossoms often survived unscathed. Those with the knowledge and skills built cider mills and distilleries, and made a good living participating in the growing market for cider brandy. Thomas Buckland Gillet, typical of a good many, had bought some craggy parcels of land in the hills just west of the village around the time of the revolution. After the war, he and his wife Rhoda moved up onto this land, planted their orchard, fenced off their sheep pasture, harvested lumber, erected a cider mill, and raised ten children in a small dwelling.[19]

So good were times for people in West Granby that even those young farmers who had had to settle in these hills before the revolution because it was the only land available had no inclination to leave for better land. In the hills west of the Gillets, Timothy and Mary Willcockson Cossitt had built a homestead before the revolution on a lot on the Barkhamsted town line. Cossitt was a millwright who had operated a saw mill. By the 1790s, he and his two sons, Timothy Jr. and Martin, had created quite a farming and milling establishment in the hills on the western edge of town. His estate record in 1795 is testimony to considerable prosperity. His furniture included feather beds, a dropleaf table and several chairs; among the rest of the inventory were listed pewterware, silver shoe and knee buckles, linen tablecloths and curtains, a sizable herd of cattle, seventeen sheep, a large stock of cider, an array of tools, some silk clothing, spinning wheels and looms, horses, pigs, and over a hundred acres of land to himself, not to mention similarly sized farmsteads owned by his sons. In the same neighborhood a number of other farmers, starting out with very modest homesteads, enjoyed similar success.[20] The topography that had once presented so many obstacles now seemed to contain only opportunities as ambitious farmers turned profits from trades and cash crops.

Other sections of town also experienced growth around the turn of the century. Ever since the tea boycott, apple cider and cider brandy had become one of Granby's principal industries. Samuel Hays and his son Seth continued to run their mill at Samuel's distinctive house, and in North Granby nearly every farmer had a distillery—whether he had a tavern or not. Even farmers who did not run stills grew plenty of surplus apples to sell to those who did. As a result, areas of town that might look today as though they could never support more than a few hill farmers hummed with activity. Aaron Post and Benajah Holcomb's taverns on the top of Popatunuck Mountain were nestled among a bustling neighborhood. Benajah Hills, an African-American blacksmith, moved in, financing a shop with Aaron Post.[21]

In the old Salmon Brook village, now called Granby Center, two men accumulated veritable fortunes engaging in a variety of businesses. Colonel Ozias Pettibone, who had moved to the village from lower Simsbury before the revolution, owned not only a major share of the West Granby grist mill but also several dwelling houses and nearly a thousand acres of land spread out around Granby (and a farm in Litchfield County). His personal inventory in 1813 filled nine pages of the probate record book and was valued at $22,373.70. He also had the distinction of being one of Granby's two slave owners at the turn of the century. His wealth was a result of years of careful attention to real estate investment, lawyer's work, storekeeping, cash-crop farming, and cider production (when he died, he had more than 150 barrels of cider in stock). A reference in his estate to "money in the loan office in Hartford" suggests the scope and type of his investment activities.[22]

Pliny Hillyer, Pettibone's partner during the 1770s, discovered after the war that there was so much growth in Granby that he could go into business for himself. He had studied law, often serving the town as selectman, town meeting moderator, and representative to the General Assembly, and manufactured cider and cider brandy. Even with his old partner as a competitor, though, his store occupied the majority of his time. In the 1790s, he took a partner himself. As well as being a licensed "spirits" dealer, Hillyer and Curtiss sold glass, wool cards, silverware, hats, gloves, cloth, buttons, kitchen utensils and gadgets, sheet lead, china tea sets, chamber pots, wine glasses, "Irish linen," tools, hardware, coffee, tea, spices, tobacco, and, to service Granby's building boom, nails by the cask. To acquire these items, they sent agents to Hartford, Boston, and New York carrying wagonloads of rye, corn, wool, cider brandy, beef, pork, and cheese, which local farmers brought to them in exchange for their new standard of living. From Hillyer's papers it is also apparent that he acted as a pawnbroker, lending money and holding as collateral such things as Thompson Kimberly's saddle (worth, it would appear, $9.86). Furthermore, his store seems to have served as a local clearinghouse for IOUs that farmers passed among one another in place of currency.[23]

Regardless of how much this local economy expanded, it was still, and would continue to be, plagued by a shortage of hard currency. Farmers, artisans, and merchants operated through an elaborate bookkeeping system in which debts would be kept on account books for years at a time, sometimes not settled with cash until after a person's death. Every so often among their papers or accounts would appear the notation "Reckoned and Setteled all our privet book akounts from the Beginning of the world to this Day and Ballanced Even by us," as brothers Increase and Nahum Holcomb declared in October 1794. Such a reckoning might involve the exchange of a few pennies after years of trading goods and services, or, more commonly, a passing on of IOUs from other cash-poor, commodity-rich farmers. In such an economy, a Pliny Hillyer was essential to help move accounts and IOUs around in a more orderly and efficient manner. And Hillyer was just one of four or five storekeepers in town.[24]

In every corner of the new town, mill wheels turned, grindstones spit out corn and rye flour, saws turned out fashioned planks, clapboards, and shingles, hammers banged against anvils, barnyards and pastures teemed with animals, men and women labored over clattering looms, oxen slogged through fields, grinders chewed up apples to be pressed for cider, stills and tanning pots gurgled, and wagons lumbered across rough tracks known as "the traveled roads" even before selectmen had a chance to survey them for town upkeep. Granby was on the cutting edge of a new world of commercial prosperity.

A New Order

One would think that a blooming economy such as this would mandate an era of peace and contentment for all the people of Granby. This was hardly the case. Even though townspeople of all classes, occupations, and backgrounds seemed to live side by side, sharing in the opportunities of the new age, everyone could see that this was not an age of peace and quiet, nor of consensus on matters of public policy or even private morality and belief. The revolution had ushered in an age of disorder, to which Granby's leaders responded, paradoxically, with concern. In the heady years of the early republic, some of those who enjoyed the benefits of economic expansion tended to distance themselves from an older world that still clung hopefully to a rough egalitarianism.

One of the more disconcerting developments in postrevolutionary Granby was the weakening of the ecclesiastical bond that Rev. Joseph Strong and church leaders had worked so hard to create in the 1750s and 1760s. Strong had left in a huff in 1779, disenchanted by his flock's unwillingness to support the preaching of the gospel with anything but devalued currency.

His eventual replacement, in 1784, was Israel Holly, who struggled for a decade with a congregation divided by petty squabbles and personal animosities. In spite of Granby's rapidly growing population, church attendance actually declined precipitously during Holly's tenure. In 1794, a younger group of lay leaders injected a fresh burst of enthusiasm into the society, resulting in decisions to enlarge and paint the interior of the meetinghouse, to "dignify the pews," and to settle a new minister, Rev. Isaac Porter.[25]

A 1788 Yale graduate, Porter had been a student of the popular tutor Timothy Dwight, who would become the college's president shortly after Porter settled in Granby. Religion, for Dwight, was the basis of morality, peace, and order in a society. He greatly feared the ideas of Thomas Jefferson, who called for an end to state-supported churches. Disestablishment, thought Dwight, was a veiled and misguided effort on the part of atheists to distract men from their duty and upset the order God had determined for society. Porter was also mindful of a recent call from the Hartford North Association for "a concert of prayer for the revival of religion." Although it is ironic that this council's predecessors had once been so unwilling to accept evangelical ministers in their midst, fifty years and a revolution had created even more threatening circumstances for the survival of the Bible commonwealth. Now the local ministers welcomed revival meetings.[26]

Porter took up the established church's call for religious revival with a passion that must have been satisfying to the New Light spirit that still lingered in the Salmon Brook congregation. From what little we have of his sermon notes, we discern regular preaching on the depravity of mankind and the need to embrace a Second Great Awakening. In one sermon he warned his parishioners that it was impossible for those "to escape everlasting punishment who neglect this gospel salvation." He reminded his audience that all who forgot Christ's suffering and death were "guilty of the blackest ingratitude towards him," and would surely meet with an ugly fate. "Mankind are in a great measure insensible of their situation," he lamented. "They are insensible of the importance of closing in with the offers of salvation they have not the least vestage of holiness remaining in them: . . . they are dead in trespasses and sins—Eyes have they but they see not ears have they but they hear not and their foolish hearts are darkened." If they were aware of their depravity for a minute, he insisted, they would "cease to be guilty of that stupidity and negligence towards religion that they now are."[27] Soon new communicants came forth to profess their faith, and church elders satisfied themselves that they had found the answer to their problems.

Calling forth miscreants of all kinds to make their peace with the church, Porter quickly established himself as a stern and forceful leader determined to restore the "church disciplyne" that had been absent too long. Fornicators, quarrelers, drunkards, and chronic absentees: all had to face the congregation and make heartfelt promises to change their ways. He even charged fines on absentees who were not church members. Unfortunately, for a good many, his passion backfired. There were quite a few who muttered about the excesses of "Priest Porter." Some tavernkeepers felt that his campaign against intoxication might limit their income. And then there were many who simply did not enjoy hearing constantly about the doctrine of election or their sinful condition. Although he made converts of many single women, newly admitted male church members were few.[28] Furthermore, attendance declined because there were alternatives, particularly with the creation of an Episcopal church in the commercial center of town.

In spite of harassment from the Congregationalists in both Hopmeadow and Salmon Brook during the revolution, Rev. Roger Viets had led a popular Episcopal (formerly Anglican) church until his departure for Nova Scotia in 1787. Thereafter, his St. Andrew's Church below the Falls struggled to survive, and his St. Ann's mission at Salmon Brook disappeared, perhaps because the bulk of its congregation consisted of hill farmers who lived at the far northern end of the parish. After a few years, though, some Granby Episcopalians began to meet and decided to build a new meetinghouse near Pliny Hillyer's house and store. This project took a few years, but by 1798 it was completed, and the St. Andrew's parish voted to divide in two, the Granby-based group to become St. Peter's Church. According to laws passed in Connecticut since the turmoil of the 1740s, persons of different denominations could be excused from both attendance and taxes assessed by the congregational ecclesiastical societies as long as they could present a certificate from their minister saying they were regularly attending their alternate church and paying for its support. By 1790, Connecticut's leading Episcopalians, some of whom were among the most prominent citizens in the state, had persuaded the legislature to refund their churches a portion of state taxes that were used to support the established church's county associations. It was almost as though there were two established churches in Connecticut. In this environment St. Peter's congregation grew quickly in Salmon Brook village.[29]

Even without favored treatment, though, people of yet other denominations maintained separate churches in Granby. Not only did the Baptists struggle on in their own independent way, but also Methodism emerged as a new faith. In the 1780s and 1790s Methodism represented a reaction against the perceived worldliness and lack of vitality in the more established churches. Probably some of those who complained about Joseph Strong's salary during the revolution were future Methodists. Before 1800 there was only a small number of converts in Connecticut, but among them was a group of people who lived along the western border of Granby. Itinerant preachers of the Granville, Massachusetts, circuit found these people had an appetite for a more populist brand of religion—they were tired of being talked down to by their more educated Congregational and Episcopalian ministers, and, like the early pioneers to Salmon Brook, felt a mild degree of alienation from the neighborhoods that had been settled longer. One Methodist society was organized in Barkhamsted just west of the Granby town line, and people who trudged into the hills to this center of heresy encouraged the ministers to spread their preaching into surrounding villages. By 1799 a Methodist society was meeting in a farmer's barn in West Granby.[30] Only fragmentary and cryptic references to these dissenting groups remain today, but they were there, brazenly defying the status quo in their insistence that religion come to them.

Another disruptive trend in the 1790s was the beginning of an exodus of emigrants departing for lands west of the Appalachians. As Granby's many newcomers and young people coming of age took their places in the town, a steady trickle of adventurous young souls packed up their worldly possessions to seek cheaper or better land. The exodus had begun, actually, on the heels of the Revolutionary War, when quite a few young families from Granby moved to Vermont. The upper Connecticut Valley offered tempting land, and the Treaty of Paris had assured, supposedly, some security to Americans moving to the frontier. In Granby, these children of large families could look forward only to small pieces of the 100–150 acre farms their parents owned. Emigrants soon looked as well to backcountry Pennsylvania, to Ohio, where land sold for twenty-five cents an acre in 1796, or to western New York State. From Canandaigua, New York, in 1800, Sylvanus Holcomb wrote to his brother Nahum of West Granby: "Enjoyed a god stat of helth

Sence we Left your hous and Had a good gurney all our way til we Got to the Ginesea and when we arrivd to our brothers was received with goy and Have ate out of one stove sence . . . have Six hogs that i expect to fat for my family and expect to have one hundred bushel of Corn . . . the small debts that you rote to me is a ly the pease and rum we had and the pig i paid . . . and the gun is at Mr. Benona buttles house . . . Seth gave us 15 lbs wool & i have 150 weight flax."[31] Although it is not clear who was calling in the disputed debts, one cannot help noting the impact of distance and the finality of separation implicit in Sylvanus's letter. Even siblings settling their affairs could be an unsettling process.

For those who remained in Granby, the turmoil of the revolutionary years also reached deep into the marrow of everyday life. Increasing contentiousness is evident in the bills for serving writs, writing letters, and arguing lawsuits and executions recorded in the account books of a growing cadre of local lawyers. The story of Hannah Phelps of Popatunuck is a good illustration of a world that community leaders might view as coming unhinged. The daughter of a man who had, himself, had to "make his peace" with Roger Viets's church for committing adultery, she married Joel Buttolph at the tender age of fifteen, in July 1773, and gave birth to their first child in December. (She did, in fact, live in that "Nest of spurious births" at the north end of the Salmon Brook Society.) After Joel died prematurely in 1786, she and her *new* husband, Aaron Post, marched into probate court and refused to accept the terms of Joel's will, by which she would not inherit any of Joel's estate if she remarried. Instead, she demanded the traditional "widow's thirds," to be added to the land she would soon inherit as the only (legitimate) child of Hezekiah Phelps. When Aaron died in 1810, she held clear title to her own land, as well her widow's thirds of his, and maintained control of it until her death four decades later. Even her son had to be content with building his new tavern on her land.[32] Sanctions against premarital sex, obedience to her husband's last wishes, deference to the norm of men being the property owners—Hannah had little use for these shackles of a former order. As Granby filled rapidly with new faces, new ambition, and new enterprises, surely there was not a little nervousness among its elite about what greater changes the future held in store.

Some of those new faces, in fact, were of a very different hue from those to which prerevolutionary residents had been accustomed. Before the war there were a few enslaved African Americans in the Salmon Brook Society, all

owned by the merchant Ozias Pettibone. The gradual emancipation law of
1783 did not affect their status, but another small group of free African Americans had moved into town by then. These were mostly the families of former
slaves who had enlisted in the Continental Army on condition of being freed
after the war, like Philip Negro, who had agreed to serve for the class of Granby
men who had paid for his freedom. Some worked trades, like the blacksmith
Benajah Hills, with whom Hannah Post's second husband entered into a partnership. Others worked family farms, and some were laborers who boarded
with white families. John and Phoebe Freeman married in 1792 and raised a
family of six children over the next twenty years. James Fuller married Eleanor
Freebody sometime around 1780 and raised their family in Granby. She died
young of consumption, but he lived in town until 1810, apparently well enough
off at one point to take in the pauper Asher Frank, a black war veteran. Even
though these people may have maintained a low profile, they served as re-
minders that the world was changing rapidly.[33]

The most public contentions of the time concerned the ongoing disputes between the Turkey Hills Society and the Salmon Brook Society to the
west. These turned largely on the growing expense of constructing roads and
bridges, and the taxes needed to pay for them. The new town was responsible
for two long bridges across the Farmington River, nine additional "framed
Bridges," and a great number of smaller plank bridges, all of which needed
rebuilding at least every decade. As town taxes climbed precipitously in the
early 1790s, Turkey Hills residents requested that the legislature divide the
town. Their list was twice the value of Salmon Brook Society's, they complained, yet they had only half the people, and nowhere near the number of
roads and bridges. Year in and year out the conflict continued. It was true
that the western part had many more bridges, steeper grades, more abundant
groundwater, more serious problems with spring runoff, and far less money
to pay for the roads' maintenance.[34] It was disturbing enough to have the
church fragmented, young people moving away, new faces everywhere, and
customs challenged. To have every town meeting divided by resentment
over taxes surely worried leaders of the new town.

As turbulence and contention gripped every aspect of life in the years
after the revolution, the community's leaders sought various ways to bring
calm to the situation. A seemingly minor change in public policy should be
seen in this light. At a special town meeting in March 1797, the town passed

"Some Regulations Relating to Restraining Horses & Cattel Swine Sheep & Geese from Going at Large on the Commons or High Way in sd Town." The highways were about all that remained of the common land once considered so abundant by covetous outlanders in the 1720s. Even so, many farmers apparently still followed the old "open field" practice of allowing livestock to roam freely, fencing in their private lands for crops and orchards. One can imagine the impediment to travel and transportation of goods that resulted when a growing population funneled its livestock to the town grazing land, alias "highways." Geese must have been the most offensive miscreants, for their retrieval after removal from a highway would cost an owner eight cents a goose—a hefty expense for the cash-poor owners of these renowned escape artists.[35] Clearly this ordinance favored the more established farmers in town at the expense of those newcomers who had been able to purchase only ten or fifteen acres. No doubt farmers with small holdings resented having to build pens for their swine on land that might have produced more apples; yet they did not seem to control the majority at the town meeting on this issue.

Thus, it became more and more difficult for people without land, or without extensive credit, to make a place for themselves in Granby. Town officials, in turn, became more diligent in dealing with people who might become a "public burden" as they assigned overseers to those who "by Reason of age mismanagement and bad husbandry [were] Likely to Come to want and be Chargable to Sd Town." One of the first acts of the new town government in 1787 was to "warn out" eight people who had no "legal settlement" in Granby and could not care for themselves. What this meant was that Micah Miller and wife, the Widow Butler, and Davis Williams, his wife and three children ("Tranchant Persons") had not been born in Granby, had no relatives living in Granby, had no employment in Granby, and owned no property in Granby. Therefore, the selectmen instructed Constable Thomas Spring to escort them to the town line and order them not to return.[36]

Those who invested in land or shops and tools in the 1790s—James Huggins of West Granby, for example—often did quite well, in spite of the slow development of roads in this town. Those who had to borrow their way into a mill business, farm, or store were in a more precarious position, for creditors themselves were not always securely established, and notes and mortgages could easily find their way into the hands of strangers or otherwise unsympathetic people. The selectmen's account book and the town meeting records are full of people who either could not make their payments on debts or never found anyone to lend them money in the first place.

The town's African Americans found themselves in the latter situation quite often as a result of emerging racial prejudices and their newcomer status. Although the land records show a good deal of lending and mortgaging to finance property purchases for white farmers and artisans, it appears that few were willing to lend money to former slaves, regardless of how much they had contributed to the war effort. Continental Army service just did not convert to capital in a town run by militiamen, where the two senior officers in that militia were Colonel Ozias Pettibone and Colonel Hezekiah Holcomb, both slave owners. Benajah Hills was one of the lucky ones who was able to get a shop and a mortgage from his neighbor Aaron Post (who, as a newcomer to town himself, probably was more sympathetic to Benajah's struggle for acceptance). Others, like Asher Frank of West Granby and Philip Negro, had to be content with renting small pieces of less-than-desirable land, and supporting their families on that. By 1800 both Asher and Philip were listed on the paupers rolls. If able to work, they were placed under the watchful eye and strict orders of an "overseer," who kept track of them from dawn until dusk. Alternatively, they suffered the ignominy of the notorious "vendue" system, a rather cruel process in which poverty-stricken individuals were "bid out" to someone who would agree to care for them for a period of time. Sometimes families were split up and divided among people who shared the common belief that poverty was the fault of the pauper. African Americans could not have missed the irony as they labored in their fields under a white man's eye, or as they stood on an auction block—although this time people were bidding down, instead of up, as the selectmen tried to find the person who would charge the town the least for the care of the paupers. Some bidders, like Jacob Pettibone, who took in Asher Frank at one point, could scarcely support their own families, and may have hoped to make a little profit by paying less for their boarder's care than they had bid. By 1810, most solvent African Americans had, not surprisingly, left Granby. Up to that point, not only did Granby have an underclass that was not much better off than the slaves of an earlier time, but there was also a ghetto (called Shacktown) for those assigned to that class who did not get bid out. Their plight represented, albeit in the most extreme way, the tendency to bring order to a chaotic world by defining new tiers of status within the community.[37]

Among solvent whites, social distinctions were emerging as well. This is surprising, since Granby was a community first settled by outsiders, developed by poor outlanders, and incorporated by Antifederalists. One would think that the town that had opposed bonus payments to the Continental elite would avoid social classes altogether. Furthermore, as the town grew in the 1790s, it became clear that it was one of those exceptional New England communities that identified with the Democratic-Republicans, the national political party that opposed the Federalists, whose merchant-nationalist coalition so dominated New England politics. Evidence of this can be found in a letter from Pliny Hillyer to Jonathan Humphrey of Simsbury, in February 1803, in which Hillyer urged Humphrey and Jonathan Pettibone to avoid controversy, for "it might give a fatal blow to *Democracy* in Simsbury, and bring about once more the arbitrary reign of Federalism, and restore things to their ancient rigid order."[38] It appears that for Hillyer to remain a town leader, in a town where increasing numbers were struggling farmers and artisans who hated taxes, it was necessary to be an Antifederalist, and then a Democratic-Republican.

Evidence of both Granby's Democratic political leanings and its parallel stratification is found on the rolls of the St. Mark's Lodge #36 of Free and Accepted Masons. In the 1790s, even though the Masons themselves expressly denied any political party commitments, leading New Englanders (like Timothy Dwight) saw them as heirs to European freemasonry and therefore linked them to the Jeffersonians as part of a national campaign against piety. By 1802, St. Mark's Lodge had eighty members, including nearly all of the town's political leaders and gentlemen farmers and businessmen, or, as Roger Viets called them in a homecoming address in 1800, "men of enlightened understanding, the strictest integrity, and conspicuous rank in society."[39] In spite of their disdain for Connecticut's "Standing Order," they were not above designing their own distinguished order to mark themselves from the common folk of their community. The lodge had its headquarters in the town's commercial center, the original site of the Salmon Brook village, where its men of "conspicuous rank" were also determined to create an "enlightened" cultural center with an academy and a revived subscription library. Mason James Kilbourn took charge of the library in the 1790s, organizing or selling off Reverend Strong's old books and purchasing over four hundred new volumes "adapted to the advancing state [and] tastes of the people." Five decades later he recalled proudly that the value of the shares in the library increased 400 percent by 1800.[40]

Another center village institution, St. Peter's meetinghouse, where Kilbourn was also an active leader, was a magnificent structure for a town of farmers, and one more example of the desire to fashion a degree of social order. Fitted out with box pews arranged along two aisles, and also in two galleries, the interior was quite handsome. Each box had paneled doors with six-inch spindle rails across the top, and the pulpit was ornate and elevated.[41] The Episcopalians, who listed among their membership the families of Ozias Pettibone, Hezekiah Holcomb, Pliny Hillyer, and probably most of the men of St. Mark's Lodge of Masons, do not seem to have felt bound by the traditional New England strictures against ostentation. On the contrary, in building a structure that must have put Isaac Porter's meetinghouse to shame, they not only attracted the now frequent town meetings to the village, but also expressed their determination to be a "Standing Order" at least in Granby if not in Federalist Connecticut.

When Roger Viets returned on a visit and spoke at this bright new structure on June 29, 1800, he took pains to distinguish the Episcopalians (and in a later speech the Masons) from the Jeffersonian Republicans and "the prevailing infidelity of the present age." He urged support for the clergy, regular attendance at church, charity for the poor, and deference to God, government, and men of "conspicuous rank." At the Masons meeting he complained that they had been "abused most outrageously. . . . Our adversaries have denied us to be either Christians, or peaceable subjects of our respective civil governments. And have accused us of inventing and propagating Atheism, and the execrable plundering, leveling principle commonly called Jacobinism." The exact opposite was the case, he argued.[42] Perhaps his old parishioners from the "nest of spurious births" in the northwest hills were not present.

In 1797, when Granby selectmen were drafting their ordinance to restrict the freedom of geese and swine, it had been a century since the Scottish indentured servant George Hays had decided to move his family into a war zone in order to get some decent meadow. There he had joined others of New England's "fringe" of society to create a community of people who would exact a price for the risks they took. For that and later for "settling their minds in peace," they would insist on substantial freeholds and almost complete autonomy.

Three generations after its beginnings, the Salmon Brook settlement would have been unrecognizable to Hays and his fellow outlanders. The elegant spire of an Episcopal church rose from a collection of spacious painted houses laid out on the "center-hall" plan and adorned with Adam-style woodwork celebrating an architectural renaissance. Men of "conspicuous rank" wore silver shoe and stock buckles, sent their children to an academy, borrowed books from a library, and attended lodge meetings as well as church and town meetings. What had once been a narrow path that virtually ended at a rough meetinghouse was now a wide main street bustling with activity as farmers carted their surplus to trade at Curtiss and Hillyer's store. Hillyer and Curtiss themselves brought in wagonloads of goods from all over the world. The surrounding hillsides, at one time heavily forested, were now nearly clear cut and dotted with houses under construction and roaming herds of sheep. Where people once turned pine sap into turpentine, they now distilled cider into brandy.

While a few of the more successful entrepreneurs, like Ozias Pettibone, James Kilbourn, and James Huggins, were fairly new to town, most of those achieving a healthy level of respectability were descendants of the earliest settlers: Hayses, Holcombs, Willcocksons, and Dibbles. It may seem odd that these sons and daughters of outlanders would aspire to refinement and social distinction, isolate and stigmatize the poor, and, in some cases, tire of the uncompromising God of John Calvin. After all, their forbears' court pleadings and petitions to the legislature had hinted at a certain sense of cultural "distance" from the proprietor and creditor class, and they themselves had sung the song of communal and ecclesiastical harmony in their objections to losing the Notch to Massachusetts. Yet those forbears had never rejected the commercial and capitalist order on which wealth and status would depend. On the contrary, with what resources they could scratch from the land, they had embraced that order, and had done all they could to thrust themselves into it.

Now, as deacons, commanders of militia regiments, representatives from a populous town, Masons, and manufacturers, they had decided to remove the livestock from their pathways to the world. In unpainted houses in the hills many people still lived a more austere life, but like the outlanders of old Salmon Brook, they too would find a way to make a place for themselves, on even more marginal land. While they no longer defended the frontier from attack, their attendance at Methodist and Baptist meetings caused more than a little concern among the leaders of the Congregational and Episcopal churches. And when they objected to high taxes and demanded help repairing their roads, the men of conspicuous rank had to listen, for the outlanders' numbers could turn an election. Thus, Granby's obedient leaders rejected the Constitution of the United States, supported religious toleration, and mostly favored the government that governed least. The quiet habit of accommodation of the outlanders continued, bringing them slowly into a great middle class as they themselves shaped the character of the American democracy.

HUNTSTOWN

Massachusetts Route 116 West out of South Deerfield begins decep-
tively. For a little over a mile I am traveling across a broad plain
south of the Deerfield River and west of the Connecticut, taking in farmland
that must rank as some of the best in the nation. There is not a rock in sight.
Fields brimming with lush vegetation stretch far to the north and south. It is
a brief vision of agricultural paradise, and then the road begins to curve
right and left.

No sooner have I begun to wonder what New England farmers ever
had to complain about than I am winding through a ravine and beginning to
climb. The engine becomes impatient after two miles of this and drops down
to low—a good thing, too, for the angle of ascent has become alarming.

There is brief respite shortly after a sign announces "Conway." This is
a village that seems stuffed into a small valley, and it ends before I realize
there is a speed limit. The front end noses upward again. Signs warn of
twists and turns, and each is an understatement. There are farms, but now I
can appreciate the complaints.

Sudden darkness is next. I have entered a tunnel of woodlands and another serpentine section of highway. Three more miles up a ravine with
banks so steep there can be no more than a few hours of direct sunlight in

each day, a large green sign is anchored in what appears to be a cliff: "Ash-field." Again the woods give way to farms. Again I do not doubt the wisdom of those cultivators who fled west over the years. I am snaking through an area locals call "the flats." They must have cows with legs of variable length.

I round one last curve and I am in Ashfield, once called Huntstown. Here is where my subjects lived. That is, near here. The town's "business district" sits on a "plain" reaching eastward from Long Pond. But in the mid-eighteenth century when settlers were first arriving in Huntstown, the so-called Plain must have been heavily wooded, for they chose instead to take up land to the northeast. To see that part of town, I am obliged to endure more sharp curves and steep climbs. According to my topographical map I have climbed over seven hundred feet from the Connecticut Valley. Out on Beldingville Road I meet my hosts, deeply loyal leaders of the local historical society. In more suitable vehicles that can manage potholes, rocks, even steeper inclines and sharper turns, I get a tour of the early lots from Bellows Hill north to Baptist Corner and westward into a wilderness that still covers the northern edge of the town. Southern New England does not get much more rugged. There are places in the region that maps refer to as "mountains," but no one ever tried to build a farm there. I myself am hard-pressed to consider anyone even imagining a farm here.

In the eighteenth century there were some who did. In small pockets between the hills, on "beaver meadows" along the Bear River where the dams had collapsed after the beavers were trapped out, and even on steep hillsides, farmers desperate for land labored long and hard to build small farms. Beginning in the 1750s or 1760s they cleared a couple of acres a year, planted grain and orchards, grazed a few animals, and built houses that amounted to little more than huts. I am standing in a field that was part of house lot number forty-nine, cleared by the town's first settler. A farmer still grows corn here in the shadow of Mount Owen, where a surveyor by that name got lost when laying out the first division. The surrounding woodlands

Mount Owen viewed from a cornfield on one of the lots cleared by the first settlers in Huntstown. Huntstown (later Ashfield) consists of small pockets of farmland tucked in among steep hills.

and the walls piled high with rocks taken from the field are documents from which one inference can be drawn: these people chose a hard life.

One would think that the world would have been happy to leave them to busy themselves with their endless project in the hills. But the world had people in it who were as desperate to "move the settlement forward" as the few settlers that they could recruit were desperate for land. It was at places like this in northwestern Massachusetts that the empires of the world were grinding together for much of the eighteenth century, and the English empire's leaders' most effective weapons in the fight were frontier farmers who would be unyielding in defense of their land.

Nevertheless, it took a great long while before a community came into being in this harsh land. Those who made it happen, like their counterparts in Salmon Brook a half century earlier, were some of the least esteemed people of New England society. Had the provincial elite not urgently needed someone to do this work, it might have treated the recruits as history has—that is, ignored them. Here the otherwise ignored struggled for survival, and in doing so the ground and isolation with which they struggled became sacred to them. It became their property, and their independence. If the commonwealth would not recognize their service in extending its domain and protecting the more settled river towns, they thought, at least it could accord them the status of freeholders and the independence of yeomen. At least it could respect their dignity.

When the better sort hesitated, the lesser sort insisted.

5. Settled Our Land According to
Your Command

Huntstown, Massachusetts. July 1, 1756: Chileab Smith leads the way, so the story goes. A gun across his saddle, swinging his gaze right and left, he urges his horse down through the ravines toward the Connecticut River. Behind him are various family members and friends, the groom (his son Ebenezer, twenty-two), and sitting on a pillion behind the groom, the bride (Remember Ellis, twenty-one). Richard Ellis, father of the bride, brings up the rear, also armed. This is the way a wedding party looks in Huntstown in 1756. Only a dozen families have homesteads in the small town back in the hills. There is not yet a magistrate among them, so the Smiths and Ellises must take their children eight miles east, and nearly a thousand feet down, to Deerfield. Two years earlier the county court recorded the surveying of the "highway" on which they travel, yet the way is rough. There can be neither carriage nor even a wagon for those attending—only horses. And the darkened woods within the ravines may well hide an uncompromising enemy.[1]

In September 1754, local magistrate and militia leader Israel Williams of Hatfield wrote to Governor William Shirley: "It is open war with us, and a dark and distressing scene opening. A merciless and miscreant enemy invading us from every quarter." Colonel Williams sent a squad of troops from Hadley to guard the Ellises, Smiths, and their neighbors scattered through the hills west of Deerfield, but the guard left when winter set in. The following summer was tense. In June, French and Indian raiders attacked a settlement just north of Huntstown. Then came news of General Braddock's defeat on the Ohio frontier, and of mixed results when three thousand Massachusetts men set out to capture Crown Point on Lake Champlain. In the spring of 1756, Colonel Williams ordered garrisons stationed in towns north of Huntstown, but this was little consolation to settlers who knew their enemy was perfectly capable of slipping through the cracks in a line of outposts to attack less fortified communities. Upon the formal declaration of war between France and England, Canada's military commander Montcalm promised, "I will as much as in my power, keep up small parties to scatter consternation and the miseries of war throughout the enemy's country." Through all of this, Huntstown's residents went about the business of farming, raising families, and now seeing a marriage carried through, but they kept their guns with them wherever they went, equipped for "the miseries of war."[2]

It would appear from the sparse scattering of homesteads in Huntstown in 1756 that the settlement is in its first years. It is not so. Huntstown is already two decades in the making—twenty years, yet barely a dozen families and no magistrate to preside over a marriage! Surely, the rough contours of the land are part of the explanation. Surely, the events of the past two years have something to do with the scarcity of willing settlers. But what of the years before that? The town is six miles square. How is it that thousands of acres of land have failed to attract a large "peaceable kingdom" of inhabitants in the manner envisaged by the colony's founders? And what sort of people have actually agreed to set up households in a mountainous region that has become a battlefield in an eighteenth-century guerrilla war?

Captain Hunt's Town

Huntstown's story begins during another war in another place—nearly seven decades before Richard Ellis and Chileab (pronounced KILL-ee-ub) Smith escorted their children to Deerfield for their wartime nuptials. The unlikely point of origin was the wetlands north of the fortified town of Quebec in Canada in the autumn of 1690. It was there and then that Captain Ephraim Hunt and a company of soldiers from the coastal town of Weymouth, Massachusetts, found themselves cold, wet, and hungry, forcing themselves to press an attack in a doomed mission.

This is not to say there was not great enthusiasm in the colony when the campaign began. The borderland between New France and New England had crackled with violence throughout the 1680s. In January 1689, when the people of Salmon Brook in Connecticut were huddling in the homes of their Hopmeadow neighbors, there was urgent talk among provincial leaders about the need to subdue the French and the Indians. That was when the Comte Frontenac arrived in Canada determined to conquer New York, perhaps on behalf of France's new ally, the deposed King James II, who had once been the proprietor of the province. Frontenac launched his crusade of terror against the English domain in the winter of 1690, sending soldiers and Indian allies to strike Albany and settlements in New Hampshire and Maine. When word of the "massacre" at Schenectady, west of Albany, arrived in Boston, the response was at once vengeful and enthusiastically opportunistic. New York, Connecticut, Plymouth, and Massachusetts authorities, still barely organized after disassembling the Dominion of New England, and all short on funds, threw together what they hoped would be not only an overwhelming response, but also a very Protestant crusade to rid North America permanently of the "popish" French.[3]

New York officials agreed to work with the Iroquois to move against Montreal while Massachusetts looked forward to overrunning Port Royal, from which French privateers had harassed their colony's merchant ships. Then the Massachusetts force was to proceed up the St. Lawrence to take Quebec. Sir William Phips and a small force captured Port Royal easily in May 1690, but they returned home to find that the English ministry would not be sending arms, ammunition, or financial support for the Quebec campaign. King William had his sights set on fighting James II's allies in Ireland. Undaunted, Phips and the General Court proceeded to outfit their expedition. The next month the order arrived in Weymouth for Captain Hunt to form his company, either by taking volunteers or by impressment. All he could offer his recruits was the hope that the quick surrender of Port Royal would be repeated in Quebec, and that there would be considerable plunder.[4]

Weymouth lies on the rocky South Shore between Boston and Plymouth. Its dubious claim to notoriety in the seventeenth century was that it had been the site of Merrymount, where, during Plymouth's early years, Thomas Morton had annoyed the Puritans with his Maypole and various other festivities. Underneath that veneer of infamy, poor farmers lived on poor land, or supplied even poorer fishermen in nearby Hingham and Hull. When townsmen chose Ephraim Hunt's father to be a sergeant in their train band in 1662, they had to get a special act of the General Court passed because he apparently did not own property of sufficient value to qualify as a freeman. This man of small means raised his son to be a fighter, and both saw considerable action during King Philip's War, especially when the Nipmucks attacked Weymouth in the winter of 1676. Young Ephraim rose through the ranks to become a captain in 1690, and in later years he would serve as selectman and representative to the General Court. Yet he was never able to buy any land for his twelve children, as many fathers tried to do at the time, and when he died in 1713, his estate, including his small homestead, was valued at only £139. The probate court decided that it was insufficient to divide among his heirs. If Captain Hunt was their leading citizen, the people of Weymouth were hardly a prosperous lot. No doubt visions of plunder were attractive to the young men of the community. Even so, with no promises of a base wage, a portion of Ephraim's company had to be impressed.[5]

The absence of Crown support for the Canada expedition was only the beginning of the provincials' bad luck. It took the better part of the summer to gather the troops. Then, when the fleet was headed north in August, storms battered the commandeered ships and whale boats, delaying them yet another three weeks as the men consumed most of their food. Guided by a pilot who had never been on the St. Lawrence River, the force of twenty-two hundred soldiers and three hundred sailors did not arrive at Quebec until early October. Fontenac had plenty of time to fortify the town and send for reinforcements. When the "Albanians" and their smallpox-ridden friends among the Iroquois did not follow through with their part of the invasion, eight hundred French troops set out from Montreal to bring Quebec's garrison to a total of three thousand.[6]

Phips would not accept failure. He held a council of war and determined to use his naval guns to barrage the town from the St. Lawrence while he put the soldiers, under Major John Walley, ashore on the north side to attack from the rear. He sent a contingent of boats on a feint south of the town, hoping to draw off some of the garrison. Ephraim Hunt's men were with Walley. It was a hopeless plan from the start, for Phips was outnumbered and even outgunned. Then more bad weather interrupted the operation. On October 8, when Walley finally landed his troops, he found himself wading through marshes at high tide, sometimes up to his waist. Although quite miserable, his soldiers pressed their attack vigorously, but the French, "by convenience of swamps and bushes," sniped at them and evaporated, inflicting sixty-four casualties. "All things considered," reported Walley, "it was a great mercy wee had no more damage done us." Unable to get dry, the men passed a cold night, some managing to find shelter from the wind in a barn. Before daybreak, much to Walley's horror, boatmen attempted to put six field pieces ashore. These promptly sank in the mud. Meanwhile, Phips's small armada was not making a dent in the east side of the fortifications, and fast running out of ammunition. That would free up more defenders to stand against Walley's weary forces, many of whom were now becoming both sick and angry. After another day of debilitating swamp fighting, the Massachusetts soldiers suffered through a bitter cold night. Still, there was little progress toward the town on the hill.[7]

Walley discovered through interrogations of prisoners that the defenders were now reinforced by the rested troops from Montreal, and these were encircling the Massachusetts men. While he went aboard Phips's boat to describe his situation, his men began to disengage, and many believed that a withdrawal had been ordered. As the swell of retreat increased, "Many precipitately and disorderly drew down to the beach, four times more than had leave, and a very great noise was made." Hundreds of troops were wading in the water, boats threatened to capsize, and the mired guns were left behind, now totally submerged. In place of a council of war, officers held prayer meetings, while the fleet weighed anchor and fled down river. "Winds and weather after proved such, as wee had never opportunity to come together," lamented Walley in his report to the council, "but the whole fleet were scattered, and such exceeding hard cold and windy weather sett in for 3 weeks or a month together, as I never was in." Two of the vessels were wrecked, one burned, and two hundred soldiers and sailors died either in the accidents or from disease. Phips returned to Boston on November 19, bringing "camp disease" with him and spreading it through the city. Some of the ships did not appear until February, having been blown as far away as the West Indies. Some never appeared at all. Captain Hunt's ship reached Cape Ann by November 22, where the soldiers presumably disembarked, preferring to walk the rest of the way home. Several of the company had died, and some were so weakened by illness that they never recovered and died within two years. Upon his return to Weymouth, Hunt's constituents sent him as their representative to the General Court to complain. The leadership appointed him to a committee to find out "what plunder may any ways be concealed, by such as come from Canada on the late expedition, and also of all stores which were brought back," and to submit a report so that whatever was left could be divided up equitably. None could be found.[8]

Even before Phips's arrival in Boston, the General Court had anticipated considerable unrest. The expedition had cost £140,000 to get off the ground, with no thought of providing wages for the troops. The government had lured poor men with dreams of plunder, and all the men had brought home were frostbitten, diseased, and maimed bodies, along with shattered egos—if they made it home at all. As Thomas Hutchinson later wrote, the expedition's outcome was "a humbling stroke to New-England," that "struck a damp on the spirit" of the people. At first, the Massachusetts General Court considered a measure to borrow money to pay the troops, but now, expecting a long and bloody war with little prospect of raising taxes from a despairing and frightened population, it simply printed bills of credit that soldiers could use to pay their provincial taxes in the future. Poor soldiers and sailors had few if any taxes to pay, however, and when they tried to exchange the bills for money or goods, they found that they could get only twelve to fourteen shillings on the pound. The government tried to make the bills more attractive by offering a 5 percent discount on taxes paid in the paper, but that served only to fuel the resentment of the soldiers who, in order to acquire food that they had not been able to harvest in the fall of 1690, had already sold the bills at a discount to traders.[9]

Having rallied their people for a campaign they had wanted even before the French attacks on the frontier, and puffed up with religious self-righteousness, the leaders of New England had jumped into a war that they did not have the money or the military acumen to fight. The cost, instead, had been borne by the poor and the powerless. There were numerous junctures where their leaders might have turned back and at least regrouped, but the venture's setbacks seemed only to make them more resolute in carrying it out, lest the efforts and resources already invested be spent in vain. It is little wonder that tempers flared in the countryside and complaints rolled in to the legislature from 1690 forward.

Border warfare raged throughout the next two decades. Meanwhile, the resentment of those involved in the 1690 expedition continued to simmer as economic distress grew. The financially strapped government chose to issue paper to cover expenses, rather than raise taxes, and that led to runaway inflation that hurt the poorest inhabitants whose ranks provided the majority of the soldiers. The colony also experienced severe crowding after the Peace of Utrecht in 1713. As in Connecticut, people were reluctant to consider moving north or west, for rumors of war parties and occasional attacks persisted into the 1720s. Meanwhile, between 1700 and 1740 the colony's population nearly tripled. All the good land in the already settled towns was in private hands, so prices for acreage rose. For immigrants and for younger people, like Captain Ephraim Hunt's twelve children who were coming of age at his death in 1713, the cost of acquiring a "competency" was becoming prohibitive. In 1727 the House of Representatives noted with some dismay the great need for "Room [to be] made for great Numbers of His Majesties Subjects to Settle who are by their Increase straightened for want thereof." Five years later the legislature repeated its concern, declaring that "by the Great Increase of His Majesty's Good Subjects, many that are inclined to Industry have not been able to obtain Lands for the Employment of themselves . . . & great numbers have removed to neighboring colonies for their accommodation." These discoveries were not the result of legislators taking the initiative and doing independent research. Petitions for relief were frequent, many from the families of the Canada soldiers who would not let the legislature forget the ordeal of the 1690 expedition. Ephraim Hunt's son Ebenezer, for example, by this time himself a militia captain in Weymouth, led his neighbors in demanding that the colony recognize that the bills of credit were hardly just compensation, and that the government ought to be doling out land "in consideration of their hardships & sufferings in the said Expeditions."[10]

Pressure from discontented farmers and concern about the outmigration of those "inclined to industry" were not the only factors motivating the legislature to take some sort of action to ease distress for poorer people, many of whom thought the government still owed them for the 1690 debacle. Even after the Peace of Utrecht in 1713, the French presence to the north posed a continuing threat, and House members could not help but think that settling their surplus population on the Massachusetts frontier would mean a more secure province. As early as 1715 the legislature discussed creating a contiguous line of settlements across the frontier for the purpose of discouraging attacks from the north and west. Cotton Mather himself even developed a liking for Scots-Irish immigrants who were so desperate for land that they might create buffer communities in the borderlands. Such settlement "will be greatly to the Honour of His Majesties Government," the House of Representatives declared in 1726 as raiding parties were striking outposts in Maine, "and tend to the Security & Protection of the Inhabitents of this Province; very much Shorten our Inland Frontiers, both *westward* and *Eastward,* and vastly lessen the Charge of the Defense of this Government in time of War."[11]

So it was, as a result of both military considerations and chronic distress, that encouraging the heirs of the veterans of the 1690 Canada expedition to take up land on the frontier became public policy in the 1730s. The legislature created nine "Canada townships" in 1735, three the next year, and one in 1738. Each township was to be divided among the survivors or heirs of a company of soldiers. These townships would be the guardians of the Massachusetts frontier, the prop for the defense budget, the net to capture farmers "inclined to industry," and the safety valve for all the steam being generated in crowded communities by farmers with smoldering resentments. All of these grants contained essentially the same terms. Each proprietor was to receive an equal share of the township on the condition that within three years he see to it that there would be settled in the township "one good family who shall have a house built on the Houselott of Eighteen feet square and seven feet Stud at the least and finished," and bring six acres of ground under cultivation. The community was also to set aside land for the support of a "learned orthodox minister," build a meetinghouse, and provide for schooling. The settlers were to put up a twenty-pound bond, which would be forfeited, along with the land, if the terms of settlement were not met.[12]

These terms deserve some comment. It is not surprising that the government would insist that proprietors of the new towns put some serious effort into "improving the land" before they could have secure title. After all, they did want people in place on the frontier, and the best way to ensure that would be to require them to do a lot of work in residence if they wanted to call the land their own. Further, the provisions for the church, ministry, and schooling were long-standing requirements for new towns. Equal distribution of land, however, was unusual. In both Connecticut and Massachusetts— even in Simsbury when the unruly "inhabitants" asserted themselves over the proprietors in 1723, towns granted land in amounts proportional to individual estates. In the case of the Canada townships, however, the Massachusetts leaders of the 1730s were not about to stir up more anger by suggesting that some soldiers were more deserving than others of recompense for suffering and then waiting all these years. Even officers were accorded the same amount of land as everyone else. Furthermore, no matter how poor the proprietor, he could still draw the most desirable piece of land in the new township. Apparently, popular sentiment had determined an uncustomary egalitarian turn.[13]

Ebenezer Hunt and his fellow petitioners, the heirs of the Weymouth soldiers of 1690, received their grant in 1735: a six-mile-square township to be surveyed on the western boundary of Deerfield. There were to be sixty "rights" to lots in the town, with each right due to receive over three hundred acres of land by the time it was all parceled out. The petitioners met with some difficulty when it came to finding legal heirs for all of Captain Hunt's men. Some soldiers had died heirless on the expedition, some of the heirs of the others were unknown, and some soldiers or heirs had moved some distance from Weymouth. Consequently, in 1737 the legislature extended the settlement deadline five years and allowed Ebenezer Hunt and his petitioners to include sailors from Weymouth or nearby towns whose "merit was as great as the Soldiers." In the meantime, the leaders of the proprietors sent a surveying team west to the grant to mark out a first division of fifty-acre homelots and three more lots to support the meetinghouse, ministry, and schooling.[14]

Actually it is a wonder that, after forty-five years, the petitioners found representatives for forty-three of Captain Hunt's sixty soldiers to draw lots at John Hubbard's inn at Braintree in July 1739. At least six of the veterans, along with perhaps three more of the mariners, were themselves present. Heirs-at-law, mostly sons with a smattering of brothers and nephews, along with some men who had purchased rights before the drawing, comprised the remainder of participants. The purchase prices of rights had been between nine and thirty pounds. Homelots ranged from fifty to sixty acres, "according to the Goodness or Meanness of the Land," and came with a right to one sixty-third of all subsequent divisions of land. Only six of the proprietors lived in Weymouth, and the rest came from all over eastern Massachusetts. In spite of the primitive state of communications of that day, word had spread and men had gathered—testimony to how long they and their families had held the government accountable for their suffering in 1690. It also speaks both to the degree to which the provincial leaders of the 1730s rightly feared the public wrath over lack of land, inflation, and long-overdue compensation, and to how much these people valued land, no matter where it was. And, indeed, the drawing was an egalitarian event. Stepping forward as the nineteenth person to draw was Heber Honestman, a former slave, who had paid twenty pounds to the son of a Weymouth soldier for a right. Heber

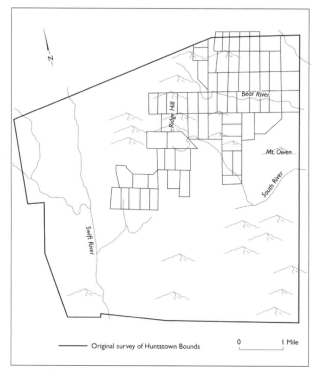

First division survey in northeastern Huntstown, done in 1738.

drew Lot #1, an already partially cleared piece of land at a "beaver meadow" on the Bear River.[15]

As it turned out, of the proprietors drawing lots that summer, Heber was the only one who actually settled in the new township.[16] Nevertheless, this examination of the events leading to the creation of Captain Hunt's town may serve as an overture for the rest of the town's eighteenth-century history. The colony's leaders had resorted to recruiting or impressing poor farmers and fisherman into military service to advance the strategic goals of the province. Few had anticipated the ordeal they would face, but those who did the work would not rest until they exacted compensation in the currency of their most valued commodity: land. It remained to be seen how valuable that compensation would become, or how the settlement on that land would take shape. Yet in achieving, on their own, an egalitarian distribution of nearly twenty-four thousand acres among sixty proprietors, even though few of them had previously owned anywhere near three hundred acres, they had

Looking north across Lots 1 and 2 of Huntstown's first division of lots. Lot 1, on the right half of the picture, was drawn by Heber Honestman and was already partially cleared as a result of a collapsed beaver dam. He purchased Lot 2 once he arrived in Huntstown in 1743.

wrested both a measure of wealth and begrudging respect from the provincial elite. These currents, generated in the cold tides of Quebec's swamps, would continue to flow through Huntstown's history.

Incouragement of the First Settlers

The proprietors met in July 1739 not only to draw their lots, but also "to doe something for the Incouragement of the first Settlers." Indeed, this was an urgent matter, for the clock was ticking against the deadline declared by the General Court two years earlier. They were all the more anxious because it was becoming clear that creating a settlement was going to require considerable investment. The committee that had worked with surveyor Nathaniel Kellogg Jr. of Hadley to lay out the lots the previous summer presented a bill for over £130. Undoubtedly, after hearing about Daniel Owen's harrowing experience being lost on a mountain while on that errand, no one was inclined to dispute the expense. In addition there were other bills connected with getting the original grant, along with one proposal to have Kellogg "clear a way" to the lots and another to offer a £30 bounty plus fifty acres of land for the first men who would build a sawmill and agree to saw boards for the proprietors at twenty shillings per thousand feet. As the proprietors assessed themselves thirty shillings per right, it was beginning to look as though those who had already sold their rights had made things easy for themselves. If settlers could not be found soon, the proprietors would lose not only the land grant, but a good deal of money too.[17]

More sales soon followed the drawing of lots, with some rights selling for as low as ten pounds. By the next spring, in fact, fewer than half of the original soldiers or heirs-at-law remained among the proprietors who attended a meeting at Hubbard's inn to discuss the future of the township. A fair number of the soldiers or their descendants were still land-poor in the 1730s, but ten to thirty pounds in cash seemed more inviting to many of them than the prospect of several hundred acres in a forest a hundred miles to the west. There was, furthermore, growing concern that few of the new proprietors appeared to be interested in actually moving to the new town. Most of those who had acquired rights by purchase seemed to be speculators hoping to resell their rights for a higher price once the settlement was established and had become a more attractive place for additional settlers.[18]

At the May 1740 meeting, though, there was little talk of profit. Instead, the proprietors considered more expenses, now including Kellogg's bill for cutting the path to a settlement in which no one wanted to reside, much less build a sawmill. Unhappily they assessed themselves another fifteen shillings per right, even though they were having trouble finding proprietors who still had not paid the tax assessed the previous summer. The bills were piling up, and summer passed into fall with only a few potential settlers identified, but no one yet in residence. Over the winter of 1740–41 there was an avalanche of sales, many to Nathaniel Kellogg or his father, who were willing to credit as much as thirty pounds for a right against the young surveyor's charges. Perhaps the Kelloggs felt more confident that they could find settlers. From their perspective it may have appeared a good risk, for at the time land along the Connecticut River in the town of Hadley was going for as much as ten pounds per acre. At any rate, by the spring of 1741, many of the rights were now in the hands of the Kelloggs and other investors in Hadley.[19]

The proprietors would have to act fast, though, for now the deadline for securing title by establishing a settlement complete with cleared fields and frame houses was little more than a year away. At the May 1741 meeting, those in attendance decided to offer £5 to each of the first ten proprietors who would clear land and build a house according to the terms of the legislature's grant. They also raised the sawmill bounty to £120 and contracted with William Curtis of Stoughton, a new proprietor and prospective settler, to "mend" the unused road Kellogg had created over a year ago. Two winters had done more damage to it than the few people who had traversed it. At this point, though, things began to take a turn for the better.

The break came with a group of friends and relatives who lived in Easton, Massachusetts. These were the families of Thomas Phillips, Heber Honestman, and Richard Ellis. Like Weymouth, Easton was not blessed with good land, although what there was of quality had been attractive enough to some of those Weymouth veterans of the Canada expedition who had moved there during or shortly after King William's War. By the 1730s, though, what was available for young people coming of age and newcomers was mostly swampland, gravel, and wooded areas with rocky outcroppings. Although John Phillips, a Canada expedition veteran, had done well for himself as a housewright, his son Thomas was able to acquire only ten acres of poor land when he married in 1738. Thomas's older brother Caleb had moved to Plymouth, but had done little better, even though trained in his father's trade. When Captain John Phillips drew Lot #6 at the Huntstown drawing in 1739, he probably had Thomas, Caleb, and his other five sons and two daughters in mind.[20]

Heber Honestman, Thomas's neighbor, was a newcomer to Easton in the 1730s, at least to the community of free farmers trying to wrest a living from Easton's miserly ground. Brought to Easton as a slave in 1711, his master's widow had freed him and his sister in 1722, "in consideration of the good and faithful service . . . for me in my age & widowhood, & for their Incouragement in well doing." She also gave them each ten acres of land. Heber took the name Honestman, which to Puritans meant pious and godly (that is, Puritan), worked hard, and purchased over thirty additional acres between 1730 and 1734. In 1735 he married Susanna Cordner of Braintree, and their son was born the following year. He improved his land and then traded all of it to an heir of a Canada veteran for sixty pounds plus a right in Huntstown. When Heber drew Lot #1 in 1739, he must have been eager to move out to this choice 50-acre parcel, with its right to at least another 250 acres. But Heber and Susanna lingered in Easton, apparently unwilling to venture forth alone.[21]

There were quite a few people in Easton who had connections in one form or another to Huntstown proprietors, for a number of the proprietors were now Easton residents, including Easton's minister, Rev. Joseph Belcher. Recruitment efforts by those proprietors, along with the growing conviction among some young people that there was no future for them in eastern Massachusetts, slowly led to interest in settlement. Be they young married couples with many siblings and fathers with few acres, or recent immigrants from towns that had already divided up the last of their productive common land, a chance to make something of three hundred acres at the other end of the province got their attention. But like Heber Honestman and Thomas Phillips, they would need more than a low price to get them to move their young families miles into a mountainous forest: they needed neighbors.[22] In regard to this need, the Huntstown proprietors, whether they were speculators, potential settlers, or just worried right-holders, were fortunate to attract the interest of one Richard Ellis in their enterprise.

Ellis was a man with a colorful history. He was born Ireland in 1703, the only son of a Welshman serving in the English army. He was still only thirteen when his father died, at which point his widowed mother sent him off to a wealthy but childless Virginia planter who proposed to bring him up, or so she must have told Richard. Whether there was such a benefactor or not, the ship captain who brought Richard to America sold him for passage money as an indentured servant to a miller in Boston. When his term was up, he moved to Easton, where in 1728 he married Jane Phillips, Thomas Phillips's sister. It is clear he was an ambitious man with a good eye for opportunities. With whatever his former master had given him and his earnings as a laborer, he spent thirty-five pounds on thirty-six acres of land and built a dwelling house, two barns, and a "hayseed mill." Over the course of the next decade, Jane gave birth to six children. In 1739 Richard sold his property for three hundred pounds. Even taking inflation into account, this represents a significant achievement for a couple with young children, and for a man whose Welsh heritage and initial status as a servant from Ireland would not have secured him much credit.[23]

Apparently it was Ellis who gathered together a small group of Easton people, including the families of Thomas and Caleb Phillips and Heber Honestman, and convinced them that they could do well in the hills west of Deerfield. Some of the proprietors may even have recruited him for that purpose, for he turned out to be both a millwright and a talented trader, two avocations that would make him valuable to proprietors trying to get a settlement off the ground. In December 1739, after selling his property in Easton, he paid twenty-eight pounds for Huntstown right #56. He then moved his family to Deerfield and spent the next three summers preparing to take up permanent residence in Huntstown. It appears that he took Easton laborers Ephraim Marble and Seth Leonard with him, although, because they were renters in Deerfield while they worked in Huntstown, the records of their travels are limited.[24]

Ellis was not simply trying to build a dwelling for his family as stipulated in the conditions of the town grant. The settlement bounty for the first ten resident proprietors did attract him, but additionally he was interested in the various inducements that the proprietors were offering for building mills. He and the other workers may have been engaged in constructing a sawmill during the summer of 1740, but probably Ellis discovered that designing a mill for the mountains posed a serious challenge. The Bear River, which in the summer appears to be a shallow brook, can become a raging torrent during snow melt in the spring, hurling boulders, logs, and ice mercilessly, and fatally, at relatively frail dams and races built by millwrights accustomed to the lazy streams of Bristol and Plymouth counties. That may explain why the proprietors raised the sawmill bounty at their May meeting in 1741. They continued to debate and fret over "the affair of the sawmill," so essential to framing a settlement, through the summer and fall, balking at the expense it seemed to require. By the following September, the proprietors decided to settle for Samuel White and Job Porter, two laborers from Braintree, cutting lumber with a whipsaw. Ellis, however, seems to have stepped in and persuaded them to continue to acquire materials for a real sawmill.[25]

Along with the Ellises and the families of laborers who had come with them from Easton, there were additional settlers who appeared in Huntstown in the summer of 1742. There was, of course, William Curtis, the laborer from Stoughton whom the proprietors had hired to work on the road to the settlement. White and Porter, the sawyers, were also on hand sawing boards at four pounds per thousand feet. Beriah Chilson, who had no land in his native town of Uxbridge, brought his wife Patience and three young children west that spring to take up Lot #25, which he had purchased partially on credit the previous fall. He was still in a tenuous position, though, for another creditor in Deerfield was preparing to take him to court for nonpayment. John Nightingale of Braintree and his elderly uncle Samuel Nightingale probably moved that summer. Samuel had been a soldier in the 1690 expedition, but missed the drawing in 1739, and eventually lost his right when he did not pay his assessments. Unlike Chilson, the Nightingales had owned some property in eastern Massachusetts, but Samuel may not have been too welcome in Braintree. According to local tradition in Ashfield, Samuel was a very learned man, perhaps educated in England. He built his house in Huntstown on his nephew's lot up against a large south-facing boulder that he used for its back wall, and his neighbors considered him so odd generally that they suspected him of being a "wizard." When he died (and no one is saying when) they would not permit his body to be buried with the other settlers. Wizard or not, he may have had one of the more comfortable of the crude huts or cellar houses then being built in Huntstown—cooler in the summer, and warmer in the winter.[26]

Between 1739 and 1742, then, investment-minded proprietors were working hard to attract settlers. They depended on Richard Ellis's enterprising spirit to recruit workers or broker lots to prospective residents; they prevailed upon less-involved proprietors to sell lots at low prices or on credit to prospective settlers; they offered bounties, and they confiscated rights of "delinquent" proprietors and gave them to workers in lieu of work on various projects. William Curtis, Ephraim Marble, Samuel White, and Job Porter all acquired full rights in Huntstown, and probably paid nothing but their labor for them. In this manner, the proprietors managed to get several men to work on developing the settlement as early as 1741, and bring their families to take up residence in the summer of 1742. Clearly a community was emerging. After convincing the legislature that winter to "allow two more years to complete the settlement," the proprietors voted in March 1743 to hire a minister to preach for the settlers.[27]

During the spring and summer of 1743 the momentum of the settlement "volgarly called Huntstown" continued to build. New families arrived, encouraged that the proprietors were considering building a meetinghouse and a cornmill. Thomas Phillips and his family, along with his brother Caleb, and Heber and Susanna Honestman moved in during the early months of 1743. Proprietors Nathaniel Kellogg and Obadiah Dickinson of Hadley were also trying to get people from the Connecticut River towns to consider residing there, offering to exchange or rent some of their now extensive holdings, or the lands of "delinquent" proprietors, for work done on roads and building projects. One of these was Ralph Way, a free African-American resident of Hadley, who became a proprietor of Huntstown.[28]

Nightingale Rock—the boulder that the alleged "wizard" Samuel Nightingale used for the rear wall of the abode he built in about 1742.

In spite of a conflict with Deerfield over boundary lines, ongoing disputes between proprietors in eastern Massachusetts and those on the Connecticut River, and instances of timber poaching, the pace of settlement quickened noticeably in 1743. Somehow the proprietors met the challenges of getting families and supplies up the washed-out cart paths to the settlers, and keeping those settlers motivated for the back-breaking tasks of cutting trees, grubbing out stumps, throwing up dams and millraces, hewing and sawing lumber, breaking up ground, and trying to build houses that would meet the General Court's specifications. Hired workers finished construction of the cornmill, and the proprietors put Caleb Phillips in charge of grinding grain in return for half the profits. Other residents continued to earn their tax money, and even additional rights to the township, by cutting new roads from Hatfield and Deerfield to the Huntstown house lots. After considerable discussion, the proprietors voted to lay out lots on all of the remaining undivided land. In case anyone had any ideas about the "gentlemen" among the proprietors getting more land because of their prominence, the majority proclaimed that the division was to be done equally among all proprietors "for Quality and Quantity" and "in no other method whatsoever."[29]

As it was with Salmon Brook in Connecticut a half century earlier, so it was with Huntstown. Promoters of New England's expansion and defense were forced to draw from the social fringe to "move the settlement forward." The community that was taking shape in the hills west of Deerfield housed a motley group—a Welshman (once an indentured servant), an African American couple (once enslaved), some poor laborers and tradesmen (some having been expelled from Deerfield), and a wizard. Whatever their backgrounds, they now constituted a scattered neighborhood and were working hard in a sometimes frightening land. Furthermore, they were generally willing to hear preaching, had a mill to grind their grain and a pair of sawyers to produce some rough boards for their rough huts, and were even becoming numerous enough to warrant a meetinghouse. And as it was with Salmon Brook, the new recruits, once landless and indebted and now landed and solvent, began to claim an advanced status. In land deeds, men who had once been laborers suddenly began calling themselves husbandmen, and husbandmen became yeomen. That might have been unsettling for the recruiters, who were careful to refer to themselves as "gentlemen" in their meetings with the county clerk, but it got the work done. As it also was with Salmon Brook, though, the early years of Huntstown were filled with dashed hopes.

Under Our Distresst Circumstances

Ominous entries in the proprietors' records for a meeting on April 4, 1744, anticipated a sudden reversal of fortunes for Huntstown. "After some debate" over the matter of building a meetinghouse, they voted to suspend the project, "for that there is great Expectation of a War with France." They did agree to create a committee to provide a "Minister To preach to Such as Inhabit at Huntstown," and perhaps even settle a minister there, "Provided the War Shall Not Come on Speedily."[30] But it did.

England and Spain had been at war since 1739, but in 1744, when France decided to enter the conflict on Spain's side, the prospect of a new round of punishing raids on English settlements in New York and New England drew away the attention of everyone along the New England frontier from such mundane issues as meetinghouse construction. Considering the fear of attacks, along with the campaign to capture the French fortress at Louisbourg, it is not surprising that the Huntstown proprietors did not meet at all in 1745. When they did finally convene in May 1746, the outlook for their community

had changed drastically. A raiding party had just attacked Colrain, a settlement of Scots-Irish immigrants ten miles north of Huntstown, killing one and
wounding two, and Huntstown was now virtually abandoned. Some of the
settlers had retreated to more protected towns as a temporary measure, some
had gone off to war, and others were nowhere to be found. Only Richard
Ellis, Thomas Phillips, and Heber Honestman and their families continued to
reside in the hills west of Deerfield. During the summer the proprietorship
underwent important changes. Major Israel Williams of Hatfield, an emerging magnate of Hampshire County who had bought a right in Huntstown in
1742, joined with Obadiah Dickinson, Nathaniel Kellogg, and other investors
in Hatfield and Hadley to wrest control of the proprietorship from the Braintree proprietors in order to revive the settlement. There would never again be
a proprietors' meeting in eastern Massachusetts.[31]

The formal cessation of hostilities in 1748 did little to dispel the fear that
plagued the Huntstown enterprise. Even Reuben Ellis, Richard's eldest son,
could not persuade his new bride to move to Huntstown with him in 1749, and
the couple remained in the Connecticut River valley town of Sunderland for
two more years. As late as May 1751, Timothy Woodbridge of Hatfield wrote
that he could tell "from the Situation of affairs that the peace will not Continue long." The Ellises, the Phillipses, and the Honestmans were living on
the edge, to be sure, with precious little support from either the proprietors or
the provincial leadership. Stories come down to us of Huntstown people subsisting on maple sugar and the buds and leaves of basswood trees, and of
Richard Ellis scrambling away from a band of Indians with a five-pail sap kettle strapped to his back. True or not, that these tales were passed from generation to generation suggests that at some point Huntstown's settlers began to
think of themselves as people who had endured much for their freeholds. For
five years after 1746, the proprietors did not even bother to meet, and during
that time there were only three land transfers recorded. Although the General
Court did not seem interested in enforcing the old settlement deadline, it remained a daunting problem to entice willing settlers to risk their families' lives
on the outskirts of English America. The General Court, in fact, seemed to
forget about deadlines altogether as nearly every western Massachusetts proprietorship grappled with recruiting challenges. For the investment-oriented
Huntstown proprietors there were no returns.[32]

In the fall of 1751, nevertheless, it appeared that there might be hope for
the unfortunate settlement. On November 20, the proprietors gathered at an

inn in Hatfield and elected Chileab Smith, a new resident of Huntstown, to be their moderator. They then proceeded to order the raising of money to pay a minister for the next several months and to repair the cornmill and the road to the settlement. Over the next three years, the peace did continue, and there was additional progress. More and more of the rights now belonged to middling farmers either in residence or planning to move their families to Huntstown soon, and that added new energy to the project. After some negotiation and investment, construction of a new cornmill began, and of a real sawmill as well. Substantial funds were voted for continued preaching, a meetinghouse, and road improvements. After a few petitions, the proprietors succeeded in getting the county court to survey a road from Deerfield that would be maintained at county expense. Most importantly, families began moving in at such an accelerated rate that the proprietors had to step back and sort out who were the first ten that would get the five pounds promised back in 1741.[33]

The new wave of settlers had diverse origins, but they were similar to the group that had come before King George's War in that their circumstances made them eminently recruitable for a hard and precarious life in the hills. The first of these to bring their family to Huntstown in 1751 were Chileab and Sarah Smith, a couple who would leap into an active and prominent role in their new community. The Smiths and their eight children, along with Chileab's twice-widowed mother, came from South Hadley, which was the poorer section of Hadley. South of Mount Holyoke, the land, albeit Connecticut River valley land, was rocky and heavily wooded when it was finally divided up in the 1720s, late in Hadley's land-division history. Chileab's father had been killed in Queen Anne's War, and although his mother received a small portion of that South Hadley division and had remarried to a fairly prominent Hadley man, Chileab had not come into much land of his own. When his mother's second husband died, that husband's children ended up with all of the property. Thus, the prospect of hundreds of acres twenty miles northwest must have appealed to Chileab and Sarah.[34]

There also were other aspects of South Hadley life that got the Smiths looking elsewhere. The "south precinct" had been the scene of considerable conflict over the Halfway Covenant during the 1730s. While the earlier settlers of that part of town, including Sarah's father, and Chileab and his brother, had been opponents of the more inclusive church championed by Solomon Stoddard of Northampton, more recent arrivals, the sons of

Hadley's more prominent leaders, favored it. A majority by 1740, the Stoddard followers dismissed Rev. Grindall Rawson, who was a devotee of Jonathan Edwards. Rawson tried to continue preaching into the next year anyway, but at one Sabbath-day gathering a group of young men literally gagged and dragged him from the pulpit while he was in the middle of a prayer. His replacement, John Woodbridge, had the confidence of both the new majority of South Hadley and the civil leaders of Hadley, including Nathaniel Kellogg and leading selectmen. Paying taxes for Woodbridge's new parsonage and watching the meetinghouse seated "by age estate or qualifications" surely rankled our Chileab, who eventually decided that "the South Hadley church was dead in trespasses and sin." After a number of angry discussions with church leaders he concluded that "they did not pretend to require persons to be converted, in order to join the church." These were dangerous words, for they were the language of the emerging "separate" movement so hated by the river valley elite. Reverend Woodbridge sent him to the association to discuss his concerns. The association declared him "wrong," and sent him to, of all people, Jonathan Edwards, who promptly told him that he was right. Thus, in 1751, Chileab traded his meager and sandy land in the "south precinct" for right #27 in Huntstown. There was probably a mutual sense of "good riddance," for Huntstown must have seemed many times more than twenty miles away at a time when "the peace will not Continue long."[35]

In Huntstown, Chileab not only had a full proprietor's right, but also served on several committees that shaped the future of the settlement. These positions also enabled him to pull in some cash income as half owner of the new sawmill and for repair work on roads and the cornmill. Furthermore, he gathered his family and some of his neighbors together and happily held separate church meetings, presumably affirming their conviction that only evidence of saving grace could result in church membership. Later in life he would mark 1753 as a year when "a Number were brout savingly home to Christ" and began keeping the Sabbath regularly as a group that recognized only heartfelt conversion as qualification for approaching the communion table. It is not clear whether they also submitted to the Stoddardian preaching hired for them by the proprietors, but they did enter into a written covenant together. Chileab's teenage son Ebenezer began "to improve among them by way of Doctrine." He apparently impressed not only his neighbors but also people in neighboring settlements with his speaking skills, for he was soon well known, and an irritant for licensed preachers in the area. Thus did Huntstown's hills offer sanctuary and fertile ground at least for religious dissent. No doubt those hills also shaped the character of that dissent: a faith in a discriminating God, who could be merciful but also allowed His followers to be severely tested.[36]

Other newcomers like the Smiths soon arrived looking for opportunities or escape in Huntstown. We know very little about most of them, except that they generally came to Huntstown from relatively desperate situations where they had little land, were being hounded for debt, or were uncomfortable with the current preaching. Moses and Philip Smith had no land at all in Hadley, and they were probably on the side of the Smith family that supported Reverend Rawson. John Sadler was a poor husbandman trying to make ends meet in Deerfield and seemingly ineligible for any of the last bits of common land parceled out there in the 1740s. Josiah Rockwood had drifted from Mendon in eastern Massachusetts to "Roadtown" in the 1740s, and finally was able to get some land on credit in Huntstown in 1753.[37]

What drew Wetherell and Jemima Wittium to Huntstown may well have been the exact opposite of what Chileab Smith was seeking. The Wittiums had moved to Easton in 1733, and Wetherell had managed to rise from the ranks of the laboring class there to become a yeoman farmer with over sixty acres of land. However, during the 1740s the tremors of the Great Awakening rippled through Easton. There was considerable division over the sort of preaching that the congregation preferred. Wittium was among the Old Lights, and when a new minister took his post in 1747 and declared a "love for none but such as are savingly converted," Wittium sold all of his property (now valued at three times what he paid for the lots) and with his wife and three children headed west. He probably worked for Richard Ellis for a time, and finally acquired his own right in the town through credit for labor. It is testimony to Huntstown's diversity that, even in a community inhabited by Chileab Smith and his evangelical son Ebenezer, the Wittiums (who, with some extra cash actually had a choice where to go to live) decided that this settlement had a place for them.[38]

It is somewhat difficult to chart Wittium's life in Huntstown, which makes one wonder how many more laborers passed through the settlement, collected wages, and kept moving. Could the challenge of finding a paper trail for Wittium, Joseph Porter, William Mack, and a half dozen other laborers' names that appear in the proprietors' records for doing work be a small candle

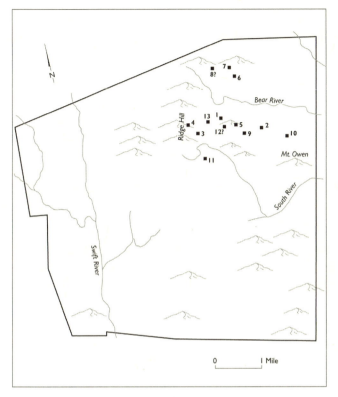

The scattered Huntstown homesteads in 1754 (approximate locations): *1.* Heber Honestman, *2.* Richard Ellis, *3.* John Sadler, *4.* Joseiah Rockwood, *5.* John Nightingale, *6.* Thomas Phillips, *7.* Chileab Smith, *8.* Moses Smith, *9.* Ebenezer Belding, *10.* Reuben Ellis, *11.* John Blackmer, *12.* Philip Smith, *13.* Wetherell Wittium.

throwing dim light on a whole class of people who are virtually invisible in New England's history? Historians investigating the social and economic structure of the eighteenth century have often said that a laboring class, at least outside the farm family structure, was almost nonexistent in rural New England because of the availability of land. Indeed, we have seen that ambitious but landless men like Richard Ellis, John Sadler, Josiah Rockwood, and even the "free Negro" Heber Honestman did not remain landless for long. But it was only crowded and barren land, or dangerous land, that was in abundance and available. If working men did not take up the offer and stay long enough to acquire land in return for the withering struggle against large trees, steep slopes, roads that were barely marked, let alone cleared, and all of the perils of living on the edge during wartime (which was often), how can we find them? The great genealogy movement of the late nineteenth and early twentieth centuries missed them because they were not of the families that put down roots and became prominent. How many "wandering laborers" were there moving about New England in the mid-eighteenth century?[39]

Whether there were more settlers than we know in Huntstown on the eve of the French and Indian War will remain difficult to determine. Nevertheless, it is clear that once again Huntstown had come alive. A horse-drawn cornmill was turning out coarse flour, Richard Ellis built himself a new frame house out of boards produced in the new sawmill, increasingly carts with supplies made their way up the mountain, and surplus lumber and flour destined for the market descended to Deerfield and to Israel Williams's store in Hatfield. Rather than huddle together as did some early settlers in eastern Massachusetts and the Connecticut Valley, these settlers boldly spread themselves out around the landscape, being both confident as well as practical in searching out the pockets of arable land among the hills. Proprietor meetings now met in Huntstown, and at a meeting in May 1754 they agreed to grant out most of the remaining undivided land in two-hundred-acre lots.[40]

The survey never happened. For the next six years, in fact, the proprietors, as a corporate entity, virtually ceased to exist. Those were trying times for the settlement. Even though Huntstown was no longer the outermost of English settlements on the province's northwestern frontier, as it had been in 1742, it was far enough away from the river valley to be in danger of attack, and in late summer 1754, the peace that had been living on borrowed time came to an end. Israel Williams, now a militia colonel commanding Hampshire County's northern regiment, learned from his scouts that raiding parties had set out from the French fort at Crown Point on Lake Champlain, and by the end of the month they had struck at Fort Number Four in New Hampshire and at West Hoosack in northwestern Massachusetts. He had his work cut out for him, for the long line of forts constructed under his predecessor and uncle John Stoddard had fallen into disrepair, and few had a garrison. Williams had recently become the Huntstown proprietors' clerk. He knew full well that there were settlements that did not even have a fortified house.[41]

Even as he wrote to Governor Shirley about his plans to rebuild and regarrison the forts along the frontier, Williams recognized that the best program for defense lay with the settlers themselves. He urged Shirley not only to think of military campaigns into the enemy's country, but to provide funds for fortifications and wages for enough soldiers to stand guard and encourage the settlers to stay in their new communities on the front line. Governor Shirley was in full agreement with Williams and had already made known his fear that people on the frontier "are in danger of retiring from their Settlements, upon the sd Hostilities, whereby the Towns of Stockbridge, Sheffield & the new Settlements between Westfield and Sheffield & the Old Towns on Connecticut River . . . will be much exposed to the Attacks and Ravages of the Enemy, than if the Inhabitants Should remain upon their Settlements." Shirley gave Williams free reign to station troops wherever they would do the most good, but it is clear that both men saw the settlers themselves as the bulwark of the defense of both the river towns and of the proprietorships that had become valuable assets in recent years. It was not until late September that Williams found that he could spare a squad of ten soldiers to go out from Hadley to guard his nervous Huntstown inhabitants as they gathered in their crops. With the arrival of winter the frontier seemed quiet, though, and the settlers themselves, doubtless unwilling to feed the detachment for months on end, sent them home.[42]

The next spring, as Williams put together his regiment in preparation for an attack on Crown Point, French and Indian raiding parties began striking frontier settlements again in an effort to keep the Massachusetts troops at home. In the early morning of June 11, they killed two and took two captive in Charlemont, a few miles north of Huntstown, demonstrating that Williams's line of forts was quite porous. Eager for the extra cash and probably convinced that Huntstown's best defense was to take the fight to the enemy, nearly every fighting-age man of the settlement was in New York with the army. By late afternoon the remaining Huntstown settlers were on their way east to Deerfield, leaving their crops to succumb to the wildlife and weeds for the summer.[43]

The campaign did claim a few successes, and was somewhat of an antidote to the depressing news of Braddock's defeat in Pennsylvania, but it did not result in the capture of Crown Point and casualties were heavy. The outcome was hardly reassuring to those at home who were hoping for fewer raids in the future. Thus, as the next winter set in and several families returned to Huntstown, they began to build a stockade around Chileab Smith's house at the northern end of the settlement. "We were in a broken situation at that time," Ebenezer Smith later recounted. Apparently Colonel Williams, with his resources stretched thin, was not willing to pay for this construction, nor to station a guard in the settlement during the winter. Angered, the settlers wrote directly to the governor about their "destresst circumstances." After all, they complained, "we . . . settled our land according to your command and have gone through great hard ship before the war by reason of the new inhabitance not coming." Now that the war was on, they were in daily fear for their lives "for want of the common defence allowed to other fronteers." Their wives and children, "in leiveing our hooses as they were casting our household stoof some of it into the weeds and bushes to hide from the enemy and so to go to sojourn wher we could find a Place and thus have been scattered husbands from there wives and children." They had asked "The Hon Con Israel William as our father for Protection" many times, "but he not being willing to put the county to charg acourded us no help." With their families spread all over the countryside they had to "come to worck on our Lands without a gard save what we made among ourselves one of us spending a considerable time in the woods of hunts town to see if he could see or track the enemy. . . . [T]ake some pitty on us," they begged. Then they attached a rough map pointing out that Deerfield lay eight miles to the east, and Williams's Hatfield eighteen miles southeast.[44]

Williams was clearly embarrassed when he got word that his settlers had gone over his head. Nevertheless, he wrote to Shirley that he thought a guard of ten or twelve men might encourage the settlers to remain in Huntstown and work their land. The issue seemed to be who would provision the troops, and whether any money could be found to pay for the construction of fortifications. Smith's fort ended up being 150 feet square with a 15-foot stockade wall, and that took a lot of logs. Yet Williams, in spite of his assurances to the governor, dragged his feet throughout the spring even in sending a squad of soldiers.[45]

Perhaps he was of two minds. On the one hand, as a merchant, a proprietor, and a military man, he wanted the settlement to grow, or at least survive, and become a good market, a good investment, and a strong piece of the defensive shield that New England needed. On the other hand, Wetherell Wittium's unmarried daughter Elizabeth had just been brought before the county court, over which he presided, for having "carnal knowledge of the Body of one Negro Male person and had there & then a child begotten on her body by Fornication." No doubt *Rex v. Elizabeth Wittium* reminded him that these people were a difficult and unruly assortment and might not be worth the expenditure of money he did not have.[46] At any rate, for the spring of 1756, when forts along the frontier were reporting daily sightings of the enemy, Huntstown people carried on with no guard.

And so it was in Captain Hunt's town, as spring turned to summer and the European powers finally got around to declaring war on each other. On July 1, Chileab Smith and Richard Ellis brought their children down the county road to their wedding in Deerfield, using markings on trees for guidance where the "road" was difficult to discern. They had much on their minds. For Ellis, Huntstown had been a seventeen-year project that had meant back-breaking labor and constant vigilance. After all that time, they could not even have a wedding in their own settlement, not only because there was no magistrate in Huntstown, but also because half the family had already fled to Deerfield. For Smith, Huntstown was, no doubt, a divine ordeal—God testing the fortitude of His people to see if they were truly worthy of saving grace. None among the wedding party were about to surrender what they had come for: land, respectability, independence, and, in Smith's case, godliness. It appears from their letter to the governor that they believed they were owed at least those things, for all they had endured. Whether the county and provincial elite was ready to allow as much to a surly bunch of debtors, former servants and slaves, religious dissenters, and people of otherwise questionable character would depend, it seemed, on how much longer it took to secure the borderlands and begin to derive some return on their investments. For that the elite was somewhat obliged to those few they had encouraged to dwell in their hill town.

6. We Ought to Obey God Rather Than Man

From his Hatfield home the world had a different look for Israel Williams. It was not Huntstown's world of mountains and ravines, towering pines and scattered beaver marshes, or deep, menacing silences on cold spring nights early in the raiding season. His village lay at the southern end of a broad alluvial plain stretching two miles west from the Connecticut River and eight miles north toward Deerfield. For another mile or two west of the plain the land rolled gently upward to a long ridge that separated the inhabited part of the town from the backcountry. He could only imagine the Huntstown settlement as he gazed northwest toward Chestnut Mountain, for it was another eleven miles beyond that—if one were to draw a straight line on a map. The eleven miles was rough country, though, and in effect the distance was much greater.

It was a cultural distance as well. Hatfield, even in the midst of war, was a town for which Timothy Dwight's phrase "order, peace, and harmony" was particularly apt. Much of the order was, in fact, attributable to the town's being Israel's home, for by 1756 Williams had become Hampshire County's most prominent citizen, and it could be said that order, peace, and harmony was the essence of his social vision. The son of the popular and beloved minister William "Hatfield" Williams, Israel rose to preeminence on his father's reputation, a Harvard education, and ties to the remarkable Williams-Stoddard clan. Elected selectman at age twenty-two, he climbed through a number of administrative, judicial, and military positions during the 1730s and 1740s. During King George's War he was chief of the commissary department for the northern regiment of Hampshire County, and when his uncle Colonel John Stoddard died after the war, Israel assumed his place as regimental commander. Both positions produced considerable revenue for the firm of Williams and Graves, of which he was the principal proprietor. As a member of the Massachusetts House of Representatives after 1748, he cultivated his relationship with provincial leaders in Boston, particularly his Harvard classmate Thomas Hutchinson, and made himself indispensable to their strategic and economic concerns. In return they helped him to consolidate his position locally. There were few who could claim to have had a greater role in ending the pastorate of the great Jonathan Edwards in Northampton. In fact, wherever Williams had any sway he urged congregations to adopt Solomon Stoddard's inclusive model of church governance.

He saw to it, furthermore, that his sway was far-flung. His proprietary right and clerkship in Huntstown was only one of several holdings that ensured that he had a finger in developing settlements scattered throughout northwestern Massachusetts, at one of which he hoped someday to establish a college that would be the western sister to his alma mater. For each town, on the river or in the backcountry, he had a vision of a well-ordered community of honest yeomen who would extend godly vigilance over all within their settlement, observe the law and rules of social decorum, work hard to produce marketable commodities, defend the frontier against the savage and papist threat from the north, and buy supplies at Williams and Graves. He was not a wealthy man by Atlantic standards, but rather he dedicated himself to presenting an august aura in order to lead his countrymen and honor his heritage.[1] Across the river in Hadley, and around the river's bend in Northampton, yeomen, tradesmen, and merchants alike gave him the respect that was due to a defender of a way of life, and the inhabitants of the backcountry . . .

. . . well, yes, there was the backcountry.

Israel Williams understood that every vision had a reality crowding into it, or he would have confined himself to Hatfield politics long ago. In his meetings with the other Huntstown proprietors and inhabitants he surely grew accustomed to being patient and accommodating toward men with rough edges. He had purchased his right a few years after the first drawing of lots, but by now he comprehended the difficulties in the task of "bringing forward the settlement." If there was to be a Huntstown, with its inhabitants trading at his store, driving up land values, slowing an attack on Hatfield and

Deerfield, and spreading the New England Way into the wilderness, he recognized that the early migrants would be mostly odd birds. In return for their discomfort, they would want credit, land, rights to more land, roads, mills, the privilege of working off their taxes and debts on the roads and mills, and, alas, a degree of respect. As he and his associate Obadiah Dickinson of Hadley, the treasurer of the Huntstown proprietors, commiserated about the slow pace of development in the backcountry, they certainly understood the concessions that would be needed to attract even more settlers, now that the French and Indian War had intensified. What they were not so aware of was that their settlers would also want autonomy—the privilege to define their own lives. And viewing the world from his house in Hatfield, Israel Williams would always have trouble understanding that.

Your Fatherly Protection

Perhaps they talked about their frustrations as they made their way down what was called the county road to the Smith and Ellis wedding on July 1, 1756. At any rate, two days later, the "faitfull and now gratly distressed" inhabitants of Huntstown had another petition ready to send off to the governor, council, and "the great and jenoral Court . . . at booston." "Have som marcy on us" they complained once more. "Notwithstanding we had such incourrigment from the govennor and Counsell and some of the settlers that new our distresses that the request we made to you the last spring for help should be answered," Colonel Williams had yet to send any soldiers to guard them. Now in the summer they were spending nearly all of their time "imployed in defence of our country" scouting from Deerfield west across their own town and northwest toward the Deerfield River. Thus, they themselves were serving as a guard for both Hatfield and Deerfield, spreading themselves thinly throughout the western hills (a long list of places scouted followed). In this work they had become "gratly impovereshed many of us that ware inhabitance are alredy broken up and in want of soport," and they would surely have to surrender their town if it was attacked. In fact, fifty-four of Huntstown's eighty-three inhabitants had "scattered away . . . for want of protection." Perhaps, they suggested, the leaders in Boston might have "some bowels of pittye . . . and send us some strenth of men and put us under the common Pay of the garoson service of this Provence from last March and forwards."

The petition was signed by Chileab Smith and three of his sons, Richard Ellis and three of his sons, and Heber Honestman. They noted that "Chileab Smith son and John Elis [who had signed] are not yet quite of age [they were fourteen] but are good soldiers able bodyed every way able to do the work of solders and have don it this sommor being expert with guns beyond som that are of full age." Whether or not that last assertion was accurate is hardly important. A fourteen-year-old was a field hand that could not be spared to patrol the outskirts of the settlement while there were crops to be tended and more land that needed to be cleared. To the petition there was also appended a list of signatures of men who said that, although they did not currently live in Huntstown, they supported the petitioners and appreciated their vigilance and hard work on the frontier.[2]

While petitions will always be suspect for a degree of exaggeration, in this case the sense of fear, frustration, and desperation is credible. Colrain, a settlement of Scots-Irish immigrants just ten miles north of Huntstown, had already sustained an attack in this season, and its settlers had completely abandoned their homes (one of which had been burned to the ground).[3] And even though nearly every Huntstown man, and some of the boys, had served in the Crown Point campaign, and now lived in a constant state of armed readiness, the "Hon Col Williams" had not yet obeyed the governor's instructions to help them. He had not even put them on his payroll. Their trepidation must be taken all the more seriously when we consider the risk they were taking in testing Williams's patience. This was the second instance in which they had gone over his head, and it was already evident that the first time had not lit much of a fire under him.

This time, though, Smith, Ellis, and Honestman must have taken a measure of the House of Representatives, which had not been in session in March, and decided that more sympathy would be forthcoming, inspiring more action on the part of Williams. Indeed, the House did respond favorably, asking that the lieutenant governor "be desired to give direction to Col. Israel Williams that he order a suitable number of Forces destined to Scout on the Western Frontier for ye Protection of ye Petitioners and Inhabitants of sd. Place." Acting governor Spencer Phips followed up with orders to that effect.[4]

Williams, however, was not to be moved. For one thing, he had far more pressing concerns. He was getting reports daily from his captains in the outer forts that they were regularly sighting and occasionally engaging enemy forces, that their supplies and ammunition were inadequate, and that they needed more men. It was important to keep residents in Huntstown, and for that he supported a measure by the proprietors to see if more delinquent taxes could be collected for "bringing forward the settlement" and to forgo taxing further for a meetinghouse at the moment. But he would not commit paid soldiers to guard the town nor pay boys to creep around in the woods. Even if he had not managed to stare down the settlers, he knew how to play the game of provincial politics. There would be no troops or funds for an inner-tier garrison unless Boston was going to send extra money for that, and for a lot of other needs too.[5]

By September 1756, he had won that game, to an extent, and had received some funding as well as authorization to impress soldiers. The presumptuous young preacher Ebenezer Smith, in fact, was among the first to be called to duty. Williams was not completely hostile toward the farmers in Huntstown, however. He gave Richard Ellis a commission in the commissary. Ellis had a head for figures and merchandise, apparently, and Williams was willing to trade pay and respect for a cessation of petitions to Boston. He also promoted Richard's son Reuben to the rank of ensign, a concession that actually paid a second dividend when Reuben almost single-handedly captured an entire squad of French soldiers later in the war.[6]

In this way, Williams held his cantankerous backcountry constituents at bay while he secured the financing he thought he needed to defend the countryside. Meanwhile, the inhabitants of Huntstown remained huddled in the fort at Chileab Smith's for the winter of 1756–57. In April 1757, the House of Representatives resolved that a guard of ten men paid at four shillings a week (plus forty pounds for every Indian scalp taken) be stationed at Huntstown, but again Williams dragged his feet. On April 19, he had a Lieutenant John Hawks of Deerfield enlist and send out nearly sixty soldiers to Northfield, Greenfield, Colrain, Falltown, Charlement, and Huntstown, but only three of them went to Huntstown. Hawks himself stopped at Huntstown on May 13 and, seeing that Smith's fort was at the north end of the settlement, and quite a climb for some of the families, suggested that another be built closer to the Ellis and Phillips homesteads. Perhaps more important, he told them that the province would pay for the construction of this fort and would be willing to send more soldiers.[7]

Hawks's visit appears to have had the desired effect of mollifying the settlers. Even Chileab Smith was willing to give Israel Williams the benefit of the doubt for the moment. On May 27, Smith wrote to Williams that "your advice and directions to buld a new fort in the middle between Ellis house and my hous is so far as I can perseive harttyly imbreaced and the worck now goeth fast on." There had, he said, been a small delay when they put their crops in, and there had also been some question among the soldiers at first as to where to build the fort. Eventually, though, he and the sergeant of the guard had settled the matter. Smith went on to say that he was concerned that Williams might have heard "of the evel speaking of one or two men in this form that he will send to the cort other men are as good as the Cornol Williams, and another saying he don't care how sone the Cornl draws all the souldiours off." Smith did not want Williams to "with draw your fatherly protection over us for the ungreatfull speeches of two or Three men," for then "our distress . . . would be very great." And besides, he added, "the peace love and unity that hath ben sence the soldiers came to my house hath ben great."[8]

Beneath the seemingly deferential surface of this letter, with its invocation of "peace love and unity," we can read the continuing concern for safety on the part of the Huntstown settlers. They had finally received some help, and Smith did not want to do anything to discourage more by seeming ungrateful. Additionally, there is a bit of an olive branch in the reference to those one or two (or was it two or three—or more?) men who were speaking unlovingly of the colonel. Williams knew Smith well. Before Smith moved to Huntstown he had a reputation among Hadley's leaders, associates of Williams, as an unpleasant devotee of Jonathan Edwards's views on conversion and church membership. And then there had been the infamous preaching of young Ebenezer Smith, who had barely a dame-school education. No doubt, both Chileab and his son had inspired among their neighbors a regularly frosty reception for the ministers that Williams and other river-town proprietors had engaged to preach in Huntstown before the war. None of that endeared Chileab Smith to Williams, and surely Smith was aware of the degree to which he had offended Williams in the past. The message in Smith's letter, then, was that Smith would back off the criticism that he apparently had been conveying here and there, and even all the way to Boston, as long as the "fatherly protection" would continue. As a sweetener, Smith had suggested that peace, love, and unity, a favorite theme of Williams's, might result from the presence of more soldiers.

Williams got the message—or so Smith might have believed when a guard of nine men arrived from Deerfield in June to help complete the fort and to remain on permanent garrison duty in Huntstown for the next two years. One of them, Nathan Chapin, stayed even longer after peace, love, and unity apparently inspired him to propose to Smith's daughter Mary. During those years the British ministry committed more regular troops to New England and New York, and Williams could afford to draw back more of his militia for garrison duty, put a number of the Huntstown men "on the country pay," and apply more funds to fort construction. This, and the willingness of the proprietors to credit the inhabitants for work on roads and mills, earned him a respite from their challenges to his authority. It appears too, that he and the other proprietors were able to entice families back to Huntstown, and even to find some more settlers who would move to the town.[9]

Nevertheless, in spite of the surface thaw in relations between Williams and the inhabitants of Huntstown, the ongoing continental conflict continued to produce tension over the next two years. Huntstown men were still called to military service, some for long periods on distant campaigns. The new fort was really only about half the size of the fort that Chileab Smith and his closest neighbors had built and continued to use. A sighting of what appeared to be an Indian reconnaissance party in Huntstown, along with the fall of Fort William Henry and the massacre of its garrison in August 1757, discouraged families from sleeping in their own houses at night, and must have resulted in increasingly crowded conditions. Finally, neither the proprietors nor Colonel Williams appeared to feel an obligation to pay anything for the construction of Smith's fort. When the Smiths protested, Williams and his friends recommended "that Every agreved person tack his Remidy as the Law hath proscribed and not come to the Proprietors for Reliefe." When they went to the county court of common pleas, they found Williams newly sworn in and sitting on the bench.[10]

In addition, as relations between Williams and the inhabitants remained cool, Williams himself seemed unable to resist asserting himself from time to time. He had the king's attorney press the fornication case against Wetherell Wittium's daughter Elizabeth after she turned up pregnant a second time by the same "Negro person." To his embarrassment she arrived in court with a sharp lawyer and the king's attorney decided not to pursue the prosecution against either Elizabeth or John Abel, her alleged partner in crime. In exasperation, the court then turned its attention to Wetherell's son for "wickedly, willingly and unnecessarily absent[ing] himself from the public worship" for a month while living in Sunderland. Wetherell Jr. found himself a lawyer too, and the case was continued for two more years. Meanwhile, the group taking refuge in Smith's fort seemed to be observing the Sabbath in its own separatist manner. Furthermore, they were ever more enamored of Ebenezer Smith, whose apparent lack of learning and orthodoxy did little to dissuade his listeners from the need for evidence of saving grace in order to come to the communion table.[11] Evidently each side was prepared to stand its ground, the inhabitants expecting protection, respect, and compensation for their defense of the frontier (yet independence in terms of adherence to doctrine), and Williams expecting a degree of patriotic sacrifice, ecclesiastical and social order, and deference to his standing.

One would think that the simmering contest of wills might subside with the fall of Quebec and Montreal by early 1760. Canada was British and the war was over for New England. Williams, however, had yet more insolence to endure. In May 1760, the inhabitants went to the legislature with a petition complaining that "the proprietors refuse to help pay for the fort," and asking that the government require nonresident proprietors to settle their lands or give them up. When the House of Representatives hesitated, perhaps hoping for an amicable solution between one of their more prominent members and these difficult people, the settlers called a proprietors' meeting in Huntstown on September 10. There they elected Chileab Smith moderator and treasurer, and Ephraim Marble clerk. Israel Williams rode up to the meeting, perhaps thinking that his personal bearing could put an end to this disorderliness, but he found himself outnumbered and not at all intimidating. To compound the humiliation, being the only magistrate present, he had to suffer through the role of swearing in the new officers, namely Smith, his ongoing nemesis, and Marble, a one-time laborer in the employ of the proprietors but now his own replacement as clerk. In a none-too-subtle statement of their determination to keep the upper hand, the inhabitants also voted to buy their own law book.[12] Williams did have a lot on his mind beyond the unruly settlers in Huntstown, but just the same, they were becoming annoying.

Ashfield

To be sure, there were numerous matters upon which both gentlemen proprietors and backcountry farmers could agree. It was important, for example, to settle once and for all the boundary dispute with Deerfield or there would always be a hazy zone on the east side of town where some of the land with better potential could not be granted out without risk of conflicting claims from Deerfield's grantees. Israel Williams and Chileab Smith both owned disputed lots there. Therefore, the proprietors consented to pay for a new survey of the town and prepared a petition for the General Court complaining of Deerfield's miscalculations.[13]

Additionally, there were other areas of general agreement. Trade between the river merchants and the backcountry farmers was mutually beneficial, and, in fact, necessary for both sides. The settlers needed tools, hardware, glass, sugar, salt, pins, and other items for the household economy, and they were building an appetite for cloth, china plates, and substantial quantities of rum. The merchants would gladly fill up Richard Ellis's wagon with such items and give him a cut of the profits, as long as he would return with livestock, lumber, and potash for which there were good markets locally and abroad. The nonresident proprietors were probably not averse to the expenditure of their assessment money on a boar and a bull in the spring of 1761, if that would encourage a livestock surplus that the settlers were eager to sell. Finally, both nonresident proprietors and inhabitants were interested in attracting new settlers and in collecting taxes from delinquent proprietors. In 1761, there was still barely a trickle of settlers moving into Huntstown. The war was over, but experience showed that a community needed to reach a threshold of about twenty families before momentum behind in-migration would build. Present and prospective residents wanted neighbors for face-to-face trade, for mutual assistance, for sharing of the tax burden, and for moral support. Nonresident proprietors wanted demand for land to rise. A surge of new settlers would signal good times to come and justify a final division of the common land.[14]

In spite of these areas of agreement, as long as Smith and Marble maintained control of taxation and the proprietors' treasury in 1761, the antagonism between nonresident proprietors and the inhabitants deepened. There was conflict over the daily rate to be paid for work on the roads, and some of the early settlers were still not content with how much they had received for being among the first ten families to set up housekeeping in Huntstown. Wartime inflation surely played a role in these disagreements. The five pounds voted for the first settlers in 1741, and the two shillings per day previously paid for road work, were not going to buy many supplies in 1761. It must have seemed unjust to the settlers, in fact, that those wanting to stick to the old rates were the ones selling store goods at inflated prices. In March, the inhabitants gathered a proprietors' meeting at Huntstown and passed a measure to set road work at four shillings per day (while allowing a mere six shillings in compensation for the recent resurveying of the town boundaries, a task that must have taken Nathaniel Kellogg many days). Then in May, Chileab Smith, who had already asked for and received two shillings to allow the public use of a bridge he had built over Bear River, began to complain that he wasn't being paid enough to saw boards at the sawmill. In response, the proprietors put together a "committee of indifferent men" to determine a fair rate.[15]

There was more hostility between the gentlemen in Hatfield and the inhabitants of Huntstown over church matters. Now that Ebenezer Smith had children of his own, he had become convinced of the error of infant baptism. He was soon finding scripture to support his contention "that true Believers and None but Such, were proper Subjects of the ordinance of Baptism—and Immersion the proper Mode According to the Scriptures." Again his speaking talents impressed his parents, siblings, and in-laws—a large number of people at this point—and, along with some neighbors, a group of separatists joined by an informal covenant became a thoroughly committed congregation of Baptists. A trio of Baptist preachers from as far away as Sturbridge, Massachusetts, and Thompson and Stafford, Connecticut, arrived in July 1761 to ordain twenty-seven-year-old Ebenezer as the "Elder" of this church, and to immerse a number of men and women. According to Ebenezer, this "made a great tumult among the people," and "all manner of evil was said about us." In their new covenant they declared "that the Gospel is to be supported by a free Contribution and not by Rates, Fines or prisons. . . . If magistrates encroach upon the Laws of Christ we ought to obey God Rather than Man." For Judge Israel Williams and the other gentleman proprietors, this formalization of dissent must have been the most disturbing element of the tension between them and the inhabitants.[16]

At a late-summer meeting at Richard Ellis's house it appears that the nonresident proprietors managed to assert themselves over their presumptuous inhabitants. The first line in the record reads that the "Method for Calling a meeting of the said Proprietors Having been attended," Obadiah Dickinson was chosen moderator and treasurer, and Reuben Belding clerk. That language suggests that the resident-proprietors had been derelict in giving notice of meetings, no doubt purposely in order to keep attendance of the river-town gentlemen low, and that the latter were not going to put up with that in the future. They then appointed Dickinson, Belding, Nathaniel Kellogg, and Charles Phelps, all river-town gentlemen, to a committee "to settle accounts with the late treasurer" and to conduct the business of selling lands of delinquent taxpayers. At the next meeting, in December in Hatfield, they followed up by adjusting the rate for road work down from four to three shillings a day and establishing a committee to build a meetinghouse. The tax sales would also be held in Hatfield, lest the inhabitants think they might acquire land and rights without having to bid against wealthier interested parties.[17]

The following spring, Philip Phillips, who seems to have allied himself with the nonresident proprietors, brought a test case before the county court in an apparent effort to check the rising Baptist insurgency. He, Reuben Ellis, and Ephraim Marble had been chosen assessors the year before, and Ellis and Marble, being Baptist, had exempted Ebenezer Smith from the provincial taxes because the law allowed exemptions for ordained ministers. Thus, Phillips sued at the Quarter Sessions for being overtaxed—that is, taxed extra to make up for Ebenezer's exemption. At the trial Chief Judge Israel Williams would not allow the Baptists to enter any evidence that Smith was a settled minister. He declared that any man with no college degree or support of the ministers of the county could not be ordained. He then fined the Baptist assessors four pounds each, ordered them to put Ebenezer Smith on the tax list, and refused to allow an appeal to the Superior Court.[18]

The determination of the gentlemen and traders among the proprietors to take a leading, even domineering role in shaping Huntstown is understandable. They had a lot at stake. Dickinson, Belding, Kellogg, and some others had made a sizable investment in rights that would pay off only if there was a viable community that others would want to join—one that would justify further divisions of land that could be sold. The longer it took to reach that threshold of families that would make Huntstown attractive, the longer their investments languished. For Israel Williams, who had only one right and seemed to be content, at the moment, to remain in the background, regaining social control and establishing ecclesiastical order was even more important than deriving profit from land sales or even settling a population dependent on his store for supplies. Probably all of these men doubted that a community of strict Baptists opposed to infant baptism was going be comfortable for the average young family looking for farmland.

As they surveyed the scene in early 1762, though, they knew that their present control of Huntstown was tenuous. For one thing, in proprietors' meetings they did not have the votes they needed to carry issues when the meeting was well attended. Obadiah Dickinson owned the most rights, with six to his name. Reuben Belding and Nathaniel Kellogg each had three, and Belding held a mortgage on a fourth. Israel Williams had only one, as did a couple of other Hatfield men who would vote with him. There were other nonresident proprietors who might have been prevailed upon to support these Hatfield and Hadley gentlemen, but they lived in somewhat distant places like Braintree, or had long since lost interest in the Huntstown project and their taxes were in arrears. Of the sixty rights, inhabitants themselves owned thirty. Some of those inhabitants may have been beholden in one way or another to Dickinson, Belding, Kellogg, and Williams, but getting them to a meeting was not always assured.[19]

In fact, during 1761 the challenge of shaping Huntstown to their liking had become more difficult rather than less. Although some new settlers had arrived during that year, they were not the sort to whom the nonresident proprietors could look for support in their campaign to establish an orderly community. Samuel Belding from Deerfield was a man of questionable reputation, having been sued prior to his marriage for not supporting his illegitimate child. Nathaniel Harvey, who had served in frontier garrisons throughout the war, and Israel and Miles Standish, who arrived from Stafford, Connecticut, immediately proved themselves suspect by joining the Smiths' Baptist congregation. These men could hardly be counted on to contribute more than the paltry sum voted in 1761 to pay for preaching by "an orthodox and gospel minister."[20]

The following summer the dispute with Chileab Smith over how much he would be paid for sawing boards came to a head when he simply shut down the mill. The proprietors dispatched a committee to ask him "why he does not Perform of his obligation . . . sawing boards for the proprietors," but they were unable to come to terms with him. This was not at all propitious, for the proprietors had settled on a site for a meetinghouse and had voted to raise a considerable sum to build it, but now they would have to bring boards into a town that was well endowed with timber. All in all, the nonresident proprietors could not help but see that if they were going to establish more firm control of Huntstown, they themselves would need to do some serious recruiting of families more amenable to their social vision.[21]

They reached out to contacts throughout the region to find suitable settlers, and over the next four years they met with considerable success. Huntstown's population more than tripled between 1762 and 1766, as twenty families became nearly seventy. An example of the people they called upon in their recruitment effort is Daniel Alden, Esquire, a prosperous Congregational church deacon of Stafford, Connecticut, who had acquired three rights in Huntstown before King George's War. Alden's far-flung network of acquaintances and kinship ties may have been responsible for as many as twenty of the new families that set up housekeeping in Huntstown between 1762 and 1765. A longtime proprietor who had been unable to persuade even one of his sons to move to his property in Huntstown before 1762, he understood the frustrations of the absentee proprietors who had been waiting long for a community to emerge. Furthermore, his experience in Stafford, where a congregation of Baptists had challenged his established church, probably motivated him to assist Israel Williams and his friends in the river towns to build a Congregational majority in Huntstown. Even though he sold two of his rights in 1761 (his son Barnabas still held the third), he worked hard alongside other nonresident proprietors for the sake of ecclesiastical and social order.[22]

The trouble was that not all of the settlers who were pouring into Huntstown were necessarily people who would conform to the social norms and deferential habits of the river towns. In fact, the two rights that Daniel Alden sold went to Stafford residents Miles and Israel Standish, who soon ended up in Huntstown's Baptist Church. To be sure, only a few of the new settlers were willing to submit to the strict discipline and high standards for admission of the Baptist Church. Yet many of the newcomers were laborers, renters, or young single men, and there were quite a few whose piety was unknown or suspect. And so, while Huntstown's population grew rapidly, the gentlemen proprietors still had to move carefully on such agenda items as locating the meetinghouse, settling a minister, and distributing land. As was true of Salmon Brook, in Connecticut, as its population began to grow in the 1720s and 1730s, the inhabitants would require a soft touch if local leaders hoped for cooperation.

One approach to this problem, again as Connecticut's leaders discovered in the case of Salmon Brook, was to assure the inhabitants that they could retain a measure of independence. Moving meetings back to Huntstown was a first step. Joseph Mitchell, a fairly prosperous farmer who had moved from Deerfield, opened an inn on the county road, and that served as a place where business could be conducted in an orderly manner. It was there that proprietors began the process of transferring the reins of local government to the inhabitants. The proprietors also began the process of establishing a local civil government with town privileges. The king had put a hold on the incorporation of new towns in Massachusetts, but Huntstown began to operate as a town in 1762. Its first officers, the tax assessors, were Ebenezer Belding (originally from Hatfield and allied with the nonresident proprietors) and Reuben Ellis and Chileab Smith (both Baptists), who became de facto selectmen. Then, as the number of families climbed, the proprietors dispatched Nathaniel Kellogg to Boston to petition first for an exemption from colony taxes while the settlers were getting their feet on the ground, and second for formal status as a town. Achieving the latter would empower the town government to collect its own taxes, survey and maintain its own roads, send its own man to Boston, and generally manage its own affairs.[23]

Also to pacify the more unruly of their inhabitants, the wealthier proprietors continued to allow proprietors' assessments to be paid in work on roads, bridges, and other community improvements. Further, they did not hesitate to share the trading business with the locals, in particular Richard Ellis, and, when he moved to Colrain in 1762 to open a new store, his son John. Both Richard and John Ellis enjoyed trading connections with river merchants who had discovered a market for potash that could be produced in abundance in the backcountry and moved to the river more easily than the trees that were burned to produce it. Finally, during the summer of 1762, the proprietors surveyed a land division of hundred-acre lots, not only parceling out equal acreage to each right, but also declaring that anyone dissatisfied with the lot he drew could exchange it for other land as long as the new lot was not located in the "Extreme parts of the township."[24]

In what appears to be a moment of overconfidence that they had lulled most of the potential troublemakers into contentment with various favors and inducements, the river-town proprietors voted in December 1762 to call Jacob Sherwin, Yale-trained and "orthodox" by Israel Williams's standards, to settle as Huntstown's minister. They plied him with a hundred-pound settlement, a proprietary right, and a salary of sixty pounds per annum, scheduled to rise as the number of families rose. The formation of a Congregational church that accepted the Halfway Covenant soon followed in February, and some of Huntstown's earliest settlers joined. The river-town proprietors were also quick to make Sherwin the proprietors' clerk.[25]

It is doubtful that anyone could have been less suited to preach to the inhabitants of Huntstown. While they were living in daily fear for their lives during the war, Sherwin was studying safely in New Haven. He had no idea what the Huntstown people had endured. To compound the problem, he must have been selected because of his virulent opposition to separatists, for once ordained, he busied himself preaching against the Baptists, and once even barged into one of their meetings and ordered them to disperse. The response of the strict Baptists at the north end of town was predictable. Not only did Chileab Smith persist in demanding a higher rate for sawing before he would create lumber for the meetinghouse and the furthering of the settlement in general, but with Richard Ellis's help, he constructed a cornmill at a location detrimental to the operation of the sawmill. In addition, the emerging Baptist congregation let it be known that they were going to make it difficult to raise enough money to cover Sherwin's settlement. There was even talk that the proceeds of the right set aside for the ministry ought to go to the Baptists since they had the first ordained pastor in Huntstown.[26]

Even with this background grumbling and mixed results in terms of recruitment, the Hatfield and Hadley proprietors could be said to have gained the upper hand by 1765. During the previous two years they had successfully auctioned off a fair amount of land belonging to proprietors who had not paid taxes, and gained a number of friends among the settlers in the process, like Philip Phillips and John Sadler, who were able to buy some of the lots at rock-bottom prices. Phillips and Sadler joined the Congregational Church. In June 1765, the legislature helped the gentlemen proprietors further gain favor with the inhabitants when it acted to incorporate "the Plantation called Huntstown . . . into a Town by the name of Ashfield." With hundreds of acres in the hands of inhabitants (from new surveys and tax sales), the ability to work off taxes on roads that they themselves used, and a town government of their own choosing, Huntstown residents seemed to have little reason to raise much of a fuss over ongoing differences with the nonresident proprietors.[27]

Coursing through all of these developments was the arrival of a modicum of prosperity, and who could complain about that? Huntstown, now Ashfield, was still quite poor by provincial standards. There were only seventeen horses in the whole town. The average farm family, according to the tax valuation done in 1765, was likely to have a house to live in, might have cleared ten acres of land, and owned five animals. About a quarter of the men on the tax roll had no taxable property at all. Those who had lived in town for some time, however, were illustrations of what could be done. Nathan Chapin, the soldier from Springfield who married Chileab Smith's daughter, had cleared nearly fifty acres, owned a horse and two yokes of oxen, and managed a herd of fifty sheep. Thomas Phillips and his son Philip were now in the sawmill business, and between them they had over sixty acres cleared. Samuel Belding, who had come from Deerfield in 1761, had a pair of oxen, a horse, six cows, three pigs, and fourteen sheep on forty-two acres of cleared land. There were some, like Joseph Mitchell the innkeeper, and physicians Moses Hayden and Phineas Bartlett, who were arriving in town with a measure of wealth, ready to trade with the locals as they got their families established.[28]

As Huntstown became Ashfield, a name selected by Governor Francis Bernard to honor his friend Lord Thurlow of Ashfield, England, it seemed that "peace, order, and unity" had spread across the rough country that the proprietors had worked so long to tame. It was a fragile peace, but a peace nonetheless. Economic growth and control over local affairs had a way of taking the edge off sharp differences in visions that remained under the surface. Dickinson, Belding, Kellogg, and Williams probably felt that Ashfield would soon become the model of decorum that its patrician name seemed to embody. But in achieving the present tranquility they had empowered people whose vision of social order did not match their own. Ashfield may have been named after a peer of an aristocratic social order, but the new town had nothing to do with aristocracy or social order.

Scandalous and Disorderly Christians

Among their agenda items listed on a warrant for an Ashfield town meeting in March 1768, the selectmen announced that inhabitants should consider "if the town will Concur with a Vot past in Boston the 28 day of Oct 1767 Consurning keeping Superfluties out of this Countwry."[29] Indeed, one might begin to wonder if, amid the excitement of a rapidly growing population and the town's incorporation, the inhabitants were at all aware of the simmering conflict between the province and the British ministry. Parliament had passed new tax laws in 1764 and 1765, raising a storm of protest in Boston and other port towns, and subsequently had repealed the Stamp Act. Yet, the imposition of the Townshend duties and the resulting boycott movement in 1767 seems to have been the first time that anyone in Ashfield paid attention to the issues that would escalate into the American Revolution.

It would also be the last time, at least for another six years. The March 1768 meeting never did take action on the proposed boycott. While colonial leaders flooded the presses with diatribes on tyranny, representation, and rights, Ashfield inhabitants and proprietors were preoccupied with their own local turmoil. Whatever harmony there was in 1765 was short-lived. In a somewhat ironic twist, actually, local antagonisms would unfold and expand to envelop the whole region. While this "obscure village," as one historian has called it, was relatively unconcerned with the regional resistance to the government of Great Britain, all New England would soon concern itself with Ashfield, and even the king of England and the Continental Congress would grapple with the tumult that began deep in the hills of western Mass-achusetts.[30]

The roots of this controversy lay in the Huntstown grant of 1736. The General Court had obliged the proprietors to set aside three of the rights in the township for the meetinghouse, the ministry, and schooling. It was not really asking much of the proprietors, for everyone knew that without these elements a settlement would not develop and grow. The idea was to use the proceeds of these rights to build a meetinghouse and a school, and to settle an "orthodox and gospel" minister. After this had been accomplished and settlers had built their frame houses to specification, the terms of the settlement would be fulfilled and, as soon as local government could be established, the town's inhabitants would assume the responsibility of upkeep and support of everything.

As late as 1767 there was still no meetinghouse in Ashfield, and its imminent construction, along with Jacob Sherwin's settlement and support, constituted quite a drain on the proprietors' treasury. The Baptist proprietors, though a minority at this point, were already resentful that the proprietors had not exempted their minister from taxation, nor paid for a meetinghouse when they had formed their church. After all, theirs had been the first church in Huntstown. Now it appeared that the proprietors would have to raise additional taxes to establish a religious society whose minister was downright hostile toward them. The proprietors among them could not claim dissenters' exemption from taxes, or so Judge Williams insisted, because they were bound by the charter as proprietors to settle an "orthodox" minister. To make matters worse for the Baptists, many of the newer settlers were taking up land in the central or southern part of town and agitating, through the town meeting, to move the partially built frame of the meetinghouse even farther from the Smiths' neighborhood. Finally, there were conflicting interpretations regarding whether the 1736 grant allowed the proprietors to collect taxes for the *support* of the ministry, or only for a minister's *settlement*. For their part, Israel Williams and his associates among the nonresident proprietors were becoming impatient with all the wrangling.[31]

In the spring of 1767, the nonresident proprietors asked the General Court to clarify Ashfield's act of incorporation and allow the proprietors to collect taxes from both the proprietors and the inhabitants for the support of Jacob Sherwin and the building of the meetinghouse. The House of Representatives sent word to the inhabitants to see if there were any objections, and the next year Chileab Smith arrived in Boston with a lengthy petition invoking the themes that had been successful in the past. First, they recounted how they had defended the province's frontier during the war. Then the proprietors installed Sherwin, they complained, and even though the Baptists had created their own church, the nonresident proprietors used the proprietors' treasury and taxes collected from the inhabitants (and even from their own minister) to fund Sherwin's "Large Settlement and Sollory" and the building of the meetinghouse. During the war Smith and his neighbors "could do little else in the summertime But Gard our Selves and Skout in the woods to See if we could make Discovery of the Enemy and there by was some Gard to the towns Below us." And their concerns had been ignored. Now "under destrest surcomstances which we think crys a loud for some pitty," they had their money taken away from them yearly "or our Lands Sold att an out cry to maintain their Worship." Attached to the petition was a deposition describing Ebenezer Smith's ordination, along with the signatures of eighteen of the inhabitants. But Israel Williams took his seat in the House the day after Smith presented his petition, and he used his extensive influence to push through what later became known as the Ashfield Law, an amendment to the town's act of incorporation empowering the proprietors to collect taxes in support of the ministry.[32]

Unfortunately for the Baptists, this session of the legislature was a chaotic one, and at the same time Williams was twisting arms to get the Ashfield Law passed, Governor Bernard had asked the House to rescind its previously passed resolution to send a Circular Letter to other colonies opposing Parliamentary taxation. Williams and his closest associates voted to rescind, but the motion failed by a large margin and Bernard dissolved the House. It was not until the spring of 1769 that the Baptists' objections could be heard again. In the meantime, the nonresident proprietors had assessed all rights for support of the ministry and the meetinghouse. With their land advertised for sale because they refused to pay these taxes, the Baptists again sent Chileab Smith to Boston to try to sway the legislature. "We shall Soon be Stript of all we have," they lamented in their petition, "for Lands are frequently Sold at the Vandues here for but a Small part of What it is worth." Smith also carried a companion petition from a group of Ashfield Congregationalists stating that "it is not all the other Society that would thus Oppress us." Signed by thirteen inhabitants, the second group of petitioners said that they had "no objection a Gainst the anabaptest societys Being set free from paying to the maintenances of the other worship which they Do not Belong unto." This was a dangerous development for Israel Williams, for it set the nonresident proprietors apart from the majority of inhabitants in whose best interest they were supposedly acting. He did all he could to keep the petition from being heard, and was successful. In the process he pushed through another measure affirming all of the proprietors' votes in taxing for the minister and the meetinghouse. And again, because of the crisis over Parliamentary taxation, the governor dissolved the House until January 1770.[33]

At an angry meeting in the fall, the proprietors voted another tax in support of the ministry and meetinghouse, and when the Baptist proprietors protested, Reverend Sherwin retorted that they would always be required to support him. In the meantime, the Baptists appealed to the Warren Association, a group of Baptist churches mainly in eastern Massachusetts, and received from them a certification that they were indeed Baptists and would be admitted to the association. They also sent Ebenezer Smith with another petition to Boston in March 1770, bemoaning that "we (or at Least many many of us) Shall be Disinherited for the support of a Society that we Do not belong unto." This gave little pause to the nonresident proprietors and their local Congregationalist allies, and again they posted the lands of the Baptists for sale for nonpayment of taxes.

In April, the proprietors auctioned off nearly four hundred acres belonging to the Baptists. Smith had already showed his certificate of ordination to members of the House, who then pronounced the whole affair "piracy" from a people who were "devilishly oppressed." Then, on April 26, the House issued orders that the sale "be staid." But the deed had already been done, and the order merely resulted in the Baptists having to pay the costs of notifying "their oppressors." Ebenezer Smith lost ten acres of his homelot for back taxes of a little over a pound. His father Chileab lost twenty acres of cleared ground, including a well-kept orchard, the Baptist burying ground (where his mother was interred), and a small dwelling house. Elijah Wells of Hatfield had bid thirty-five shillings for it, and he arrived on May 4 with surveying equipment and a shovel (to dig up some of the smaller trees). Before he left he delivered a mock sermon ridiculing the Baptists and boasting that he looked forward to another sale soon.[34]

At this point the Warren Association churches decided to become much more active in supporting the Ashfield Baptists and in protesting treatment of the Baptists throughout the province. They followed the example of the Massachusetts legislature itself (although they claimed to be acting as the early Christian apostles) and began corresponding regularly among themselves and with the Philadelphia Association to discuss grievances. They also resolved to petition the king for redress. When they were dissuaded from that by members of the House of Representatives who were hoping to maintain a united front in the dispute on Parliamentary taxation, they wrote a biting petition to the House in September in which they threw the House's own rhetoric in its face. Invoking the principles that many of the province's leaders had hotly proclaimed in the wake of the "Boston Massacre" in March, they wrote "That No Taxation can be equitable where such Restraint is laid upon the Taxed as takes from him the Liberty of GIVING his *Own Money Freely*. . . . With what Equity is *Our Property* taken from Us, not only without Our Consent, but violently, contrary to our Will; and for such purposes, as we cannot, in faithfulness to that Stewardship with which God hath Entrusted Us, favour." They then returned to another useful theme, reminding the legislature that "the revd Ebenr Smith, a regularly Ordained Baptist Minister, . . . together with his Father and others, their Bretheren, in the last Indian War, built at their Own Expence, a Fort, and were a Frontier; and this they did for two years without any help from any Quarter; from which, we beg leave to say, that they deserve at least the common privilege of the Subjects of the Crown of England." In a section that anticipated the cadence of the Declaration of Independence, they recalled, "they have taken from Us Our Dead—They have also sold a Dwelling House, and Orchard, and pull'd up Our aple Trees, and thrown down Our fences, and made our fields waste places." What Baptists, they argued, would want to move to a "New-settled" town if this is the treatment they would have to endure? In other words, the Great and General Court was behaving as an ungrateful, hypocritical despot that did not seem to recognize who it was that was doing the work of settling the province's backcountry.[35]

The conflict now escalated to a regional issue, and a flurry of essays in the Boston papers threatened to distract the public from the enthusiasm for the Whig cause that the House leadership hoped would be the only issue that concerned anyone. In fact, at one point one writer accused the Baptists of being unfriendly to America in its dispute with Britain. Finally, in March 1771, the Congregationalist proprietors submitted a lengthy response to the legislature, hoping to put an end, once and for all, to the Baptist insurgency. This ten-page argument was probably written by Israel Williams himself, but it was signed by five inhabitants, including Philip Phillips. Surely there would be no government at all, they insisted, if the Baptists of Ashfield were freed from paying taxes. These people were not Baptists, in fact, but "were originally separates, as they were vulgarly called, from the established churches, without other name or appellation than that of *Separatists*. The causes or springs of whose separation have been such as these—to wit: with some it was an unconquerable desire of being *teachers;* a privilege or indulgence which could be not otherwise insured to them but by a disorderly separation from the churches to which they belonged." Furthermore, they chided, "Some have left the Churches and gone to those people because they had been guilty of such offences as justly exposed them to a kind of discipline to which they could not feel themselves willing to submit." Their church, therefore, has become "a kind of receptacle for scandalous and disorderly Christians," and "a sink for some of the filth of Christianity in this part of the country." They are of "that religion that rejects men of learning and ability for teachers; and altogether chooses such as are illiterate and men of ordinary abilities."[36]

The petitioners went on to complain that these so-called Baptists, as proprietors, had always been slow or delinquent in paying their rates, and often had "worked out their rates upon the ways (heedfully, however, spending that labour upon those ways which might more immediately benefit themselves, which ought to have been laid out on the ways in general in the Town) And by this means they have frequently brought the proprietors into their debt and received orders upon the treasury." They went on to ridicule both Ebenezer and Chileab Smith for their lack of education and odd behavior, saying that for some time these two and their followers "neither knew what they were nor how to name themselves—Pride and vanity . . . having caused them irregularly and unwarrantably to leave the humble post of the ordinary and modest Christian for that of teachers."[37]

There was far more here than a dispute over religious doctrine or who ought to be paying taxes. Williams, Phillips, and the other Congregationalist proprietors were arguing that the Baptists were disruptive, immoral, disorderly, selfish, ignorant, and, worst of all, trying to be more than they really were. They were "ordinary" but trying to be leaders. It was unnatural. They were a threat to social stability, to harmony, and even to prosperity. The Congregationalists' impatience and exasperation was abundantly evident. They were right about Ebenezer Smith having no formal training, and in some cases they were right about some of the Baptist converts being more interested in escaping from Jacob Sherwin, or paying taxes, than in submitting to the even stricter discipline of the Baptists. But the Smiths and most of the adherents of their church were clearly sincere in their faith, and understandably resented the way the leading Congregationalists characterized them.[38]

A committee made up of members of the House and the Council was moved, nevertheless, by the Congregationalist proprietors' petition and, in spite of intense lobbying by the Baptists, announced in late April that the proprietors had done nothing wrong in auctioning lands of delinquent proprietors and inhabitants. This was a matter of civil obligation, they concluded. The "plantation" had always been required to provide for the ministry, and those unwilling to do so should not have purchased a right in it. In accord with the general patriarchal attitude evident in the proprietors' petition, the committee also said "That if [the Baptists] had in the Petition treated the General Court with more good manners and truth," they might have been more persuasive. (Perhaps certain members of the General Court had not appreciated being branded as hypocrites and tyrants!) They went on to say that the Baptists were lucky that the proprietors did not take all of their lands for not living up to the terms of the grant. The legislature's response was a severe blow not only to the Baptists of Ashfield, but also to the whole denomination throughout the province. It appears that a coalition of social conservatives and patriot leaders who resented the distraction from the greater cause of liberty had joined, temporarily, at least, to bring the issue to a close.[39]

It did not end there, however. Lieutenant Governor Thomas Hutchinson, hoping to divide the troublemakers in the House, embarrass the opposition to Parliament, and curry favor with the backcountry, secretly urged the Smiths and the leaders of the Warren Association to follow through on their plan of the previous year to petition the king to disallow the Ashfield Law. At that time John Davis of the association had asked Hutchinson about the possible "evil that our going to England might do," evidently implying that Massachusetts would be cast in a bad light. In reply, Hutchinson had said "he did not think it would do any, for said he, it is as bad as can be already." Now Hutchinson also wrote to Governor Bernard, who was in England, to suggest that Bernard could support the disallowance of a law he had signed by saying that he had not known that the original charter of Huntstown had not contained the word "support" in regard to the ministry. When the petition to the king reached England, Dr. Samuel Stennett, a Baptist minister who was close to George III, supported it as well, and on July 31, 1771, with advice from the Commission for Trade and Plantations, the king disallowed the Ashfield Law.[40]

Fewer than half a dozen people in all of New England knew of the efforts of Hutchinson and the Warren Association to get the Ashfield Law disallowed. When the news arrived in October, it jolted provincial leaders and had the legislature scurrying to restore lands and revise statutes. Those in the House who had opposed the Ashfield Law all along pressed the issue further and succeeded in exempting the Ashfield Baptists from both ecclesiastical and civil taxes for three years to compensate for all their trouble. And that truly should have been the end of it.[41]

Not for Israel Williams, however. If actions speak loudly of a state of mind, Williams must have been enraged to have been abandoned not only by the king but, even worse, by his friend Thomas Hutchinson. No sooner had Chileab Smith returned from Boston ready to recuperate from his long ordeal of being embroiled in provincial politics than he discovered that his adversaries had "filled this part of the country with slanders against me, and our minister in particular, and also against the whole church, villifying and reproaching us; but me they called the Old Devil of all." And who should appear at his door but Elijah Wells—he who had defiled Smith's orchard and burying ground—with a warrant signed by Israel Williams to arrest Chileab for counterfeiting and to search his property for evidence. Wells set to his task with unsurprising vengeance, and even shocked the constable who had accompanied him with his virulent determination to find something— anything—incriminating. He finally settled on a lump of boiled brine as just what he needed to call Chileab to account, and ordered the constable, against the latter's better judgment, to remand Smith to the Hatfield jail to await Judge Williams's pleasure.[42]

At trial Smith, though in poor health, had to stand while the prosecutor examined, at length, ten witnesses, including a number of Baptist communicants. Then an enraged Judge Williams turned his attention to Chileab and demanded to know why there was smoke coming from his shop chimney on the Sabbath (the Baptists met there), and what he used mercury for. Finally he said, "I know you of old, Smith, you are cunning," and he bound him over to Superior Court, setting an excessive bail. Smith spent the winter in jail. In the long run, though, there was little the judge could do, and he realized he was only damaging his already flagging reputation and standing among even the more prominent of his colleagues on the bench. In frustration, he wrote Hutchinson in late 1772 to find out what his friend had been thinking when he advised the Baptists to appeal to the king, but Hutchinson replied by asking why Williams had been so long absent from the General Court, leaving Hutchinson virtually alone to deal with the "absurdities" that were being passed unanimously. "As to Ashfield & the case of the Anabaptist Laws in general," he continued, "they require more thought than I am able to afford. I have no other interest in them than as the Publick is interested & am open to any beneficial measure." The tax on tea was still on the books. There were still soldiers stationed in Boston. Hutchinson had enough on his hands.[43]

It is a strong reminder of how complex colonial politics had become when we consider that on the eve of the Boston Tea Party the Ashfield Baptists had been "set at Liberty" by the king of England. As Ebenezer Smith said of the General Court at one point, "they were calling themselves the sons of liberty and were erecting their liberty poles about the country, but they did not deserve the name, for it was evident all they wanted was liberty from oppression that they might have liberty to oppress!" Indeed, the questions raised by the Ashfield affair regarding the commitment of Massachusetts leaders to the cause of liberty troubled notable men in other colonies, such as Ezra Stiles of Connecticut, and even reached to the Continental Congress in Philadelphia in 1774. Stiles noted a "coolness" of Congress toward the Massachusetts delegation because of the persecution of the Baptists. The Baptists were holding a convention in the city at the same time (attended by Chileab Smith), and they approached the Congress complaining of the poor treatment of religious dissenters at the hands of so-called defenders of liberty.[44]

While all of this was percolating, Jacob Sherwin's pastorate was in serious trouble. The town's population grew, though more slowly, throughout the late 1760s, most of the immigrants being of the Congregationalist persuasion. In 1771 they completed construction of the meetinghouse, but disciplinary issues and defections to the Baptists constantly distracted the church and drove a wedge between Sherwin and many of his parishioners. Some also found it offensive that he owned a slave. Finally, in 1773, the town refused to raise Sherwin's pay above fifty pounds and Sherwin protested. After a council of ministers met on the issue, the congregation dismissed him from the pulpit and in late 1774 installed Nehemiah Porter.[45]

Porter was a Stoddardian, just as Sherwin was, but it hardly mattered anymore. The disagreements in Ashfield had long since gone beyond the issue of what it meant to be converted. The Baptists had made a place for themselves not only as dissenters and adherents to an articulate faith, but also as a legitimate social constituency within a fast-growing town. Between 1765 and 1774 there was always at least one Baptist among the town's three selectmen, and on occasion two. Among the inhabitants, there cannot have been too much hostility toward the group. Chileab Smith's part of town became known as Baptist Corner, and, although it was a good hike from what became the center of town affairs, for the remainder of the century it constituted one of the foci of an elliptical local polity. Nor did the local economy reflect any divisions between the Baptists and the rest of the town. The Baptists, according to the provincial and local tax valuations of 1771, were about as well off, as a group, as the rest of their backcountry neighbors.[46]

Israel Williams undoubtedly suffered many sleepless nights fuming over what he perceived to be disorder and disrespect for orthodoxy to his northwest. He certainly had not cowed Smith and his neighbors into a deferential state, and it is doubtful that a great many of Ashfield's inhabitants held him and the other nonresident proprietors in high regard. Had the river-town gentry been more accommodating from the start, they might have gained at least a measure of cooperation in building the meetinghouse and in developing more advantageous roads. But the early settlers were not about to let anyone forget how they had risked their lives with little assistance for the sake of the colony's frontier. And all of them, whether newcomers or first settlers, were well aware of the distinction between those who truly worked the land and those who hoped to have it work for them. With the exception of a few who were on good terms with the nonresident proprietors, the inhabitants were largely poor and middling folk who did not seem to mind if disruption, disorder, and disunity became a way of life. For many of them a faith in a God that allowed such turmoil to test the mettle of His true followers made a hard life tolerable and challenges to the judgment of "the better sort" justifiable. And that applied not only to the residents of Baptist Corner, but also to the Congregationalists who had tired of the imperious Jacob Sherwin.

Huntstown's story at this point had become a bit of a variation on Salmon Brook's. Connecticut's leaders had accommodated their backcountry constituents in Simsbury's northwest quadrant with such extensive land grants that the former "outlanders" had, in effect, become the proprietors of their community. The legislature had set them up with their own ecclesiastical society, and, even though they had turned defiant during the Great Awakening, the minister they eventually settled tolerated their New Light tendencies. As a result, Salmon Brook's Separatist, Baptist, and Anglican dissenters were few in number, the inhabitants were willing to delay their campaign for a separate town, and the commonwealth was not embarrassed by a petition controversy that compromised its standing with both the king and the Continental Congress. In Ashfield, on the other hand, backcountry people had demonstrated how persistent they could be when authorities would not respect their independence.

In 1774, though, both Thomas Hutchinson and the Sons of Liberty had suspended their support for Israel Williams and the patriarchy he had hoped to establish. There had been no compromise. In fact, Ashfield's Baptists and unruly Congregationalists had won. For the six hundred or so persons who called Ashfield their home, a new era had opened. There were inns, mills, a store, a meetinghouse, more cleared land, some good roads to the river towns, and a town government that was about to send its first representative to the provincial legislature. The Baptist controversy had ended with the Baptists "set at liberty," and most of the town in support of their right to be so. It remained still to be determined whether it would be the king of England and his governor or the Sons of Liberty who would eventually earn the loyalty of the backcountry.

7. We Do Not Want Any Goviner but the Goviner of the Univarse

On March 6, 1773, the Massachusetts General Court declared that, because of all of the "perplexities and difficulties" brought on by the late controversy and the consequent inability of the town of Ashfield or its proprietors to collect taxes, certain remedial measures were in order. It authorized the proprietors to levy a tax to cover all expenses to date. Baptists would not have to pay for the minister's salary or the meetinghouse and would not vote on these matters, but all other inhabitants, whether proprietors or not, would be subject to the tax for those purposes. In addition, because of "their poverty" as a result of the "difficulties," the inhabitants would be exempt from province and county taxes for three years.[1] Overall, it was a far-reaching settlement, designed to obey the king, fund the local church, and appease the hard-pressed inhabitants—that is, designed to restore "order, peace, and unity" to the town.

That the people of Ashfield had been so mired in the issue of taxing the Baptists, and consequently so impoverished, goes a long way toward explaining why they seemed to take little notice of the other controversy of their times—the dispute between the British Parliament and the colonies—over taxation. During 1774, with the Baptist controversy behind it, a more united Ashfield did turn toward the patriot cause. While at first affirming loyalty to the king, the great majority of the town, just as in Salmon Brook, fell into step with those throughout the colonies who eventually took up arms in resistance to Parliamentary taxation, blamed his majesty for all of their troubles, and declared independence. During the war, a large proportion of Ashfield men served in numerous military campaigns, leaving their families behind to work day and night to supply them and keep hearth and home from falling into ruin during their absence. What accounted for this dramatic embracing of the revolutionary cause? Did they appreciate the three-year tax break passed by a legislature dominated by opponents of Parliamentary policy? Did they become convinced of the theories of representation and popular sovereignty advocated by those patriot leaders? Or were they always, at heart, anti-British, or anti-authoritarian, but simply more involved in their own struggles with the wilderness and with each other until 1774?

None of these explanations are entirely satisfactory. Once Ashfield's inhabitants had cooled down after years of "perplexities and difficulties," the Whig argument that the Parliament was threatening their liberty did begin to resonate with them. They were somewhat selective about what elements of that argument they subscribed to, though. What made sense to them was the insistence on equality and collective autonomy. In addition, they had seldom demonstrated the respect for authority that people like Israel Williams believed was necessary for an orderly society. These habits and sentiments they had inherited from the town's brief history. Whether early settlers or recent immigrants, most of the inhabitants in the 1770s understood themselves to be backcountry people, different from those who lived along the rivers and on the coasts of New England. They thought of themselves as long-suffering and honest folk who worked hard on hard ground. In the crisp mountain air they communed with one another and with their Maker in their own ways, and those who threatened their independence and the high regard they had for their labor would have to face their wrath. Ashfield was now their town's name, but in fact, they were still Huntstown men and women who had little use for a gentrified class structure, outside interference, or any threats to their status as freeholders. These were the sentiments that propelled them into the patriot cause and kept them fighting for that cause for seven years. During that time they became so committed to their own brand of revolutionary ideology that they later launched into open rebellion against even patriot leaders who seemed to them to be abandoning the cause.

Defending Our Rights and Privileges, Civil and Religious

There is something to be said for economic explanations. The decade before the American Revolution was a time of sluggish growth for the town. No doubt both in-migration and the local economy suffered from the "perplexities" of the Baptist crisis. And besides, it was just rough country requiring more time to tame than other places. The trees were bigger, the slopes steeper, and the damage done to roads by the winter ice more severe. Between 1760 and 1765, the town's population had more than tripled. During the next five years, as petitions and pamphlets about church taxes multiplied, there was only a 16 percent increase. There was more land cleared by the 1770s, but in terms of estate value per acre, Ashfield remained one of the poorest towns in the colony.[2] Ashfield's inhabitants were simply struggling too hard with the business of creating farms to be concerned with resistance to British taxation.

It is in the small measures of growth, however, where there may be found, perhaps, another explanation for Ashfield's silence in the conflict with the British ministry prior to 1774. The hints lie very subtly in tax and land records, and in the account books of Richard and John Ellis for the previous decade. While economic development may have been slow for a new town, it appears that some inhabitants were just beginning to experience an improved standard of living. Work on road construction and repair, and then on the meetinghouse, continued to keep laborers solvent, even if the town was paying only two shillings per day. Farmers who already had pasturage and tillage by 1766 slowly became more active producers of surplus lumber, grain, hay, and livestock, and thus were able to participate more in the regional marketplace. Finally, resident proprietors began to sell some of their new division land. All of this had the effect of putting a little more money in the pockets or on the accounts of struggling farmers.

While most of John Ellis's business involved local exchanges of labor and farm products, on occasion he traded ribbon, tape, rum, tea, cloth, "plats," "Tobacken," pins, and other "wares," to customers who could produce some extra butter, flax, wheat, rye, ashes, and cattle. He traded locally with men like John Sadler, who had managed to clear thirty-nine acres since his arrival in Huntstown in 1753, or Jonathan Taylor, originally of Cape Cod, who had moved from a renter's status to the owner of eleven cleared acres and nine animals. Generally, tax and land records reveal a rising standard of living. The differences would not strike us as particularly astounding, but for families who had lived for a decade or two in survival mode, the newfound capacity to purchase "ribbons, tape, and cloth," or "five plats" was a turning point.[3]

It was exactly at this turning point that the Boston Committee of Correspondence was asking the people of the countryside to join them in "keeping Superfluties out of this Countwry." It is little wonder that Ashfield's response was mute. Probably the call for a boycott in 1767, and subsequent efforts to keep the flames of resistance burning in spite of the repeal of most of the Townshend duties, seemed to be one more imposition by the Sons of Liberty upon the dreams of beleaguered and "oppressed" people. The Baptists already thought the Sons of Liberty were more properly called, as Chileab Smith put it, "the Sons of Violence." The Congregationalists, most of whom could not afford to bid for Baptist land, pay taxes to build a meetinghouse, or support a steadily increasing salary for Jacob Sherwin, must also have been resistant to sacrificing their hard-won ability to purchase a small "Superflutie" that might grace their mantel, fill the one teacup they could offer a guest, or make themselves feel more presentable when dressing for a Sabbath meeting. As in-migration began to pick up again after the king disallowed the Ashfield Law in 1771, even more people were engaged in the market for consumer goods, or soon expected to once they cleared their new land.[4]

The "perplexities and difficulties" of the people of Ashfield, then, encompassed not only the Baptist controversy, chronic poverty, and ambivalence or even hostility toward the Sons of Liberty, but also resentment over deferring dreams of becoming respectable at the moment when those dreams appeared to many to be within reach. Backcountry people who took pride in their ability to endure distress would not admit that they cared much for anything but essentials, but the nascent consumers of Ashfield betrayed themselves with ever-so-slightly improved incomes and estates, sales of excess produce and land, small purchases, and utter silence, until 1774, on the question of boycotts.[5] Then, in May of that year, news arrived that the Parliament had passed a number of bills in response to the destruction of East India Company tea in Boston harbor the previous December. That changed everything. For one thing, it was now not the boycotts of the Sons of Liberty but the ministry itself that had closed the port of Boston, through which passed fine textiles, tea, spices, and all manner of manufactured goods from building materials to porcelain plates.

It was not as though the tiny beginnings of a consumer culture in Ashfield made so much difference that the townspeople were suddenly all of one mind when it was the ministry that was preventing them from their purchases.

It is just that the hesitancy on the part of a considerable number of inhabitants to oppose Parliamentary taxation evaporated quickly. In the place of apparent indifference, though, was a fair amount of confusion about how to respond, not only to the closing of the Boston port, but also to Parliament's other measures designed to put an end to sedition. A number of historians have argued that the Massachusetts Government Act was especially galling to the New England countryside. This law restricted self-government by limiting town meetings to annual election meetings and by giving a royally appointed governor (in this case General Thomas Gage) complete power over the appointment of judges and provincial officials. There were, indeed, some in Ashfield who were still bitter about their own dispute over taxation, and for whom these two provisions combined could only mean more interference in their lives by the likes of Israel Williams. Distrust of such appointed officials is evident in the nearly unanimous aversion on the part of Ashfield families to deal with Williams's probate court. Seven adult males died in Ashfield between 1764 and 1775, but Williams saw only two of their estates come before him as judge of probate.[6] On the other hand, there were still some among the elected leadership and the town's more prosperous inhabitants who had allied themselves with Williams and the river-valley proprietors. Thus, the response in Ashfield to the Coercive Acts was not as instantaneous and resolute as it was in some other towns.

During the summer of 1774 there was considerable discussion of the current state of affairs, and finally on September 8 a group of inhabitants pushed through the town meeting "Articles of Covenant and Agreement relative to Resistance to the Tyranny of the British Parliament." This document was an altered version of the Solemn League and Covenant that the Boston Committee of Correspondence had sent to all of the towns in Massachusetts in June, calling for enforced boycotts of British goods. In fact, only eight towns adopted the Solemn League and Covenant, suggesting colonywide disagreement on the best way to deal with the crisis of the Coercive Acts. A majority in Ashfield agreed with it in principle, but in their own "Covenant and Agreement" they made their particular collective concerns clear.[7]

They began by asserting that they were motivated by "Self preservation, the Dictates of Natural Conscience, & a Sacred regard to the Constitution & Laws of our Country, which were instituted for the Security of our Lives, Liberties, & Properties." While they professed themselves subjects of the king and "Duty bound to yield Obedience to all his good wholesome &

Constitutional Laws," they still felt compelled to "bare testimony against all the oppressions and unconstitutional Laws of the British Parliament whereby the Charter Priviledges of this Province are struck at and Cashiered." The use of the word "Cashiered," unique to Ashfield, is interesting, implying that the authors of this version of the Solemn League and Covenant saw the Parliament as a bunch of corrupt and greedy merchants who had sold out the interests of loyal and principled country folk.

The Articles went on to declare solidarity with "Neighbouring towns in this province, and sister Colonies in America" in support of boycotting "any trade with the Island of Great Britain, until she withdraw her oppressive hand, or until a trade is come into by the several Colonies." In preparation for this fight against oppression, the town also agreed "that we may be equipt with ammunition and other Necessaries, at the Towns Cost." In a carefully worded section they maintained that they were "Contending for and Defending our rights and priviledges, civil and religious which we have a just right to both by Nature & Charter." The inclusion of "civil and religious" is a distinguishing mark, echoing the recent fight over taxation of Baptist lands, and connecting the particular concerns of these backcountry people of Ashfield to the resistance to Parliament. Ashfield people saw themselves as perpetual opponents of oppression and violation of not only charter privileges but also natural rights. This time their oppressor was the Parliament, but there was a history here that had prepared them for resistance. To punctuate their determination to put forth a godly fight, they promised "that we will do all we can to Suppress all petty mobs, trifling and causeless." As for mobs with a worthy cause, apparently they were acceptable.

Sixty-six residents signed the covenant. Notably missing were the signatures of Philip Phillips, Joseph Mitchell, Thomas Phillips, and Ebenezer Belding, leading men in town who had lined up with Israel Williams and other nonresident proprietors in support of conformity to the Congregational Church. In the debate over the location of the meetinghouse that had paralleled the Baptist controversy, Williams and the nonresident proprietors had supported building it near their houses. Living near a meetinghouse was not only a convenience, especially in hilly country, but also advantageous for certain professions, such as an innkeeper and aspiring merchant (Mitchell) or a lawyer hoping to become a local magistrate (Phillips). Of the friends of the nonresident proprietors, only Samuel Belding, apparently a consummate politician who had risen far above his initially blemished reputation to become a regular town officeholder, joined this resistance to "tyranny." Also among the non-signers were Chileab and Ebenezer Smith, and many other Baptists. They may have helped to shape habits of resistance to a commercial elite, central authority, and religious oppression, but, for the moment, they were reluctant to challenge the authority that had set them "at Liberty." Perhaps they still suspected that the Sons of Liberty wanted the "liberty to oppress."[8]

Those who did put their names to the covenant were, in large part, men who had moved into Ashfield within the previous five years or young men who had recently come of age. They had very little land as a group. The newcomers hailed from a variety of places, but in nearly every case, whether they came from Yarmouth on Cape Cod, or West Hartford or Guilford in Connecticut, their home towns had become overcrowded and land prices had soared. They came to Ashfield as renters, and their co-signers among the young men coming of age had not come into much land from their fathers. Some were a little better off than others, although it is hard to talk about differences in wealth in a community whose most prosperous person would not rank in the top quarter of taxpayers in a more established country town like Concord. Suddenly these people found themselves very active in town politics. They were principally the ones who brought Ashfield into conflict with Parliament, not only in constituting a majority, but also in defining an ideology that connected local sentiments regarding religious freedom, autonomy, and backcountry distress to the patriot calls for boycotts and potentially armed defense of "Lives, Liberties, & Properties."[9]

It appears that there were many who were determined to press the case further than the adoption of the "Covenant and Agreement." On October 17, 1774, the selectmen issued a warrant for a town meeting "to Chuse a number of men, to Settle & determine all matters Relitive to Mobes, Rioates, and Briches of the pece, within the Limets of sd Town." Perhaps, as was happening in other communities, those who had not signed the covenant were still buying and selling goods that came from "the Island of Great Britain," and that had provoked an angry response. Or, it may be that there were no riots yet in Ashfield, but the town's leaders were preparing for the eventuality. A month earlier a mob from a number of Hampshire County towns had descended on Springfield and forced the judges of the county court, including Israel Williams, to renounce their commissions. Then a week later another mob assembled around a liberty pole in Williamsburg (formerly the west end of Hatfield) and marched to Hatfield ready to deal with Williams, Obadiah Dickinson, and other social and political leaders "in Severity."[10] Whether or not there were actual riots in Ashfield, town leaders appear to have been determined to confine crowd action to the European tradition of restraint.

The method of maintaining restraint appears to have been to incorporate the young, the landless, and the angry into orderly discussion at the town meeting, for one article under consideration at the October 1774 town meeting was whether "to Give Liberty for all men to vote in this meeting that are town Inhabitence that are twenty one years old & upward." In 1771, 40 percent of the taxpayers on the town list (not to mention an unknown number of others who were too poor to pay even a poll tax) were not qualified to vote in town meetings. Many of those who could not vote signed the covenant of 1774. Perhaps they too did not think that the covenant was strong enough and took to the streets. In any case, they were eager to be part of the decision-making process, and apparently their leaders preferred them to participate with a vote rather than a riot. It was disorderly enough that the October town meeting was illegal under the Massachusetts Government Act.[11]

The town meeting continued to accommodate the concerns of the more rebellious elements in the community in early 1775, first by electing Aaron Lyon, a Baptist, and Elisha Cranson and Jasher Taylor, both relatively new to town, to the post of selectmen, and second by devoting town funds to a large stock of ammunition and to the support of the families of ten men who would stand ready as "Minit Men," presumably authorized to make use of that ammunition should the town's "rights and priviledges, civil and religious," be threatened. In February a mob had actually found Israel Williams at home in Hatfield and took him and his son across the river to Hadley, where they "smoked" them for a night in a house with a plugged chimney. These incidents outside of Ashfield, particularly the humiliation of Israel Williams, surely encouraged more radical sentiments locally. Month by month the proportion of the town that favored active resistance was growing. If it was questionable which way the Baptists would go, Chileab Smith and Reuben Ellis answered that question on April 3, 1775, when they joined a committee to oversee the organization and support of the Minutemen. At that meeting, when someone asked if the town really did mean to spend six pounds on ammunition, as it had voted in March, the town voted to spend that and six more.[12] With the exception of a few people who were still loyal to Israel Williams, and thus to order and respect for the authority of

Parliament, an overwhelming consensus had emerged by the April 3 meeting that opposition to "the oppressions and unconstitutional Laws of the British Parliament" corresponded to their own desire for autonomy.

They would not meet for another three weeks. By then "the embattled farmer" had made his stand at Concord's north bridge.

Duty to God and Our Country to Opose the Least Apearanc of Them Old Tiranical Laws

News of the fighting at Lexington and Concord on April 19 raced across Massachusetts. As thousands of militiamen from eastern towns converged on Boston, Ashfield's Minutemen began packing up and preparing to march. By the time the town met on the 24th, Ashfield had a company already encamped outside Boston. The townspeople voted to send supplies and to set up a five-man committee of correspondence. In a curious action, they created another committee that would have "full power to remit all rates that they shall finde to be erecoverable and to give dischardges to shuch as they shall think proper."[13] Was this measure designed to be considerate of the needs of the more financially stretched farm families? For those families, the now certain increase in taxation to finance the colony's resistance to military rule would only compound the problems posed by the likelihood that their sons would be the ones "goin as minet men."

Ashfield inhabitants, in fact, living in one of the poorest towns in the province, might reasonably have assumed that the burden of defending rights and privileges should fall on those with greater privilege. That did not seem to occur to them. Perhaps as many as 80 percent of the fighting-age men in town were in military units or served in campaigns of varying length during the war. To be sure, some of the enlistments were no longer than five days, and so, some of that 80 percent represents men standing by, waiting for calls from the General Court to face some emergency situation. Just the same, in one way or another it can rightfully be said that the great majority of Ashfield was "up in arms" about the perceived threat to their liberty, as they defined it.[14]

Participation in military actions was heaviest and most enthusiastic during the first two years of the war. Ashfield people were as caught up as residents of any town in the *rage militaire*. As many as thirty-two soldiers took part in the siege of Boston throughout 1775 and early 1776, while those at home made coats and sent Philip Phillips "to Albenah [Albany, New York] to procure Guns & amanison upon the towns Credit." Meanwhile, Elisha Cranson, who had been sent to the provincial congress at Watertown as Ashfield's first representative in the Massachusetts government, recruited a company to join with Benedict Arnold in the ill-fated campaign to take Canada.[15]

Although the siege of Boston ended successfully, Arnold's disastrous Quebec expedition soon became more typical of the course of the war. At least two who went to Canada from Ashfield ended up as prisoners, and in the late summer of 1776, three Ashfield soldiers died in the fighting in New York City. As we know from the experience of the Salmon Brook soldiers, that battle amounted to a string of defeats and retreats that nearly resulted in the annihilation of the Continental Army. The following spring, General Burgoyne initiated a British counterattack from Canada, and in July overran Fort Ticonderoga, where substantial numbers of Ashfield men had been stationed since December 1776.[16]

After the debacles of 1776 and the arrival of news that Burgoyne was poised to move south from Lake Champlain during the summer of 1777, interest in soldiering began to diminish somewhat in Ashfield, as it did everywhere. Besides the defeats and misery suffered by the soldiers, there were also increasing problems at home. Soldiers returning from service brought back the smallpox epidemic that ended up spreading across North America during the late 1770s and early 1780s. On top of this trouble, the frequent absence of farmers, the uncertainty regarding their pay, shortages of all sorts of necessities, and the impact of surging inflation, or what locals called "the sink of money," all took their toll. In late 1776 the town resolved "to Chuse a Committee to consult upon Some Proper Measures for regulating Prices and put a Stop to the Groth of Oprission." The committee recommended that the Committee of Safety be empowered to call for a county convention to regulate prices and to outlaw "ye carrying of Grain out of town." The use of the term "regulate" here is significant. Americans of the 1760s and 1770s associated "regulation" with backcountry uprisings from North Carolina to New York—a form of vigilantism practiced by backcountry people against the privileged. Resolutions like Ashfield's must have made the leaders of the revolution anxious about their cause disintegrating as it succumbed to economic distress.[17]

More evidence of hardship filled the town records during 1777. In the winter Ashfield applied to the state government to abate its state taxes. The town strained to supply its troops with such basic items as coats and blankets, and took to fining (ten to twenty pounds per year) those men who could not or would not serve when called up. The town's leaders could not even collect their ministerial taxes, particularly with continuing defections to the Baptists, and tried to raise revenue by selling pews in the meetinghouse or by earning credit with Reverend Porter for clearing his land. Porter, unhappy with how little his salary could purchase, decided, against the town's wishes, to take his chances with the army and left for the Hudson in the summer of 1777. In his absence, Congregationalists had to be content with sermons delivered by Jacob Sherwin, the man they had fired three years earlier.[18]

Meanwhile, some of the more respected men of the community, including Philip Phillips, Samuel Belding, and Samuel Anabel Jr., decided that rights and privileges were one thing, but the independence of the United States declared in July 1776 was quite another. In addition, they were perturbed about the choices the town was now making for civil officers and militia leaders—that is, the town was not choosing them. In fact, there must have been raging debate about military service and the direction that the rebellion was taking, for in August 1777 the town selectmen charged nine men for appearing "unfriendly to ye American states," Philip Phillips and Samuel Belding, former allies of the now disgraced Israel Williams, among them. Aaron Lyon, a Baptist and now a selectman, gathered the evidence against them. The town meeting ordered them to be placed in confinement at Samuel Bartlett's house.[19]

In spite of all that was working against their resolution, the majority of Ashfield families seem to have remained as devoted as ever during the later years of the war to fighting for independence. At the same meeting in which the town ordered the alleged Tories confined to Captain Bartlett's house (a confinement that lasted only seven days, it turned out—the town could not afford to pay the guards), it voted to "do all yt lies in their Power to Suppress vice, and especially yt they will use their Endevours to prevent profane Cursing and Swearing that the Name of God be not blasphemed amoungst them." Townspeople may have tolerated a degree of civil disorder in the name of rights, and even believed in religious toleration, but as one historian put it, they had entered "dark and trying years" and wanted to maintain the moral high ground. A sizable contingent of Congregational ministers in Hampshire County had Tory leanings, and were no doubt castigating the rebels for their disrespect for authority in general. Besides, Burgoyne was threatening to split the colonies. The provincial congress had called for one of every six fighting-age men to be sent "to the northward" to stop him. They needed God on their side.[20]

The situation took a turn for the better at this point. A detachment of Hessians met defeat at Bennington, Vermont (Ashfield's company arrived a day late to join the action). In western New York defenders at Forts Stanwix and Oriskany turned back an invading British force that was to join Burgoyne in Albany, and General Howe decided to move against Philadelphia instead of marching north to add to Burgoyne's numbers. The result was that Burgoyne found himself slowed and finally stopped by a superior force, including an Ashfield company, at Saratoga, where he surrendered on October 17. With Rev. Nehemiah Porter on hand to pray with the troops before the battle, it must have seemed that they had indeed achieved God's favor.[21]

After Saratoga, the war became more a matter of expense, scarcity, and sacrifice than military action close to home. The British turned their attention to the middle colonies and the South, and to chasing Washington's army. For Ashfield, this did not mean much respite, for the rest of the war was spent recruiting or forcing young men to sign on for longer and longer enlistments in the Continental Army, and then scraping for money and supplies to support them. The numbers of participants declined, but the expense of keeping them in the field multiplied. Enlistment bounties (at thirty and then fifty pounds per recruit) and supplies became so expensive that Ashfield petitioned the General Court "to regulate the prices of the several Commodities and Articles of Traffik among us." When there was no response, the town took to drafting men for the army and paying bounties in the form of livestock. At home the costs of routine town activities and even interest on money lent to the town were increasingly difficult to meet.[22] It had to be discouraging to persist as rebels.

Inspiration for this persistence lay in strong commitment to a set of revolutionary ideals that appeared with startling clarity in Ashfield's response to the proposals for a new state constitution. The Massachusetts House of Representatives opened the discourse over a new constitution a few months after the Declaration of Independence with a query to the towns about whether the General Court, as it was composed at the moment, should enact a new constitution. Most towns were unhappy with the idea. In Ashfield, inhabitants met on September 26, 1776, and then again on October 4 for considerable discussion, and like many towns, suggested that the House of Representatives, exclusive of the upper house, could draft the document, but that it should be returned "to the Several Towns for their Exceptanc." The attendants went on to say that they would "take the Law of God for the foundation of the forme of Government for as the Old Laws that we have Ben Ruled by under the British Constitution have Proved Enefectual to Secuer us from the more then savige C99alty of tiranical Opressars and Sense the God of Nature hath Enabeled us to Brake that yake of Bondage we think our Selves Bound in Duty to God and our Country to Oppose the Least Apearanc of them Old Tiranical Laws taking place again."

Indeed, the people of Ashfield not only wanted to answer the question about who should draft the constitution, but they also wanted to provide the House with considerable guidance as it framed the new government. In particular, they declared, "we Do not want any Goviner but the Goviner of the Univarse." Beyond that, they might accept a "States General, elected annually from the towns, to consult with the wrest of the united Stats for the Good of the whole." Any law that this body passed for the state should require the approval of the towns, the Ashfield town meeting announced. Mainly, government should be conducted at the town level, and that included the settling of all disputes in courts presided over by judges who should be elected locally. Furthermore, the town clerk should be the register of deeds, and the selectmen should probate all estates. Only in the case of murder would it be "Nesesary to Call in Eleven men from Eleven Nabouring Towns that Shull be Cose for that Porpos Anuly to Joge and Condem Such Moderrers." They insisted that they "Do Not want any Laws made to Govern in Eclasastics Afairs fairmly Believing the Divine Law to be Safficiant and that by which we and all Our Religion Affairs aught to [be] Governed by." Finally, they wanted taxes "Colected of the whole state" to pay the salaries and expenses of the representatives of the towns—that is, they desired to free themselves from the burden that had made it too expensive over the past decade to have their voice heard above those of men who came from more prosperous towns (like Hatfield).[23]

Clearly, this was a far more substantive response than the House of Representatives had sought—or wanted, probably. In phonetic spellings that revealed both their New England twang and their backcountry schooling they offered up a bold and succinct statement of their political principles and presumed to instruct the state legislature on the proper foundations of good government. They wanted to run their own affairs without interference, and they did not hesitate to announce that they knew what divine law was as well as anyone, or perhaps better. In any case, their history dictated adherence to no particular religious denomination, but rather to religious toleration. It had also taught them that county judges like Israel Williams, appointed indefinitely by the governor, did not serve their interests, that courts should be community institutions, that the registrations of their freeholds were best kept close to home, and that when they died the distribution of their meager estates should be in the hands of one of their own. Probably these resolutions had Sons of Liberty in Boston scratching their heads wondering what sort of political theory informed the minds of these country folk. It seemed that Ashfield had forgotten that the present conflict was with Great Britain and not with the state's own leaders. At once egalitarian, anti-authoritarian, theocratic, localist, populist, and totally uncalled for, the advice from Ashfield was extraordinary. In fact, Ashfield's inhabitants knew very well that they were almost as much at odds with the Massachusetts leadership as they were with the British government.

The state's leading politicians might have simply ignored these comments from one of their poorest and smallest towns, if it were not that negative responses were coming in from all around the countryside. Most town meetings were content to answer the question the legislature had asked, and were, as one commentator has put it, "less than enthusiastic" about the General Court enacting the constitution by itself.[24] A number of towns resolved that a special convention should be called for the sole purpose of drafting a constitution that would then be subject to approval or amendment by the people at large. Several towns in Worcester County met in a late November county convention to express their united disapproval of the present legislature enacting a constitution. Few towns suggested principles by which a plan of government should be formed, and no town was quite as radical as Ashfield in its insistence on local autonomy. Some in Ashfield itself may have been shocked at what the town had asserted. When Jacob Sherwin became town clerk in 1778, he seems to have decided against copying the resolves of the October 1776 town meeting into the new official town book that he bought for the town, even though he copied all of the other records of 1776 and 1777. Perhaps it was because Dr. Phineas Bartlett, the elected town clerk, had not been at the October 1776 meeting and the minutes had been taken by Aaron Lyon, an apparently unschooled Baptist.

The town met again on March 7, 1777, and retreated a bit from its radical stance. "Notwithstanding the former Instructions we gave our

Representative," they declared, "we do now Instruct him to use his Influence yt the general Court adopt the Plan of Goverment agreeable to wt was transacted by Worcester Convention." The Worcester Convention had not really put forward a "Plan," but it had made one of the more assertive statements calling for a special convention to frame the constitution. The delegates were concerned about the "many errors" that had "crept in and been supported with the remains of the late constitutions," as well as "the undue influence or power of individuals in monopolizing incompatible offices in the hands of particular persons." Perhaps Ashfield's leaders decided it was better strategy simply to get a convention called. In fact, the legislature did relent and established a constitutional convention that began meeting in June (although its delegates were the same men who had been elected to the House of Representatives).[25]

When the convention produced its draft and sent it out for approval in the spring of 1778, most towns rejected it for various reasons ranging from its plan of representation to its lack of a bill of rights. There is no record that Ashfield even met to consider it, which is not surprising, since there was very little in it that promised to prevent "them old Tiranical Laws" from continuing. Throughout Hampshire County, in fact, there was general discontent with what little change was taking place in the structure of government. Even though Israel Williams was under house arrest and stripped of power, there was still only one probate court and registry of deeds for the whole county, and in spite of growing populations, justices of the peace were few and far between. In Ashfield the only justice of the peace was Samuel Belding, and as a former ally of Israel Williams and one of the nine suspected Tories that would have been confined longer had the town had the money, he probably was not the person before whom the town's inhabitants wanted to argue their cases.[26]

In early 1779 the legislature asked the towns once again if they wanted a new constitution and if they would empower their representatives to call a convention. Once again, numerous county conventions and town meetings, Ashfield's included, insisted that, yes, they did want a new constitution that would put an end to all of the "evils" of the old system. And yes, they did want a convention of delegates, separate from the representatives, to be called solely for the purpose of drafting a constitution that would then be sent to the people for their "acceptance Rejection or Final amendment," as the Ashfield town records read. And so, in June, the legislature called just such a convention.[27]

Ashfield selected two delegates to attend the convention, and instructed them to be sure that nothing was actually enacted until the towns had seen the new plan and "approved or Disapproved." The convention began meeting in Cambridge in September, but when Samuel Bartlett was unable to attend, the Ashfield town meeting to choose an alternate gave radicals in town an opportunity to be even more specific about the way they expected their representatives to exert their influence. On October 22, they instructed their delegates to push for a "Legislative Court" to be the government of the state. The members of this court would be chosen by "ye Several Towns & . . . every Man being 21 years of Age who has not by his own Act forfited his Freedom Shall be accounted free and have a Right to Vote." That is, even slaves should vote. (In fact, there was strong anti-slavery sentiment in Ashfield, which may have been one of the reasons Jacob Sherwin, who owned a slave, had been fired.) Furthermore, there would be "no Power formed to negative [the Court's] votes." They wanted the representatives paid out of the state treasury, and each one "Sworn not to pass any Acts or Laws whereby their constituents shall be in any Sense Name or Nature whatsoever Oppressed or forced in Matters of Religion. But their Business shall be to protect all Persons in ye free Enjoyment of their religious Sentiments So far as they are good & peacibul Inhabitants or Members of Civil Society, and that any Encroachment of one Denomination upon another Shall be detected & punished by Civil Authority." In addition, they wanted all civil and military officers chosen annually, and no one allowed to hold more than one office. Again, they insisted that registries of deeds and probate courts be town institutions, and that the local town constables, not county sheriffs, be tasked with serving all writs and warrants.[28]

The convention worked throughout the winter and adjourned in March to let the towns consider its proposed constitution. The plan was to meet again in June and make any changes that a large proportion of the people wanted. Ashfield's instructions to its delegates were among the most radical, and few of those that seemed most important to the town found their way into the new constitution. The convention did make an effort to respond to concerns in general that the old order was unacceptable and that assurances of individual rights were necessary. In fact, the first chapter of the document was a bill of rights, and Article III came close, for Massachusetts, to religious toleration. The legislature would have the power to make laws requiring support of a Protestant church in each town, but the constitution did not require a particular denomination, or that everyone in town attend that church (although church attendance of some sort would be required). In actuality, most of Article III constituted an essay justifying the need for some religious institution that was supported by local government. James Bowdoin, John Adams, and Samuel Adams, who drafted the document, were probably responding more to criticism from other delegations in the Continental Congress than to advocates of religious freedom in their own state. The rest of the document betrayed the influence of the "Essex Result," a set of conservative resolutions that a convention of easterners put forward in 1778 protesting the more democratic features of the first proposed constitution. In establishing a governor with a veto, an upper house based on wealth, substantial property requirements for voting and officeholding, and a ream of state officers all appointed by the governor and council, the convention came down heavily on the side of order, centralized authority, and strong executive rule. It was not a happy outcome for backcountry towns like Ashfield.[29]

For five days between May 16 and June 2, 1780, Ashfield inhabitants met and undertook a minute examination of the document. By the time they were done, barely a dozen people were left in the meetinghouse, but the near unanimity of all the votes taken throughout the discussion suggests that the great majority of the town was firmly behind the numerous criticisms and amendments that this town meeting sent off to the adjourned convention. Many towns had problems with the wording of Article III, Bowdoin's and the Adamses' attempt at providing religious "freedom." Ashfield flatly rejected it, declaring simply that "it is unconstitutional to human Nature and [there is] no Precept in the word of God to support it." This was essentially the long-held Baptist position that had pervaded the town by the time of the revolution. For the most part, Ashfield inhabitants made an effort to show how much of the document was acceptable to them by recording vote after vote in favor of the rather mundane sections. Their objections, however, were fundamental. Once again they criticized and even proposed amendments to clauses regarding the structure of the court system and the method for choosing judges. They made it clear that they continued to support annual election of justices of the peace, who would be town officers, and even annual election of judges for the state's Supreme Judicial Court. They repeated yet again their desire for universal male suffrage, along with local control of probate and deeds, and they thought that a state senate was "unnessary and Burdensom to the Commonwilth."[30]

It was a wonder that their response was so measured, deliberate, and meticulous and that they bothered to vote at all for the clauses that they found acceptable. After all, they had been asserting their autonomy and anti-authoritarianism for five years, and expressing similar attitudes for far longer. To the majority of the people of Ashfield, it must have seemed that, bill of rights or not, the state's leaders had no appreciation for the accountability they were supposed to feel and the people's desire to manage their own affairs. They might justifiably have felt that all they had endured during the war, and even in the twenty years prior to it, was for naught. They had sent all the way to Albany to get their arms and ammunition at a reasonable price. They had suffered through smallpox, the absence of one of their ministers and much of their workforce, huge tax increases, and price gouging. Their community had once again been threatened from the north. Their sons had fought in one campaign after another and suffered through winter encampments with the Continental Army. They had scraped together all they had to send their two delegates a hundred miles to the eastern end of the state because they were serious about what the revolution meant to them. Yet, aside from offering a few superficial compromises built into the latest version of the constitution, the new state's leaders seemed to pay no attention. To make matters worse, the convention reconvened in June 1780 and, unable to see a consensus in the many objection-filled returns from the towns, simply declared the constitution ratified. In effect, the majority of delegates ignored the carefully considered concerns of backcountry towns like Ashfield. That would turn out to be a mistake.

Expect Trouble

One interpretation for the dwindling numbers at the town's deliberations in May and June of 1780 is that most Ashfield citizens never expected the state convention to take their objections and suggestions seriously. By the votes taken, it seems that those who objected to various articles in the proposed constitution wanted to be sure to maintain a two-thirds majority over the seven to nine men who might have voted to accept the constitution as written had its opponents not attended the meetings. But throughout the town, there was already, perhaps, a clear sense that the authors of the new constitution were deaf to what was important to them.[31]

Two months earlier, in fact, the town meeting had created another Committee of Correspondence and Safety made up of the town's most radical leaders. It had then proceeded to instruct the town's constables not to collect a substantially increased state tax for the year, and guaranteed that the town would stand behind them. With bounties now at three hundred pounds, the town had all it could do to recruit the year's quota of twelve Continental soldiers. And money was depreciating so fast that selectmen had to create a committee to figure the difference between what the town voted for support of the soldiers and what would be the equivalent when the money was actually paid a few weeks later. It is understandable that most of Ashfield thought that any state tax was not only burdensome, but also unjust, particularly when it was assessed on all but three-year soldiers. With Continental soldiers still in the field and the war still raging, Ashfield inhabitants were preparing for what was to them an equally important struggle against what appeared to be a revival, under a new government, of "them Old Tiranical Laws."[32]

Some scholars have actually labeled backcountry responses such as Ashfield's to the 1780 constitution as "anti-republican." The backcountry, they say, rejected the idea of a balanced government and simply wanted a weak state government that could not act without risking the ire of a tyrannical majority devoted only to its local interests. Whatever the label, Ashfield's patriots did have a good understanding of the drift of current affairs. No sooner was the new constitution ratified than the legislature began enacting policies that would create even more distress in the backcountry and raise suspicions that the revolution had simply replaced the old "court party" with an equally arrogant and perhaps even more greedy standing order. In 1780 and 1781, while Ashfield continued to struggle to put together enough hard currency to purchase its quota of beef for the army (ninety silver dollars), to pay six thousand pounds for road repairs, and to give Reverend Porter money owed him since 1774, the legislature and the state treasurer proceeded to consolidate the immense public debt incurred during the war and made efforts to pay interest on it in hard money. These were expensive undertakings, and the initial measures to raise revenue with an excise tax fell far short of the leadership's goal to pay off the state's notes at face value. Thus, in 1782, the legislature enacted a huge increase in property taxes and sought to collect poll taxes on all males sixteen years and older.[33]

To yeomen, husbandmen, and laborers throughout Massachusetts, these taxes seemed not only unduly burdensome but also evidence that under the new constitution a privileged merchant class now controlled the government. By the early 1780s the state's notes had fallen into the hands of a smaller and smaller group of speculators who had purchased them for as little as four shillings on the pound, often from soldiers or farmers who had received them as wages or payment for supplies. As a result of the new tax and credit policies, the speculators stood to make a fortune at the expense of the taxpayers. In Hampshire County the new taxes combined with resentment against the Court of General Sessions, whose judges, according to the new constitution, received their appointments from the governor, and whose cost schedules were set by the legislature.[34]

Ashfield had plenty of company in its bitterness. Two county conventions inspired by the radical anti-elitist outpourings of Samuel Ely of Conway, the town just east of Ashfield, met in Hadley and Hatfield in early 1782 to petition in protest of the governor's salary and the cost of maintaining the county courts. Ashfield sent delegates, including its militia captains Elisha Cranson and Benjamin Phillips, to both of these conventions. Nearly all of the backcountry towns wanted court functions transferred from the county to the towns. Shortly after the Hatfield convention a mob clashed with militiamen in Northampton in an effort to close the Court of Common Pleas. During the late summer and early fall tempers flared and scuffles between militias loyal to the state government and "regulators" multiplied. Regulators were jailed, only to be rescued by their supporters, hostages were exchanged, and near chaos reigned. In the four years that followed, more than a dozen county conventions met to complain about taxes, courts, and the increasingly unpopular constitutional order that had been established in 1780.[35]

Ashfield citizens came down on the radical side in all of these protests, although it is not clear how many participated in the more militant actions of late 1782. At a meeting in February 1783, the town resolved "that we will not pay the five & twenty shilling State Tax on the pole Nor no other State Nor County Tax or Taxes is or may be Assessed upon the Town of Ashfield until we are informed by Genl Cort or Some other Authority the perticular use the said Money is Designed for." Again the inhabitants voted to protect their constables against any action that might be taken against them for refusal to collect taxes. In addition they created a committee to draw up a "covenant for the People to Signe," and recommended that all the town's militia officers

"Resine their Commissions" lest they be caught in the middle and ordered to use their authority to restore order. It almost seems, in fact, to have been disorder that the Ashfield people intended. The town continued to send delegates to county conventions throughout 1783. It also passed measures to raise money to support debtors threatened by financial ruin at the hands of the Court of Common Pleas and the Court of General Sessions. In the summer of 1784 the town agreed to collect a "Continental Tax" and a "small county tax," but Elisha Cranson continued to attend sessions of the General Court to protest the more burdensome tax policies. By then the war was officially over and the town no longer had to meet the costs of supplying soldiers.[36]

While Captain Cranson carried petitions and complaints to the General Court, Ashfield remained in a difficult financial position. The town's population began to grow rapidly in the early 1780s. Most of the newcomers arrived without title to property in town, and when they did find land they could buy instead of renting, all they could afford was in the rocky hills and ravines of the southern and western parts of town. The result was that a growing number of people who did not have wealth enough to enhance the town's grand list still had a growing need for meetinghouse space, schooling, roads and road maintenance, and care for indigent residents (unless the town could get away with classifying the latter as "transients"). Selling pews in the meetinghouse gallery or renting the school and church lands produced some revenue, but as the selectmen surveyed mile after mile of new roads in order to give new yet habitually impoverished residents opportunities to get their grain to the mill and cattle to market, the town's bills continued to mount. It even had to finance a four-dollar-a-head bounty on wolves, as a town that would be productive nevertheless seemed to be forever on the frontier. It is little wonder that in May 1786 the townspeople instructed Captain Cranson to threaten to "leave his seat" in the legislature if that body agreed to a "suplimentery supply for Congress for Twenty-five years." They also asked him to "use his influence that the Genl Court be speedily Removed out of the town of Boston," no doubt hoping to bring to heel what they considered a renegade government that might listen to them only when sitting within earshot of the mobs of Hampshire County.[37]

Finally, matters came to a head in late 1786 when Ashfield joined angry farmers across western Massachusetts in an effort to close the courts until their views had an effect on public policy. In addition, the town voted to send two companies of its militia in support of the regulators who attacked the Springfield arsenal that winter. It also turned the town's powder magazine over to these units. More than fifty men, led by Lieutenant Pelatiah Phillips and Lieutenant Samuel Allen, joined the rebels in their battle against General Benjamin Lincoln's troops.[38]

There is considerable debate among historians about the mindset of those who sided with "the regulators" in the mid-1780s, and the extent to which farmers were truly oppressed by government policies and hard times in general during and following the Revolutionary War. Some attribute the regulator movement that culminated in 1786 with the so-called Shays's Rebellion to a combination of high taxes, hard times, harsh punishments for debtors, and a justifiable effort to reclaim a revolution that had become less democratic than its fighters had intended. Others see the regulators as either nearsighted, overspending ingrates or fundamentally conservative people trying to save their traditional peasant social order from the onslaught of the new commercial economy.[39]

In one way or another all of these explanations apply to Ashfield, but none of them quite account for the ferocity of anti-government sentiment that apparently even predated the 1780 constitution. On the one hand, Ashfield was a community devoted to traditional rural ideals, such as consensual politics and local enforcement of an accepted moral code. Town meeting leaders worked hard to create outcomes virtually everyone could accept and seldom resorted to taking vote counts. Efforts to maintain social concord are similarly obvious in the records, such as Rev. Jacob Sherwin's acquiescence "to live in peace with his neighbors" when the town asked that he give up the pew that had been assigned to his family before his dismissal as minister. That they lived by the ideal of a tight-knit and even corporate community is also evident in how seldom young people ventured beyond their local acquaintances in choosing a spouse. Finally, Ashfield's response to the arrival of Mother Ann Lee's Shakers on the town's northern border raises questions about how receptive its residents were to new ideas. At a 1782 town meeting they voted to send a delegation to warn the "Stragglin Tremblers" to "depart in twenty-four hours or Expect Trouble."[40]

Perhaps we might see the hostility toward the Shakers as more a fear of transients threatening to become town charges or luring away productive workers than a reaction against challenges to religious consensus. After all, Ashfield's people had settled into a culture of religious toleration with clear distinctions in doctrine. And even if their horizons were somewhat constrained, they were not hostile to the world of commerce and consumer goods, as Richard and John Ellis's account books have shown. Furthermore, Ashfield's steady stream of objections to the republicanism of the eastern elite contain a bold foray into a radical political culture that was neither traditional nor peasant-minded. The town's voters demanded strict accountability from their governing officials, and although they habitually elected a small number of men again and again to their higher offices during the 1770s and 1780s, their inclination to instruct them carefully with town meeting votes and to form special committees of five to nine men for every major issue reveals a desire for ongoing rule by the people at large. They stood for religious toleration, for a vote for every man rich or poor, and against slavery. It did not take a firebrand like Samuel Ely to stir up these sentiments. In fact, Ely may have picked up a few of his phrases from his western neighbors. If an element of a communal, "peasant" mentality still lingered in the minds of Ashfield's inhabitants, most seem as strongly committed to an egalitarian vision that defied tradition and challenged the future.

One approach to understanding the "Shaysites" has been to examine lists of the men who accepted amnesty after the rebellion by taking an oath of loyalty to Massachusetts. The Ashfield men who marched with the other regulators of Hampshire County are hard to classify. They were not primarily debtors, nor were they mostly Revolutionary War veterans. The Hampshire County Court Records do contain actions against some of these men for debt, but no more in the 1780s than in previous years, and few of these ended up in debtors' prison. As for Revolutionary War veterans, one of the militia leaders, Samuel Allen, appears to fall in this category. A poor man originally from Deerfield, he had worked hard to build a homestead in Huntstown in the 1760s, and had emerged as a leader during the revolution. Samuel Allen's story, however, applies to fewer than half of those who took up arms against the state. Many of them were too young to have fought in the revolution, and, in turn, there were plenty of veterans who were not on Ashfield's list of Shaysites. A significant number of the regulators were young or landless men, unqualified to vote under the new constitution, and perhaps unhappy with the reemergence of an older order symbolized by Philip Phillips's appointment as a justice of the peace. These factors may have played a role, but even this profile of the landless, voteless, and resentful young man does not fit fully a fifth of the combatants.[41]

There is one category that does cover all of the regulators of Ashfield: they were the town's 1786 militiamen, and here is the point. They were, in short, a segment of a much larger entity that was itself as committed to the rebellion as any pardoned regulator in Hampshire County, and that entity was the town of Ashfield. The town meeting had sent these young and land-less men into battle just as it had sent troops off to Boston in 1775 to repre-sent their resistance to the British empire. The town meeting had armed them, had sent delegates to countless county conventions with instructions embodying their deeply felt principles, had drafted a covenant of mutual protection, and had already defied the state government's tax laws. The mili-tiamen were the executive arm of a whole town in rebellion.

Even with the rebels humiliated and disenfranchised in 1787, the re-mainder of the town continued to display its localist and anti-authoritarian inclinations. In December, Ashfield elected Ephraim Williams Sr., who had marched with the Shaysites, to attend the convention to consider the new constitution for the United States and "use his influence to see that the said Constitution doth not take place." Ephraim had moved to Ashfield before the revolution to land that his father, Daniel Williams, Esq., of Easton had in-herited or purchased from absentee proprietors. Carting his sawmill equip-ment across the colony, Ephraim not only established a successful lumber business but also came into possession of over fifteen hundred acres of land that he now rented out. In spite of his instructions, Williams voted in favor of the Constitution. It narrowly passed in Massachusetts, and only after John Hancock, the new governor, had thrown his weight behind it.[42]

By most accounts, Shays's Rebellion was a dismal failure. Not only were the rebels defeated in battle, their leaders persecuted, two of them exe-cuted, and all forced to swear an oath of loyalty if they ever wanted to vote or hold office again, but in the end many historians attribute the framing and ratification of the new Constitution of the United States, which those of Shaysite inclinations had hoped would not "take place," to the fear of disor-der that the Shaysites created among the leaders of the new republic. From Ashfield's point of view, however, the result was not so clearly negative. James Bowdoin's administration went down to defeat at the polls in 1787 and John Hancock, the man that Ashfield had supported throughout the 1780s, became the new governor. Under his administration the more burdensome taxes were repealed or lowered, particularly after federal assumption of state debts, and the legislature generally became more responsive to the concerns of the countryside. It did seem that the residents of Ashfield and their counterparts in places like Colrain and Pelham had wrung a few concessions from the eastern establishment.

In the background of all the political turbulence of the 1780s was considerable social change. Ashfield was a rapidly growing town. In 1776 its population had stood at 628. By the time of the first federal census in 1790 there were 1,460 inhabitants. A postwar baby boom was responsible for some of that growth. During the 1780s there were 347 births recorded in various town and church records, and only 18 deaths. The third generations of the Phillips, Ellis, and Smith families were coming of age. Few of the members of these families had died young or left town. The bulk of the population expansion, however, was a result of a postwar surge of migrants from towns all over eastern Massachusetts, Rhode Island, and Connecticut that were so full of people that even the rugged land in southern and western Ashfield looked inviting—and for many it was land that they would have to rent, at least at first. The town began selling "pew ground" in a gallery of the Congregational meetinghouse, and with some of the proceeds fashioned windows that went up behind the seats in the gallery all the way to the upper plates of the house. The Congregationalists and Baptists were even able to work out an amicable distribution of the revenues from the rental of the church lands.[43]

Notwithstanding all of this change, Ashfield had remained true to itself throughout the 1770s and 1780s. It was as though a dedication to independence, religious freedom, and security of one's freehold represented a qualifying attitude for admission to the town. Or perhaps it was a legacy passed along from the earliest settlers to the young families who arrived in droves once the Revolutionary War ended—families who hungered for land and presumed to share in the collective management of community affairs no less than those who had arrived during the French and Indian Wars. Ashfield's history was a story of repeated expectations of improvement and empowerment. Surely, along with those expectations, the terrain itself shaped the sentiments of the inhabitants. Once they had managed to carve out a few acres on high ground hundreds of vertical feet above the Connecticut River, they did not see why anyone in the valley, or in Boston or Braintree, for that matter, should look down upon them or think them any less in touch with God. An imbalance of power in favor of river or coastal merchants simply made no sense. When the 1780 constitutional drafting committee of Adams, Adams, and Bowdoin included a lecture on morality in their article on religious "freedom," and created a powerful executive, a state senate, and a judiciary that was completely independent of popular control, these Sons of Liberty should have known to "Expect Trouble" from the backcountry. "Liberty" had different meanings for different Americans. The people of the backcountry felt that they had sacrificed mightily for their vision of a new world. Considering the speed at which the backcountry towns were growing while still understanding themselves to be backcountry people, those who presumed to take charge of that new world would have to take that vision into account or become politically irrelevant.

8. As They Shall Judge Necessary

If Philip Phillips, Israel Williams, and the other Congregationalist proprietors had wanted to remove the Baptist thorn from their sides in the 1760s, they might have stopped harassing Baptists for taxes and then agreed to share the income from the ministerial lands with them. Clearly this solution was not likely to have occurred to them, but no sooner had the town passed this very gesture of religious toleration in the mid-1780s than the Baptist Church nearly disintegrated. Given the healthy state of the church in 1785, Elder Ebenezer Smith decided it was time for him to have a regular salary as an ordained minister of the gospel. It should have been a joyous moment. The church had built its own meetinghouse and had more communicants than ever. Instances of "disorderly walkers" had declined as it had become clear that church discipline among the Baptists was more rigorous than in the Congregationalist Church. And the Baptists had found a place of acceptance in the town—to the point where the town meeting had agreed to share its rent money with them, an act that might have produced a groan from old Israel Williams that could be heard in Ashfield.[1]

The noise they heard, however, emanated from none other than Elder Ebenezer's seventy-seven-year-old father, Chileab Smith, who was firmly opposed to ministers becoming "hirelings." After all, Chileab's contention that Christ had not sought out college-educated men for his disciples had nearly "disinherited" him years ago when his lands were sold at auction, and now his son was beginning to follow in Jacob Sherwin's footsteps! No doubt he saw the income from the ministerial lands, as well as the growing prosperity of his church's adherents, as so much temptation—a test of faith. Ministers ought to rely on voluntary gifts from the congregation, he believed.

Throughout 1785 there was much "solemn labor" as church members tried to reconcile the contending parties. No doubt, there was also considerable family anxiety. The church records, which had become blissfully sparse except to record numerous baptisms, now consumed many pages detailing the breach. At the same time that the clouds of tax rebellion were sweeping across western Massachusetts in late 1786, the Ashfield Baptists were calling in neighboring clergymen to advise them on how to deal with a bitter disagreement between father and son. A council that convened in December declared "That the Elder was justifiable in his conduct," and that he should receive "Reasonable Compensation for his Labours." In response, the church voted to reject the council's advice because it "wanted the Testimony of Scripture for its support." Ebenezer and a number of followers occupied the old meetinghouse as the Baptist association withdrew its support from those who refused to pay him a salary. Chileab gathered a separate church just over the town line in Buckland. Attendance in both groups fell sharply, and days of fasting and prayer failed to retrieve a disturbing number of "backsliders." It was "a dark time with us," wrote Ebenezer's younger brother Enos, who stood by his father, "we being Despised by men . . . and . . . turned out to meet where we could find a place."[2]

For Ashfield the years after Shays's Rebellion, rather than calm after a storm, were filled with change, some of it welcome, some of it troubling. Gradually the town opened new connections to the state and nation, and with that came demographic and economic growth. Even if some, like Chileab Smith, would have had his family and neighbors move more slowly into this new world, most had always wanted to become part of the New England mainstream and enjoy a measure of respect and material comfort. On the surface it did seem that, in spite of a more democratic and disorderly past, Ashfield settled into being the sort of community that Israel Williams might have dreamed of long ago: tranquil, orderly, and respectful of able leaders. Yet, beneath the surface there was a different story, one involving both adjustment to change and persistence in old ways on the part of people who knew what they wanted and who expected their leaders to be attentive to their needs. The town's inhabitants had been very clear over the past two decades about their vision of a good society, and as much as they were now conforming to New England, they still thought New England should conform some to backcountry standards.

New People

While the Baptists were engaged in soul-searching in the late 1780s, Ashfield's population was growing rapidly, and continued to grow during the next decade. In-migration of young people did not continue at quite such a high rate after 1790 compared with the previous five or six years, but families grew in size so that the total number of inhabitants in 1800 had increased by nearly 300, to 1,741. Additionally, a third generation of natives was starting families. Except for 1784, the year after the war ended, when there were twenty-one marriages, there had been an average of twelve marriages per year in the 1780s. In the 1790s the average rose to nineteen per year, and even with all of those young families, average family size rose from 5.6 in 1790 to 6.6 in 1800. In both decades, births outpaced deaths by a ratio of twelve to one. About half of the families listed in the 1800 census were not listed in 1790, and half of those were new to town. The other half was composed of young men who had come of age and set up their own households, as well as a few widows.[3]

The 20 percent increase in the population during the 1790s, as opposed to the approximate doubling of the population in the 1780s, could hardly be considered a sign of a more stable community. Underneath the aggregate figures there is also a story of considerable out-migration. Only nine of the family heads listed on the 1790 census died during the next ten years, yet 124 of the 261 family heads' names from 1790 are absent from the 1800 schedule. Although it appears that as many as twenty of those missing family heads were older people who were absorbed into the families of their children, that still leaves nearly a hundred families that moved out of Ashfield during the decade.[4] In short, during the 1790s nearly half of Ashfield's population moved away, and over a fourth of its 1800 population was newly arrived. A high marriage and birth rate created a net gain.

Local histories, which focus on the town's more permanent families, tend to ignore this subsurface instability. In the census reports, names like Arms, Bacon, Bowker, Gay, Lazelle, Olcott, and Osgood disappear from the town's story and are replaced, briefly, by others like Bathwick, Bishop, Clough, Collins, Dasby, Dunbar, Keyes, Putney, and Sanderson. Many of these people do not appear even in the land records, and we would not know that they stayed for a while in Ashfield were it not for the federal census created by a government that many in town had hoped would "not take place." There is much more information about the Aldens, Bements, Beldings, Howes, Lillies,

Phillipses, and Williamses. They owned a large proportion of the land, and even expanded their holdings after the revolution. Generally, in late-eighteenth-century Ashfield, there was not as much pressure on fathers to acquire enough land to divide among four or five sons as there had been before the revolution. Often all but one son moved out of town as they came of age. In turn, newcomers were seldom well enough endowed to purchase land.[5]

Where did all of those emigrants go? They mingled with former residents of other backcountry towns like Granby, Connecticut, in new settlements ranging from Windsor County, Vermont, to western New York state. Many may have been attracted to these lands when they served in the army during the Revolutionary War. They found there the kinds of low spots among hills that had served as farm sites for their parents and grandparents in Ashfield. Traveling in groups of neighbors and kin, they did not need to make extensive adjustments in their new communities. Along with the families who remained only a few years in Ashfield, there were enclaves of Ellises, Beldings, Forbushes, and Annables filling the upper Connecticut and western Mohawk River valleys in the 1790s. "It is a general time of health here," wrote Edward Ellis from Sempronius, New York, to his "honored parents" back in Ashfield. "Our friends are all well. My cousin, Benjamin Ellis, has bought him a farm, about a mile from here. Peleg Standish lives with me this summer, and has bought land adjoining Mr. Ellis and Mr. Stafford, and now there is a lot to be sold a mile west of him. I think it is as handsome land as ever I saw. There is a great deal of valuable timber on it and is well watered by a number of very fine springs." Land could be had for two dollars an acre, he reported, and purchased on credit as well. "I should be glad to purchase one hundred acres myself," he continued. "Crops look promising. The distance is so great that we can seldom see each other. . . . I am haying and in a hurry and must close my letter." Other letters home from the town's former residents recorded similar enthusiasm for land that contrasted sharply with Ashfield's rocky terrain and recounted happily the numerous relatives who had joined in the beginnings of the famed "yankee exodus."[6]

As for the people coming into Ashfield, the other side of the demographic turmoil at the century's end, there were a variety of sources. The continued migration from Cape Cod accounted for a number of the new farmers who were willing to take up some of the less desirable land in the northwestern part of town. The Yarmouth people came to dominate that area with their apple orchards, and some began to refer to the section as

"Nobscusset," the original name of a part of Yarmouth. There was also significant growth in the number of people involved in trades and professions who came to live in long-settled parts of town. Although we do not have occupational information on every family head as we do for later years, it is clear that the number of manufacturing, commercial, and professional establishments was growing during the 1790s. Lawyers Elijah Paine and Thomas White arrived from Hatfield. Lot Bassett settled in as a cobbler. Selah Norton, formerly of East Hartford, Connecticut, opened a general store, having apparently bought out the partnership of Murray and Bennett, the latter also a woolen hat maker. Dorrus Graves, a clothier, moved in from Hatfield. Others were engaged in manufacturing broom handles. And, of course, every entrepreneur opening a mill, store, or shop was a potential employer for newcomers who did not or could not own or rent enough land to sustain their families.[7]

The local land market responded in short order to all of this change. Land values climbed when there was greater demand, even though that encouraged some older residents to sell out and move to better land in other regions. In the mid-1780s (after the inflationary period at the end of the war) land among the first division lots was selling for one or two pounds per acre. Ten years later prices ranged from three to six pounds per acre, and pieces with buildings on them at intersections could go for as much as two hundred pounds for an acre. In Sempronious, New York, Edward Ellis was finding valley land for a tenth of what people were paying for Ashfield's low places among the hills. Newcomers looking for a farm of reasonable acreage drove part of this demand, and so did older inhabitants wanting to rent to those who could not afford to buy. The town itself found that it could count on substantial rental income from its school and ministerial lands to support its annual budget.[8]

That large numbers of the in-migrants of the late 1780s were landless laborers who could not afford to buy land, especially at rising prices, became evident as the town had to grapple with increasing numbers of paupers. In order to reduce the town charges from one hundred pounds in 1790 to thirty pounds the following year, the town meeting in December 1790 directed the selectmen to "warn out" nearly a hundred men and their families "to prevent the town from Cost & Charge." Apparently, residents were afraid that there was not enough work for all of these people. Two years later a town meeting authorized another series of evictions, "as [the selectmen] shall Judge necessary," for newcomers and their families who had not established residency and who did not seem able to support themselves. By 1796 the state legislature recognized that transient paupers had become a major problem all across Massachusetts and began to allocate money to towns that would keep nonresident paupers instead of carting them from one town line to the next. By then Ashfield and other towns had resorted to auctioning the care of their resident paupers "at vendue to the lowest bidder," a solution that pleased neither paupers nor town officials.[9]

There are a number of other signs of the strains of population growth and change in the early 1790s. Not only did expenses for upkeep of the town poor climb, but so did the cost of upkeep on the town roads. The town spent fifty pounds on its roads in 1789. By 1797 that expense had quadrupled. The increase is even more startling given that throughout those years the town had devoted considerable energy to getting the county to discontinue its old highways, resurvey new county roads over town roads, and send county funds Ashfield's way to aid in upkeep. In addition, as the town hired more and more laborers, rather than have all inhabitants work off their taxes on highway upkeep, the town meeting cut the rate of pay for road work in half during the 1790s. The problem was that with every new family there seemed to be a need for another quarter to a half mile of town road. Between 1788 and 1800 the town meeting discontinued seven roads and approved the surveying of twenty-seven new ones in their place.[10]

Similarly the budget for schools was on the rise, reflecting the growing number of families with young children. During the Revolutionary War there were only four school districts in Ashfield, but by 1790 the town had resurveyed itself and had five more. Each required its own teacher and schoolhouse, and each received town money according to "the number of scholars between the ages of 4 and 21." It was good that there was more rent money coming in from the school lands, for expenses nearly quadrupled between 1789 and 1797. The town's expanding youth sector was filling its recently built schoolhouses to capacity.

The difficulty was that young families were hard pressed to pay taxes, and on a number of occasions the town had to authorize the selectmen to remit "what taxes they shall judge Reasonable," to give their constituents a chance to become not only solvent taxpayers but producers and consumers as well. Probably Ashfield was not alone in struggling with ways to meet expenses. Throughout the 1780s and 1790s the selectmen were not only quite busy surveying roads and determining which people could be supported by the town, but also they seemed to be involved in endless negotiations with the neighboring towns of Conway, Buckland, and Goshen over town lines. As expenses soared, every hill town needed to know exactly what property it could assess for taxes. At least Rev. Nehemiah Porter was cooperative. In lieu of part of his salary he was willing to accept a 999-year lease on a prime lot for the yearly payment of one peppercorn.

The rapid growth of the town required a more sophisticated government. To the regular collection of town officers—selectmen, clerk, treasurer, surveyors of highways, tithingmen, and fenceviewers—were added new regulating officials. In 1789 the town chose a sealer of leather for the first time, and two years later a packer of beef, a surveyor of lumber, and a "clerk of the market" appeared in the records. Over the next decade field drivers and measurers of wood joined the roster of elected—or perhaps it would be more accurate to say "recruited"—officials. The town had been accustomed to choosing a hog reeve every year prior to 1790, but the swine population grew so rapidly that by 1796 there were seven chosen to oversee the various ordinances regarding yokes and rings and when and where the swine were allowed to "run at large." Pork had become a marketable commodity for even the poorest of inhabitants, and town officials wanted to encourage as much production as could be regulated in an orderly manner.[11]

After the revolution, life changed substantially for the town of Ashfield. Unsettling population turnover and growth called for expensive public projects, new regulations, schools for a decidedly younger community, and a slew of new officials to ward off chaos. In addition, an emerging underclass of transient paupers threatened to divide the town both socially and through debate over what should be done with them. The future was falling on Ashfield with accelerating speed.

Order, Peace, and Harmony

In spite of all the time that Ashfield's leaders spent dealing with the complications of a community in a fair degree of turmoil, for most longtime residents and for those who arrived with money to buy land or invest in a business, the end of the eighteenth century seemed to be an era of contentment and even relative prosperity. Ashfield's formerly rough roads descending through ravines into Goshen, Hatfield, and Northampton, or east to

Deerfield and west into other hill towns, carried increasing commercial traffic that smoothed down not only the road surfaces but also the rough edges of those who chose to stay on their farms in the hills. Salutary change of this sort was evident both in the records of the local economy as well as in the town's collective behavior during town meetings and at the polls. A more democratic society and economy oddly became a more tranquil polity.

As noted above, even though Ashfield experienced the exodus of a significant number of its young people who were coming of age, and only the temporary stay of many others, land values climbed. Even lots in the fourth and fifth divisions of land brought profits for those who had been able to hold on to them through the revolution and the early 1780s. Cuts in state taxes further benefited these people. Not only did the new Hancock administration reduce taxes in 1787 to counter the distress that had led to Shays's Rebellion, but after the federal assumption of state debts, poll taxes in Massachusetts dropped from their high of three pounds per head in 1786 to one shilling eight pence in 1795. Young men became less hesitant to become landowners and taxpayers, and their purchases pushed many longtime residents out of debt. Where before the revolution Ashfield inhabitants had been reluctant to bring the estates of their deceased parents to probate court, they now appeared more regularly to divide quite solvent estates that seemed to require the settlement of few outstanding notes. For those who still found themselves behind in their payments, a local court under Philip Phillips, who apparently had no interest in a repeat of Shays's Rebellion, handed out extensions and continuances in abundance. Some could even avail themselves of the services of the new lawyers in town, who would not charge too much because they had other, more prosperous clients to make up the difference.[12]

New grist mills, packers of beef, and friendly regulations on the grazing of livestock meant that farmers could begin to garner some credit and even cash from merchants, as opposed to hard looks when those farmers had done nothing but take away supplies for years. For those who had not yet obtained carts and wagons sturdy enough for the trek to market towns, newcomers Selah Norton, Gad Wait, and John Bennett joined John Ellis in the trading business and set up stores in the scattered neighborhoods across town. Ellis's account book suggests that the recently arrived merchants were perhaps more efficient than he, for while he still did business with local farmers in beef and grain, he did not have as many consumer goods to trade as he once did. Instead he and his sons supplied their horses and carts, as well as their own labor, to acquire produce that he could then trade with the local merchants. Many of the merchants of Hatfield that he had dealt with in the past were out of business and new networks had emerged.[13]

The opening of a canal around the Holyoke Falls on the Connecticut River in the 1790s meant that manufactured goods from American shops and Europe became more available. In a Springfield newspaper that was apparently circulating in Ashfield by 1793, Selah Norton advertised that he had "all sorts of dry goods, also Old Jamaican Spirits, New England Rum, French Brandy &c. will pay 8 pence per pound for butter, part cash." His dry goods included cloth of all sorts, plain and fancy, housewares, tools for farmers and craftsmen alike, and tea and spices. Postal routes began to thread their way through Ashfield along with the commercial traffic, and storeowners and taverners transformed their enterprises from centers of local socializing to portals into the river valley and beyond. Whoever had the edge in the mercantile business, Ashfield farmers were more connected than ever in the regional marketplace and culture, and many had more extra cash or credit, as long as their wives and daughters could churn enough butter for trading. These trends were reflected in the construction of a number of spacious two-story houses with decorative molding and paneling to replace the rough cabins that many had endured so long.[14]

As the issue of poor relief demonstrates, there was another side to the changing local economy of the late eighteenth century. Only a few families had houses like Reuben Ellis's sons, while most continued to crowd into one-story dwellings with only two or three small rooms. As some grew more prosperous and able to achieve at least a modicum of freedom from debt and independent living, others continued to be dependent on landlords or creditors and less able to live comfortably. Not only were there disturbingly increasing numbers of people who could not support their families, but there were also quite a few families who could barely pay climbing rent costs, let alone purchase store goods.

These emerging lines of social and economic division within the town are subtly apparent when comparing the tax list of 1793 with a town valuation done before the revolution. In both cases, the upper quartile of taxpayers owned more than half the assessed wealth in town. However, in 1793 the median assessment was eight times the average for the bottom fifth (as opposed to four times in 1771), and the average for the wealthiest fifth was four times the median (as opposed to under three times in 1771). Additionally,

Aaron Lyon's house, built circa 1765. Although it has been considerably altered since then, the structure still has its original frame. This and the following photograph show the contrast between houses built by the more prominent families before the revolution and the sort of architecture that characterized the better-off residents in the 1790s.

"the bottom fifth" in 1771 refers to seventeen people, most with no taxable estate. In 1793 the bottom fifth consisted of fifty-five people with little or no taxable estate. In other words, the economic distance between the middle and the extremes on the tax list was growing. There were many people who were enjoying a higher standard of living, but a growing number lived as poorly as people ever did in Ashfield.[15]

One might predict that the unrest of the previous decade might crop up anew, if so many were to become frustrated with the apparently growing inequities. A look at the politics of the period, however, would suggest widespread satisfaction with current affairs. There were no county conventions, no marches on Philip Phillips's courtroom, no petitions other than town efforts to get the county to pay for the maintenance of some roads, and little evidence of simmering resentment left over from the 1780s. Year after year, voters returned Ephraim Williams, by far the richest man in town, to his seat in the House of Representatives, apparently forgiving him for ignoring his instructions in 1788 to "use his influence to see that the said constitution doth

The house of David and Jonathan Ellis, sons of Reuben Ellis, was constructed in 1795. This and Aaron Lyon's house are discussed in an architectural study of the town, "Survey of Ashfield Houses Before 1960," by Norma Harris and the Ashfield Historical Commission for the Massachusetts Historical Commission, 1985, on file at the Ashfield Historical Society, Ashfield, Massachusetts.

not take place." Between that year and 1800 he served as selectman nine times, and Rowland Sears was elected for eight terms. Abner Kelley, Joshua Howes, Abiezer Perkins, or Chileab Smith Jr. filled in the third slot in various years, but voters showed little interest in anyone else for the town's highest offices. In fact, on numerous occasions, votes on the most important issues, such as the surveying of roads, the management of schools, and the determination of which paupers to send packing, the town meeting gave few instructions beyond urging the selectmen to take action "as they shall judge necessary."

Even in voting for state officeholders and representatives to the U.S. Congress, Ashfield appeared quite satisfied with the existing order. Voters chose Theodore Sedgewick, a man who had been sympathetic to the complaints about taxation before Shays's Rebellion, as their congressman in 1789, but soon William Shepard won the vast majority of Ashfield votes in succeeding congressional elections. Shepard was the commander of the militia in Hampshire County who had joined with General Benjamin Lincoln in putting down Shays's Rebellion in 1787, and he did so apparently with an even greater vengeance than Lincoln himself. What is more remarkable is a vote taken in 1795. The once detested state constitution contained a provision that in that year Massachusetts citizens would decide if the constitution should be revised. In a relatively quiet meeting, Ashfield voted 56 to 12 against revision.[16]

Apparently having an established church was not as offensive as it once was. And yet, the Congregational Church had hardly become a dominant institution. Reverend Porter of Ashfield did not enjoy growing numbers of communicants, prominent or otherwise, as did Isaac Porter, the minister in Granby. One historian has said that in 1800 there were only three horse-drawn vehicles at Sunday meetings, and they were lumber wagons. Nehemiah Porter certainly tried hard enough to awaken his people, and he addressed the theme of election often. In one sermon apparently delivered on numerous occasions in Ashfield as well as surrounding towns, he warned against the temptation to "draw back" from the gift of faith that God offers. He instructed his listeners to "take heed to yourselves, lest a deceived heart turn you aside and you perish." Then, he tried to lighten things up with a joke about a man who promised on his sickbed to "make Reformation." Once recovered, the man lapsed again into sinful ways. When admonished by his minister, he replied, "he did make promises on Reformation it was true, but he never designed to keep them."

If the audience did not respond with enthusiastic conversions to Porter's jocular renditions of Calvinism, at least he did not have to deal with the tension that had gripped Ashfield before the revolution. When he traveled about town on home visits trying to get people to give more thought to the state of their souls, he was greeted with affection and hospitality. Every household served him a glass of "flip" or "toddy," and he must not have been too frustrated with the condition of his parish as he staggered home each night. It would be four decades, after all, before a constitutional amendment disestablished his church. And besides, his farm cost him only a peppercorn a year.[17]

Meanwhile, a village center developed near the Congregational meetinghouse, complete with taverns, Selah Norton's store, and two lawyers' offices. One of the lawyers, Elijah Paine, was well known for his gentlemanly attire, complete with ruffle flowing out of the front of his coat. Inside the meetinghouse, cushions appeared in the pulpit, and there was enough money to hire a "singing master." Nearby the town constructed a pound, thirty feet square with walls seven feet high.[18] Politically quiet yet economically energetic, Ashfield had transformed itself in the space of a decade. If Timothy Dwight had wanted yet one more example of a harmonious and orderly "world within itself," he might have spurred his horse up one of the somewhat improved county roads to "the Plain" in Ashfield and had a pleasant conversation with Reverend Porter or Esquire Paine.

Arguments Against Worldly-Mindedness

Impressed by Ashfield's new look, one might reasonably ask what happened to all of those democrats and separatists who so fervently despised established religion, appointed county courts, a state senate, and the Constitution of the United States? Had Ashfield become, as historian Michael Zuckerman once phrased it, "a democracy without democrats"?[19]

Here it is instructive to study, once again, the so-called Shaysites—the fifty-two men who took up arms in the rebellion of 1786–87. Certainly these militiamen may be representative of the democratic-thinking constituency of Ashfield in general. What happened to them? Did they simply leave the town, and even the state? Were they so defeated that they became politically invisible or economically marginal?

Surprisingly, after the rebellion, the Ashfield Shaysites did not simply disappear and leave behind only the meek and deferential to accept the likes of Philip Phillips as their natural leaders. By 1793 only nine of the fifty-two Shaysites were not listed on the town's tax rolls. Two of those had died, two had been resurveyed into the town of Buckland, and the other five had left town. Otherwise, forty-three rebels and their families (with some children who had since come of age and begun their own families) were among the more permanent half of Ashfield's rapidly changing population. Furthermore, with the exception of a few, like Lieutenant Samuel Allen, who had refused to take the oath of loyalty, nearly every one of these men could be found participating in town meetings when elections of officers took place. Even though voter turnout was fairly low (in 1794 less than half of the qualified voters cast ballots in the gubernatorial and congressional elections), these particular men were in the habit of attending town meetings and taking part in public affairs. Where were their democratic voices in 1795 when it came time to consider revisions in the state constitution?

One clue is in the qualification for voting itself. In 1785 fewer than half of the future rebels qualified to vote. In 1794 only four of the forty-three former rebels were not on the list of eligible voters. This is an astounding development that echoes the days when town leaders hoped to forestall "mobes and rioates" by allowing everyone to vote in town meetings. It is reasonable to think that rebels would not stay rebels for long if they felt they had some say in the community. Another development that may help to explain the relative tranquillity in spite of the continued participation of former rebels in politics is the standing of these people in the community. Whereas many of the Shaysites owned no land in the 1780s, by the time of the 1793 tax list nearly three-fourths of them had estates assessed above the median, and some of them, like David Ellis, were among the more prosperous farmers building fine new dwellings for their families. In the six years following their armed resistance, the Shaysites had been quite busy becoming an integral and prosperous part of the new order—they had good reason to feel contented. Any worries they might have had at one time that an equally oppressive aristocracy was replacing the old British "court party" could easily have evaporated as they considered their thriving farms—land that was unlikely to be attached for debt.

Finally, although Abner Kelley seems to have been the only one of the regulators who served more than a single term in the town's higher offices, at one time or another most of the former rebels occupied the position of surveyor of highways. The year after the rebellion half of the ten surveyors of highways were former Shaysites, and in 1793 Philip Phillips, who had testified against Samuel Allen after the rebellion, gave Allen the oath of office as surveyor. Surveyors could ensure that work got done on their own roads and that tax money was credited to them and their neighbors according to the records that they themselves kept. And since the town was surveying more roads every year, there was more need for additional overseers. That was empowerment, and credit, that made a great difference to farmers loading up their wagons with surplus butter, pork, beef, and lumber to trade at Selah Norton's store for French brandy, "all sorts of dry goods," and "part cash."[20]

The town meeting records suggest even more that might not be apparent from the names of major officeholders alone. Regardless of how many times the meetings deferred to the selectmen's judgment, the inhabitants were not about to cancel town meetings altogether. Between 1788 and 1800 there were at least four, and sometimes as many as seven, town meetings each year. Two of those meetings were annual election meetings, one for town officials and the other for state legislators and the governor. Nevertheless, most meetings involved between thirty-five and fifty residents (about a third of the eligible voters)—many of them former Shaysites, discussing roads, bridges, schools, paupers, expenses, the town treasury, livestock management, income from town lands, and taxes. Residents never left these matters in the selectmen's hands longer than a few months without review and comment. If they appear to have been generally approving of "the doings of the selectmen," it was probably because the selectmen were particularly good at anticipating what would meet with their approval, and knew that they would soon answer for it if their "doings" did not.

It should not be assumed either that being a selectman was a particularly privileged position bestowed as an honor upon "deserving" men. Miserly town meetings allowed a few shillings a year for the completion of their duties, which included not only care of the poor, the management of the town budget, and determination of the tax rate, but also the surveying of new roads, the seemingly endless perambulation of town boundaries and wrangling with neighboring towns about them, and the drawing up of the annual assessment for town, state, and ministerial taxes (the latter task involving door-to-door visits to take inventory of taxable property every year). Surveyors of highways got more credit against their taxes in proportion to time spent than did the selectmen. And even though they were called "surveyors," they did not need surveying skills, as did at least one of the three selectmen, to say nothing of knowing the tax code and the residential history of every poor working family in town. In Ashfield, the selectmen could truly be called public servants.

In addition to their becoming more prosperous and feeling that they ultimately had control over public affairs should they need to exercise it, many of Ashfield's former radicals may have been taking time off from active participation in politics because they had other problems to deal with that neither the expanding economy nor the town meeting could solve. This was particularly true of the Baptists who were struggling to reunite their congregation after the association had sided with Ebenezer Smith and withdrew its recognition from those who would not pay him a salary. On September 5, 1788, Enos Smith wrote, "The Spirit of the Lord began to come down in a Powerful manner among us—sinners began to Cry out under a sense of their Lost undone condition which continues to increase for some time." In January 1789, Enos, his father Chileab Smith Sr., and a few others joined with Baptists in Buckland to form a new congregation of forty-six communicants and built a meetinghouse just north of the Ashfield town line. Enos and Chileab were ordained as elders. "Several Backsliders were Returned, and saints Quickned &c," Enos wrote with greater confidence.[21]

It took some time, though, to bring about a reunion with Elder Ebenezer's group. Perhaps one of those responsible for the eventual reconciliation was Chileab's daughter Eunice Smith. She was born in 1757, the year after Ebenezer married Remember Ellis. Still unmarried in 1791, she decided to take on a more public role in her father's church. In that year, with the help of Zadock King of Conway, she published her first of several pamphlets, "Some Arguments Against Worldly-Mindedness and Needless Care and Trouble." A popular work, it went through four printings over the next six years. She married Benjamin Randall of Shelburne in 1792, but she continued to write pamphlets under her maiden name. In one year there were two printings of "Practical Language Interpreted: in a dialogue between a believer and an unbeliever."[22]

In "Arguments Against Worldly-Mindedness," Eunice created a dialogue between two women, Mary and Martha. Poor Martha is overwhelmed "with the cares of this present life, which makes [her] unfit for the service of God or man." Mary, however, seems to find it far easier to engage in the service of God and labors at length to convince Martha that the same could be true for her. "Come sit at the feet of the lovely Jesus," she urges, "and first wash his feet with the tears of true repentance, and then sit and hear his sweet voice, saying, Daughter be of good comfort, though thou art a great sinner, I am a more great Savior." Martha protests, "there is so much necessary Service for me to do in the affairs of this world." It takes all her time and mental energy to keep up with it, "and causes many troubles." Alas, "Providence works so that it looks as if all was against me," she laments.

Mary is very patient with her forlorn and despairing companion— pages and pages of patience. She tells Martha that she does not have to take time out to "sit at the feet of Jesus," but can incorporate praying into every activity of the day. At long last Martha sees that she is "a foolish child, and I have troubled myself about things that did not belong to me." Mary rejoices, for she desires "to assert nothing for truth in matters of religion but what can be proved by the Scriptures," and she feels that in quoting that scripture to Martha she has brought her to the truth about what really matters. Martha admits that she had immersed herself too much in her own cares to realize the importance of the truth of the scripture and its redeeming gifts. "Self is an unpleasant field indeed; but I am so foolish that I stay there sometimes until my soul is almost starved to death." Mary replies, "Let us be speaking of the glory of [God's] kingdom," and not waste time with anything else.

The dialogue does not reach its resolution there, however. Martha is concerned about backsliding, for no matter how joyous she feels when thinking about Christ's mercy with Mary, she is "often swallowed up by worldly cares or carnal security, or something as bad, and carried down the stream against my will. . . . It seems like mockery" to then return and ask for forgiveness "when the Lord knows my heart is not engaged therein." Fear not, assures Mary, for every time you return the Lord will take you in. "He pities them and sees them toiling all night for nothing; and he is pleased with their earnest endeavors, tho' he knows that without him they can do nothing. The love of our Redeemer is such, that when he sees we can live no longer without him, he will appear and turn our night into day." Keep at it, keep coming back, urges Mary, and one day, you will be with God forever. "Free Grace! Free Grace! My soul doth sing! Glory to God! my heavenly King!"

There is considerable crescendo and cadence at the end of what has become, it seems, a hymn of rapture for the moment of triumphal reclamation of lost Martha. It is not surprising that this work would succeed in attracting widespread readership for Eunice Smith. For an essay set in the rather old-fashioned dialogue form, it is quite moving. But anyone who knew what was going on at Baptist Corner could not help but recognize in it an anguished sister and daughter crying out for her brother and octogenarian father to start concentrating on what should be of greatest importance to them. How could their own dialogue be so caught up in worldly-mindedness? What kind of example did their quarrel set for either congregation? How would their mission of bringing souls "lovingly to Christ" fare while they bickered about a minister's salary? Certainly there were many around Baptist Corner who spoke these thoughts, if not with so much passion, for by the end of 1793 the church had reunited under Elders Chileab, Enos, and Ebenezer when Ebenezer confessed his wrongs. Many who had been disillusioned because of the argument returned as well.[23]

That was not the end of Baptist Corner's difficulties, however. There were arguments about whether to have "dancing meetings," and continued problems with "church discipline" as "wanderers," absentees, and "disorderly walkers" occupied the agendas of church meetings. Zadock King of Conway, Eunice Smith's sponsor, left to join a Methodist church, and Elisha Smith, who would not respond to "solemn labor" after he joined the Freemasons, was excommunicated. Ebenezer himself resigned from his position as elder in 1798 and occupied himself as an itinerant preacher. Eventually he moved on to

Stockton, New York. The legislature did incorporate a joint society composed of the Ashfield and Buckland Baptist churches in 1800, thus securing the Baptists' continued freedom from ministerial taxes. Yet in the early years of the nineteenth century, out-migration from both Ashfield and Buckland destabilized the new society, and Elder Enos Smith contended again with the Ashfield town meeting over the proceeds of the troublesome ministerial lands—which meant more exchanges of petitions and more trips to Boston.[24]

For some Ashfield residents of the 1790s a sense that they had control over their lives and a voice in their community was sufficient to "quiet their minds." For others, achieving a measure of respectability and material comfort satisfied them that the new republic would not be an oppressive regime. Perhaps even some of the renters were content with visible evidence of opportunity. There were still some who felt conflicted about being too worldly-minded, but the world let them work that out for themselves. In the wake of Shays's Rebellion, New England had reached out to the backcountry and gathered its people into the fold. Or perhaps, when coming halfway down the mountain themselves to meet the new age, the backcountry people had shaped New England into something in which they felt comfortable.

On August 19, 1800, Chileab Smith breathed his last. The great logs of the palisade around his house had long since become firewood. His apple trees spread out unmolested, and the small burial ground where he was laid to rest on the hillside near his house and tavern was secure. County officials appeared in Ashfield not with execution warrants, but rather with surveying chains to see if they could reach a settlement with the town's agent, Ephraim Williams, Esq., regarding the routes of the county roads. The congregation no longer had to squeeze into Chileab's shop, but enjoyed its own meeting-house where it probably discussed his daughter's other-worldly pamphlets with some pride.

He had not been able to bring an end to all of the challenges of backcountry living. The hills were no less rugged, and the frost in the plowland pushed up a fresh crop of rocks each year. Just the same, his son Chileab Jr. and fellow Baptist Abiezer Perkins occasionally took oaths with the other selectmen to oversee public affairs. Surely they and the former Shaysites who crowded into town meetings brought to the town agenda a devotion to what they considered the truth as well as their particular understanding of authority. For the moment the people of Ashfield were satisfied that New England had taken them in. Yet no matter how serene the town's agenda may have appeared after the revolution and Shays's Rebellion, the radicals who had once insisted on direct governance by the people, equality, local independence, and religious toleration were still ready to step in and insist that their concerns be addressed wherever and whenever their leaders dared to ignore them. In Ashfield, and on into western New York and Pennsylvania, or wherever Ashfield's children took their families, leaders had to judge it necessary to pay attention to those who let them be leaders. Ashfield people had thought that this should be the rule for a half century, ever since Chileab Smith had decided that Hadley's society was "dead in trespasses and sin" and headed northwest into Huntstown's hills.

Epilogue
A Hazardous State and Condition

In ancient times glaciers scarred the rippled topography of New England and scattered oversized debris as they retreated. Millennia passed, but the early English settlers of the region's backcountry could still sense the grinding of ice sheets and boulders. In the hills they found the remnants: rocky outcroppings, and gravel and stones beneath a thin layer of topsoil. Their roads replayed the ice age each spring. Here and there a few heavily wooded "plains" and occasionally some open brook land they called "meadow" greeted those who arrived first. Even for these eager frontier people, the seven or eight miles of rugged terrain between their rough abodes and a more established and fortified town seemed endless during wartime, or even during peacetime in most seasons.

In this harsh and often fearful environment, the words of Salmon Brook's David Sherman Rowland undoubtedly echoed through every task when he discussed his people's "hazardous state and condition" and the unhappy outcome if the "brittle thread" that tied them to their miserly bit of earth should snap, as it likely would. In Huntstown, Chileab Smith and his family concluded that they had "little to commend themselves" to God and set about constructing a palisade for when God's wrath descended from Canada. These were the messages of choice for many in the backcountry. Hardened souls made their living on a hard land. "So far distant" are they from the twenty-first-century inhabitants of their towns. In what way can their story possibly have meaning in our own world?

We should be careful in presuming, when we ask that question, that there is a single story that emerges from the miscellaneous tedium of the daily lives of these plain people. After all, Salmon Brook and Huntstown are clearly very different places. When Salmon Brook's first settlers were venturing into the woodlands northwest of a burned-out Simsbury in the final days of King Philip's War, Huntstown was not even an idea in anyone's mind in Massachusetts. Salmon Brook's struggle for existence consumed decades while the leaders of Massachusetts tried to appease their bitter veterans with discounted bills of credit. By the 1730s, when the Massachusetts General Court was at last ready to give land grants to the families of its soldiers from 1690, Salmon Brook was a growing parish of freeholders who had already secured hundreds of acres of free land for themselves and their children and were on the verge of establishing their own ecclesiastical society. Salmon Brook then turned to New Light separatism, while Chileab Smith was still living in the "south precinct" of Hadley. During the Great Awakening of the 1740s, most of Huntstown's property owners had no interest in moving to their "house lots," and not much more in paying laborers to "mend the way" through the ravines.

When Chileab Smith arrived in Huntstown, he and his neighbors gradually leaned toward the Baptist faith, while Salmon Brook settled into a peaceful compromise between separatism and the Halfway Covenant. In Salmon Brook the Baptists were but a tiny sect, and the main challenge to the Congregational Church came from the members of the Church of England who created St. Ann's mission. In Huntstown, incorporated as the town of Ashfield in 1765, there were hardly any Anglicans. After some years of indifference to the rebellion against British taxation, both communities participated actively in the Revolutionary War; but while Ashfield's revolutionary generation offered radical suggestions for a new state constitution, Connecticut citizens, including those at Salmon Brook, were happy with the way the first settlers to the colony had framed its government in 1639. After the war, at the moment that two companies from Ashfield were marching on the Springfield armory, two ecclesiastical societies in Connecticut, Salmon Brook and Turkey Hills, were quietly and contentedly convening for their first annual town meeting. In the 1790s the two towns of Ashfield and Granby began to resemble each other in appearance, complete with steepled meetinghouse, schools, a town commercial center, and increasingly distinct social classes. But by then they were beginning to resemble every other town in rural New England. Can these two towns illustrate one story that gives history something to say?

After examining the two stories from the ground up, it is clear that there is a common pattern in the relationships and arrangements that evolved between our plain people and leaders at the county and provincial level. Particularly, as distant as they are from our own outlook on the world, for the better part of the eighteenth century the people of both of these communities were also considerably distant from the visions of many of their contemporaries. Hatfield's Israel Williams, for example, or Connecticut's presbyterian hierarchy as represented by the Hartford North Association of Ministers, wanted to shape New England into an orderly and deferential (albeit more godly) facsimile of English society. For decades they met resistance from the backcountry people of Salmon Brook and Huntstown.

This tension is understandable. After all, the earliest inhabitants of these two settlements would hardly have been the first choice of the region's social and political elite to extend the New England way into the wilderness. Welshmen, sons and daughters of Huguenots, "churchmen," "separates," former servants, former slaves, debtors, fornicators, suspected wizards, or just plain laborers who had never had any experience working their own freehold, they were the only ones that the legislative committees, proprietor-speculators, and county magnates could find to endure the conditional five to eight years that somehow stretched into decades before either place could be said to be permanently "peopled." At Salmon Brook in the late seventeenth century and at Huntstown in the mid-eighteenth, it took time and much incentive to get the periphery of society to settle on the periphery of the colony.

The promise of a freehold or even a proprietorship in New England's backcountry seemed to attract mainly those who found the river and coastal towns unwelcome or unpromising places. And when these people of New England's social fringe, in a hazardous yet well-armed condition, managed to survive and even produce a little extra for the market, they began to see themselves as "yeomen"—and even called themselves such, insisting that their leaders accord them respect, all the while passing on to their children and to newcomers the legacy of a hard-pressed people who had secured the English domain against predators and invaders. In their petitions to their respective legislatures, in their agreements among themselves, and in their sometimes assertive and sometimes subtly threatening communications with nonresident proprietors, the first generations of Salmon Brook and

Huntstown leveraged a place for themselves in New England. What choice did the colonial elite have but to tolerate the idiosyncrasies and presumptions of their outlanders? Between 1690 and 1725, and again between 1744 and 1760, New England was under attack. Its leaders needed frontier settlements: a picket line of farmers determined to defend their homesteads. And in times of peace, those same leaders wanted an emerging population of taxpayers, producers, and consumers "inclined to industry," sustaining the mercantilist dream and promoting the rising value of thousands of acres of land.

Petitions from the backcountry played on these concerns, never failing to recount the ordeals of frontier living, hinting at the gratitude the elite owed those who had taken up land and followed orders to reside upon it even though exposed to attack. And some even contained veiled threats that disorder would ensue if measures were not taken to accommodate the outlanders further. "In a Town Way" Salmon Brook people stood up to Simsbury's proprietors, some of them quite prominent men in the colony, and divided the common land among themselves. Later these backcountry farmers expressed their preaching preferences in the face of the stern opposition of the ministers of their county association. Huntstown settlers did not hesitate to go over the head of Israel Williams to the General Court, or even to the king of England and the Continental Congress, when Williams and his associates did not provide them with "country pay" for military service, properly compensate them for roadwork and fortwork, or tolerate their dissenting faith. Even after the collapse of Williams's authority, they issued sharp criticism of the new order that the likes of John Adams and James Bowdoin were planning.

Still, the eighteenth-century inhabitants of Salmon Brook and Huntstown were hardly rebels. What generations of outlanders hoped for all along was simply a place of respectability, and perhaps prosperity in New England society. They always framed their petitions in the most respectful manner, seeking "fatherly protection," and hoping this "honorable committee" or that "esteemed Council" would condescend to take their "impoverished condition" into consideration. They joined the rebellion against Britain only after most of their colony's leaders had taken their stand in resistance. From the start they had high hopes of participating in the market economy, and as soon as they could afford it they became consumers of all sorts of goods, from hardware and tools to china plates and silver buckles.

Admission to the mainstream was not all that they wanted, though. New England society would have to change for the outlanders to commit fully to becoming an integral part of it. When colonial resistance to Parliamentary policies reached a climax in 1774, the people of the backcountry decided that the ideology of the revolution—the fight for the security of property and "darling Liberty," challenges to the authority of people that they had not elected, and talk of independence—sounded very much like their own long-standing ideals regarding social and political relationships. In Salmon Brook a decade of voting against taxes for bridges and roads at the opposite end of town, and recent arguments in favor of Salmon Brook becoming an independent town, were an extension of old causes and prepared its inhabitants to join in the protests against the Coercive Acts and to arm themselves in the face of British "tyranny." On the heels of Ashfield's two decades of quarreling with absentee landowners and the Hampshire County leadership, inhabitants easily transferred their resentments to the royal governor and ministry that now resembled those institutional magnates. Backcountry people joined the Whig cause because its advocates seemed to be promising what they had wanted all along.

As the Revolutionary War came to a close, citizens in both Ashfield and Salmon Brook seemed disappointed, and even angry, that those who had led their states through the struggle might not go far enough in opposing "them Old Tiranical Laws" and create what, in their minds, would be a more just and equitable social and constitutional order. In response to this dissatisfaction Salmon Brook people rallied against pensions for Continental Army officers and punitive measures for those who had not supplied a soldier to the armed forces at the same time that they rekindled their own local independence movement. Ashfield residents went further, protesting against state taxes and marching on the county courts.

Inhabitants of both communities articulated their long-held principles more clearly than ever and insisted on their own vision of relationships between the leaders and the people. For most people in Salmon Brook an ideal world would be one in which people chose their own leaders—their own ministers of the gospel, their own selectmen, and their own military officers—and those leaders would be making the most important decisions for the lives of their constituents (and *not* requiring attendance at a particular church). It would be a world in which one town had as much clout in a representative assembly as any other, and in which the state and national government had very limited power, particularly when it came to taxing. Similarly, in Ashfield's elliptical polity, revolving around both Congregational and

Baptist communities, there was a consensus about local control, equality, and religious freedom. Their people hesitated to pay even a county tax. These were not inclinations and ideals that appeared suddenly as a result of participation in the Whig cause of the 1760s and 1770s or exposure to revolutionary ideology. They had taken shape well before the protests against the Stamp Act and the Townshend duties—well before even John Adams thought the "hearts and minds" of his countrymen were experiencing a great change. In fact, few leaders of the American Revolution, including John Adams, wanted to make the radical social and political changes that would live up to the ideals of so many of their backcountry contemporaries.

In late 1786, the two communities seem to have set divergent courses. Ashfield's town meeting armed its militiamen for an attack on the Springfield arsenal. Salmon Brook had its first town meeting and simply elected officers. But the contrast demonstrates the dynamics of the relationship between elites and the backcountry in the eighteenth century. When backcountry people got what they wanted—in Salmon Brook's case, their own town government and, eventually, equal representation in the legislature and a rising standard of living—they settled into peace, order, and unity. The leaders of Massachusetts had yet to learn that lesson. In fact, it could be said that some of the Sons of Liberty were no more accommodating to backcountry concerns than was Israel Williams in days past. Hence western Massachusetts dissolved into rebellion, with Ashfield in the forefront. The Bowdoin administration collapsed. Governor John Hancock did not repeat the mistake of ignoring the backcountry when he entered office in 1787. In contrast to Connecticut, the arrangement with the elite that the backcountry found acceptable broke down in Massachusetts, but only briefly.

The price that both Granby and Ashfield residents exacted for orderliness was not only land, independence, and respectability, but also a new social structure that was less deferential, more egalitarian, less centralized, more democratic, and less homogeneous and institutionalized concerning religion than what many revolutionary leaders in Connecticut and Massachusetts would have preferred. It was also a system that contained growing economic opportunity for a population with fewer and fewer acres of arable land per capita. The two states continued their established churches and strong nationalist politics even into the nineteenth century, but politicians had to work harder for votes, and leaders of business and society had to be more inclusive. They also had to tolerate itinerant preachers, some like

Ebenezer Smith without even a grammar school education, roaming their hills. In the long run religious freedom remained such a nagging issue that it unseated the Federalist standing order.

It would be a mistake to conclude that it was the ideology of the revolution that opened the Pandora's box of these changes. The lesson from Granby and Ashfield is that backcountry people had long since decided on the kind of society that they wanted. They passed these notions along from generation to generation and from settled inhabitant to newcomer. When the Sons of Liberty and Connecticut's patriots expressed compatible thinking during the revolutionary crisis, the residents of Ashfield and Salmon Brook erected a liberty pole and marched to war for the cause. And then they held their leaders accountable until they felt comfortable in a social order that they had had a hand in creating.

Even though Granby today is a growing suburb with much of its farmland transformed into housing developments, a discerning eye can glimpse connections to a backcountry past. The town meeting still debates the budget, and when leaders forget to consult constituents on building projects, turnout is high at the next election. Cellar holes and stone walls inspire curiosity for hikers in the town's game refuges, and historic districts and scenic roads still show off their artifacts and symbols of a time when poor farmers struggled to make a living on this difficult land.

The five-century-old Granby Oak that sprawls on a ridge west of the original Salmon Brook settlement is a massive living connection to the town's past. Having survived the fires that Native Americans once set to make its hillside more suitable for hunting, as well as the clear-cutting of eighteenth-century English settlers and today's suburban developers, it has a rightful claim to be the town's official icon. Whenever I drive past it, I hear it speaking of what history has to say for the people who lived here when it was three hundred years younger. Its limbs twist and turn, some resting elbows on the ground and others bursting out in every direction. Like American society, the oak is complex and fascinating. We can only imagine the equal complexity of its roots. We know that there are many, as American society has many roots, and that they run wide and deep into glacial rubble not far beneath the surface. At least a few of those reach north and west into the hills, where for centuries they have drawn sustenance and character from New England's backcountry.

Notes

ABBREVIATIONS

APR   Proprietors of Ashfield, "Proprietor's Records, 1736–1803," Ashfield Town Hall, Ashfield, Massachusetts

ATR   Ashfield Town Meeting Records, Ashfield Town Hall, Ashfield, Massachusetts

BCLR   Bristol County Land Records, Bristol County Registry of Deeds, Taunton, Massachusetts

CA   Connecticut State Archives, Connecticut State Library, Hartford, Connecticut

CHS   Connecticut Historical Society

CSL   Connecticut State Library, Hartford, Connecticut

GLR   Granby Land Records, Granby Town Vault, Granby, Connecticut

GPR   Granby Probate Records, Granby Town Vault, Granby, Connecticut

GTR   Granby Town Meeting Records, Granby Town Vault, Granby, Connecticut

FCLR   Franklin County Land Records, Abstracts for Ashfield, Franklin County Registry of Deeds, Greenfield, Massachusetts

HCLR   Hampden County Land Records, Hampden County Registry of Deeds, Hampden County Hall of Justice, Springfield, Massachusetts

MA   Massachusetts Archives, microfilm edition, Sterling Memorial Library, Yale University, New Haven, Connecticut

R   Used before a page number to designate a page in the reverse section of a volume where some pages are numbered from the back to the front

SBHS   Salmon Brook Historical Society, Granby, Connecticut

SCLR   Suffolk County Land Records, Suffolk County Registry of Deeds, Suffolk County Courthouse, Boston, Massachusetts

SLR   Simsbury Land Records, Simsbury Town Vault, Simsbury, Connecticut

SPR   Simsbury Probate Records, Simsbury Town Vault, Simsbury, Connecticut

STR   Simsbury Town Records, Simsbury Town Vault, Simsbury, Connecticut

WCLR Worcester County Land Registry, Worcester, Massachusetts

PROLOGUE

1. David S. Rowland, "Ministers of Christ Freed from Blood-guiltiness" (Boston: Benjamin Mecom, 1761).
2. Hartford North Association, Records, CHS Manuscript Collection, 1:28–38; Harry S. Stout, *The New England Soul: Preaching and Religious Culture in Colonial New England* (New York: Oxford University Press, 1986), 62–63, 75–76, 96, 197–232.
3. Thomas Jefferson to Comte Diodati, March 29, 1807, *Thomas Jefferson Papers*, series 1: General Correspondence, 1651–1827, Library of Congress.
4. For discussion of the backcountry that emphasizes unrest, turmoil, and rebellion, see Gary B. Nash, *The Unknown American Revolution: The Unruly Birth of Democracy and the Struggle to Create America* (New York: Viking, 2005), 72–87; and Gordon S. Wood, *The Radicalism of the American Revolution* (New York: Knopf, 1992), 124–34. For the "new social history" on "the countryside," see Michael Zuckerman, *Peaceable Kingdoms: New England Towns in the Eighteenth Century* (New York: Knopf, 1970); Kenneth Lockridge, *A New England Town, the First Hundred Years: Dedham, Massachusetts, 1636–1736*, expanded ed. (New York: Norton, 1985); Philip J. Greven, *Four Generations: Population, Land, and Family in Colonial Andover, Massachusetts* (Ithaca: Cornell University Press, 1970); and Robert A. Gross, *The*

Minutemen and Their World, American Century Series (New York: Hill and Wang, 1976).

5. For backcountry rebellions, see David P. Szatmary, *Shays' Rebellion: The Making of an Agrarian Insurrection* (Amherst: University of Massachusetts Press, 1980); John L. Brooke, "To the Quiet of the People: Revolutionary Settlements and Civil Unrest in Western Massachusetts, 1774–1789," *William and Mary Quarterly*, 3rd series, 56, no. 3 (1989): 425–562; Richard M. Brown, "Backcountry Rebellions and the Homestead Ethic," and Charles Tilly, "Collective Action in England and America, 1765–1775," both in *Tradition, Conflict, and Modernization: Perspectives on the American Revolution*, ed. Richard M. Brown and Don Fehrenbacker (New York: Academic Press, 1977); Edward Countryman, "'Out of Bounds with the Law': Northern Land Rioters in the Eighteenth Century," in *The American Revolution*, ed. Alfred Young (DeKalb: Northern Illinois University Press, 1976), 37–70; Barbara Karsky, "Agrarian Radicalism in the Late Revolutionary Period," in *New Wine in Old Skins*, ed. Marie-Luise Frings, Erich Angermann, and Hermann Wellenreuther (Stuttgart: Klett, 1976), 97–114; Pauline Maier, "Popular Uprisings and Civil Authority in Eighteenth Century America," in *Interpreting Colonial America*, ed. James Kirby Martin (New York: Free Press, 1973), 3–35; Thomas P. Slaughter, *The Whiskey Rebellion: Frontier Epilogue to the American Revolution* (New York: Oxford University Press, 1986); and Alan Taylor, *Liberty Men and Great Proprietors: The Revolutionary Settlement on the Maine Frontier, 1760–1820* (Chapel Hill: University of North Carolina Press, 1990).

6. In making oblique reference to theories on the origins of American democracy, I have a number of works in mind besides those cited in note 5: Paul Boyer and Stephen Nissenbaum, *Salem Possessed: The Social Origins of Witchcraft* (Cambridge: Harvard University Press, 1974); James A. Henretta and Gregory N. Nobles, *Evolution and Revolution* (Lexington, Mass.: Heath, 1987); Rowland Berthoff and John M. Murrin, "Feudalism, Communalism, and the Yeoman Freeholder: The American Revolution Considered as a Social Accident," in *Essays on the American Revolution*, ed. Stephen G. Kurtz and James H. Hutson (Chapel Hill: University of North Carolina Press, 1973), 256–88; Jesse Lemisch, "The American Revolution Seen from the Bottom Up," in *Towards a New Past: Dissenting Essays in American History*, ed. Barton J. Berstein (New York: Pantheon, 1968); and a forum on deference in *The Journal of American History* 85 (June 1998): 13–97.

SALMON BROOK

1. Simsbury Probate District, "Estate of Captain Samuel Hays" (1801), CSL; *Simsbury, Connecticut: Births, Marriages, and Deaths,* transcribed from the Town Records by Albert C. Bates (Hartford: Case, Lockwood, and Brainard, 1898); Rev. Charles Wells Hayes, *George Hayes of Windsor and His Descendants* (Buffalo: Baker, Jones, 1884); SLR, 9:247, 10:216, 12:113; Mark Williams, "Gossard's Grant," unpubl. ms. (written for James and Sherred Urner, 1982), on file at SBHS.

2. Mark Williams, "The Samuel Hayes II House (1769)," National Register of Historic Places nomination study, Connecticut Historical Commission, September 1, 1991.

3. T. H. Breen, *The Marketplace of Revolution: How Consumer Politics Shaped American Independence* (New York: Oxford University Press, 2004), chapters 2–4; Richard Bushman, *The Refinement of America: Persons, Houses, Cities* (New York: Knopf, 1992); James Deetz, *In Small Things Forgotten: An Archaeology of Early American Life* (New York: Doubleday, 1996), 38–67.

4. Mark Williams, "Yeomen and Scholars: Owners of the Cossitt-Godard House (c. 1769) on Godard Road in North Granby," unpubl. ms. (1982), on file at SBHS.

CHAPTER I. A PLACE CALLED SAMMON BROOKE

1. For Simsbury's story, see Noah Phelps, *History of Simsbury, Granby, and Canton from 1642 to 1845* (Hartford: Case, Tiffany, and Burnham, 1845); Dr. Lucius I. Barber, *A Record and Documentary History of Simsbury* (Simsbury: Abigail Phelps Chapter, Daughters of the American Revolution, 1931); William M. Vibert, *Three Centuries of Simsbury* (Simsbury: Simsbury Tercentenary Committee, 1970).

2. Barber, *Simsbury,* 24.

3. *Public Records of the Colony of Connecticut* (Hartford: Case, Lockwood, and Brainard, 1873), 1:71, 161, 246–47; Phelps, *History,* 10, 56. On commodity markets, see John R. Stilgoe, *Common Landscape of America, 1580 to 1845* (New Haven: Yale University Press, 1982), 48; and John Frederick Martin, *Profits in the Wilderness: Entrepreneurship and the Founding of New England Towns in the Seventeenth Century* (Chapel Hill: University of North Carolina Press, 1991).

4. *Public Records of the Colony of Connecticut,* 1:146, 364; Barber, *Simsbury,* 15–20, 26–31; Phelps, *History,* 9–15; SLR, 2:21; Howard S. Russell, *Indian*

New England Before the Mayflower (Hanover, N.H.: University Press of New England, 1980), 14, 185; Frank Thistlethwaite, *Dorset Pilgrims: The Story of West Country Pilgrims Who Went to New England in the 17th Century* (London: Barrie and Jenkins, 1989), 155–56, 208–9, 218.

5. Henry R. Stiles, *The History and Genealogies of Ancient Windsor, Connecticut* (Hartford: Case, Lockwood, and Brainard, 1891), 1:33–39.

6. *Public Records of the Colony of Connecticut,* 1:420; Barber, *Simsbury,* 133–36; on the Welsh Anglicans, see Donna Holt Siemiatkoski, "Connecticut's Early Welsh Community, or Connecticut Yankees from King Arthur's Court," *Connecticut Heritage Press* 1 (October 1990); Douglas C. Richardson, *The Eno and Enos Family in America: Descendants of James Eno of Windsor, Conn.* (Sacramento, Calif.: the author, 1973), 1–7; Thistlethwaite, *Dorset Pilgrims,* 46, 179, 200, 225–33; Bruce Colin Daniels, *The Connecticut Town: Growth and Development, 1635–1790* (Middletown, Conn.: Wesleyan University Press, 1979), 18, 101; Stiles, *Windsor,* 1:67, 172–89; Harry S. Stout, *The New England Soul: Preaching and Religious Culture in Colonial New England* (New York: Oxford University Press, 1986), 58.

7. STR, 1:84; *Public Records of the Colony of Connecticut,* 2:73, 97, 113, 127, 214; Barber, *Simsbury,* 16–43.

8. CA, "Wars, Colonial," series 1, 1:197; *Public Records of the Colony of Connecticut,* 3:296; Barber, *Simsbury,* 61; Phelps, *History,* 23–25; Thistlethwaite, *Dorset Pilgrims,* 229–30. The statement to the Board of Trade may be too pessimistic—see Glen Weaver, "Industry in an Agrarian Economy: Early Eighteenth-Century Connecticut," *Bulletin of the Connecticut Historical Society* 19 (June 1954): 82–92.

9. For the Talcott plan, see STR, 1:22; Barber, *Simsbury,* 68–71, 92–93.

10. On Talcott's background, see Harold E. Selesky, *War and Society in Colonial Connecticut* (New Haven: Yale University Press, 1990), 27.

11. STR, 1:6, 8, 14, 15, 47; SLR, vol. 1 1/2: 106–7.

12. STR, 1:22.

13. Barber, *Simsbury,* 78–88.

14. STR, 1:23; Hannah McPherson, *The Holcombes: Nation Builders* (Washington, D.C.: the author, 1947), 101.

15. STR, 1:20.

16. STR, 1:72.

17. STR, 1:22, 70.

18. The history of the spread of ordered, covenanted communities has been well documented in the pioneering works of "the new social history." Kenneth A.

Lockridge, *A New England Town, the First Hundred Years: Dedham, Massachusetts, 1636–1736*, expanded ed. (New York: Norton, 1985); Philip J. Greven, *Four Generations: Population, Land, and Family in Colonial Andover, Massachusetts* (Ithaca: Cornell University Press, 1970); David Hackett Fischer, *Albion's Seed: Four British Folkways in America* (New York: Oxford University Press, 1989). For an alternative view, see Stephen Innes, *Labor in a New Land: Economy and Society in Seventeenth-Century Springfield* (Princeton: Princeton University Press, 1983).

19. STR, 1:18; McPherson, *The Holcombes*, 9, 10, 101; Stiles, *Windsor*, 2:395; Barber, *Simsbury*, 70–74, and SLR, 1 1/2:77, 164; *A Digest of Early Connecticut Probate Records*, compiled by Charles William Manning (Hartford: R. S. Peck, 1904), 1:130; Seth Holcombe, *The Descendants of Phinehas Holcomb (1759–1873) of New Hartford, Connecticut* (North Granby, Conn.: the author, 1988), vi–vii; Richardson, *The Eno and Enos*, 1–7; Joshua W. Lane and Donald P. White III, "Fashioning Furniture and Framing Community: Woodworking and the Rise of a Connecticut River Valley Town," *American Furniture* (2005): 155–66.

20. SLR, 1 1/2:112–13, 131, 134–35; STR, 1:20, 70; CHS, *Some Early Records and Documents of and Relating to the Town of Windsor, Connecticut, 1639–1703* (Hartford: CHS, 1930), 53, 59, 88, 71, 91, 116, 120, 175; Rev. Dudley Woodbridge, *His Church Record of Simsbury in Connecticut, 1697–1710*, ed. Albert C. Bates (Hartford: CHS, 1894), 15, 16, 19, 24, 27; *Simsbury, Connecticut, Births, Marriages, and Deaths*, transcribed from the town records, and published by Albert C. Bates (Hartford: Case, Lockwood, and Brainard, 1898), 13, 150; Henry Adams, *George Adams of Watertown: Facts, Questions, Conjecture*, Typescript (1974) at CSL; *An Index of Ancestors and Role of Members of the Society of Colonial Wars* (New York: Connecticut General Assembly, 1922), 2, 3.

21. STR, 1:21, 23, 33; SLR, 1 1/2:134–35, 226–27, 2:71, 5:186–87, 191, 286, 336, 7:588, 650. On the frequency of temporary summer residences and the crudeness of early houses, see Richard L. Bushman, *From Puritan to Yankee: Character and the Social Order in Connecticut, 1690–1765* (Cambridge: Harvard University Press, 1967), 55, and Barber, *Simsbury*, 178.

22. *Public Records of the Colony of Connecticut*, 1:59–61; STR, 1:42, 43, 45, 59, 65, 68.

23. I have pieced together my conclusions on who lived where and when from Phelps, *History*, 103–4; SLR, 1 1/2:35–36, 38, 61–62, 71, 74, 94–95, 97, 112–13, 131, 133–35, 137, 139, 149, 156–57, 175–77, 193–95; and on a list of

men from Simsbury "propowned for freemen" in *Public Records of the Colony of Connecticut*, 3:199. Freemen qualifications are given in Daniels, *Connecticut Town*, 128–29.

24. For the breakdown by individual settler and a discussion of sources, see Mark Williams, "The Brittle Thread of Life: The New England Backcountry in the Eighteenth Century" (Ph.D. dissertation, Yale University, 2006), Appendix I-A.

25. Windsor Land Records, Windsor Town Hall, Windsor, Conn., 1:24, 2:341. For the stigma attached to family members of accused witches, see John Demos, *Entertaining Satan: Witchcraft and Culture in Early New England* (New York: Oxford University Press, 1982), 351–59, 509–13.

26. Selesky, *War and Society*, 29–30; George Madison Bodge, *Soldiers in King Philip's War* (Leominster, Mass.: the author, 1896), 122, 128, 372; *Society of Colonial Wars*, 2, 3.

27. STR, 1:30, 36, 49, 56, 65, 2 1/2:R56.

28. STR, 1:48–49, 59, 61, 65, 68, 2 1/2:23.

29. Daniel K. Richter, *The Ordeal of the Longhouse: The Peoples of the Iroquois League in the Era of European Colonization* (Chapel Hill: University of North Carolina Press, 1992), chapters 5–8; Richard White, *The Middle Ground: Indians, Empires, and Republics in the Great Lakes Region, 1650–1815* (New York: Cambridge University Press, 1991), chapters 1–3.

30. STR, 1:70, 72–73; SLR, 1 1/2:219–20, which shows the exchange of land was temporary; Phelps, *History*, 32–33; Barber, *Simsbury*, 116. John Matson did not exchange his lot, but moved to "Scotland" with his partner James Miles; see their agreement in CA, "Private Controversies," series 1, 4:108; Selesky, *War and Society*, 33–44.

31. STR, 1:50, 71–72, 89, 2 1/2:42, R21, 27; SLR, 1 1/2:33, 62, 64, 66, 94, 107, 133–34, 155, 162, 188–89, 195–96, 228, 246, 248, 253–54, 256–57; Bushman, *Puritan to Yankee*, 31–32.

32. STR, 1:88, 2 1/2:1, 21, R17, R26; SLR, 1:229, 233, 1 1/2:101, 219–20. For family information on Matson, who was in business, until 1695, with James Miles, his mother-in-law's husband, I am indebted to Diane Delbridge of Yukon, Oklahoma, who wrote me in 2001 with information that she had found on Matson's relation to James Miles and the Addams family of Windsor.

33. STR, 1:33, 36, 39, 54–55, 78–79, 2 1/2:1, R18, R22, R26, R39; Barber, *Simsbury*, 103, 157–59, 173–78; SLR, 1 1/2:181; John Langdon Sibley, *Biographical Sketches of Graduates of Harvard University* (Cambridge: Charles William Seever, 1885), 3:306ff, 400ff.

34. STR, 2 1/2:3, 21, R35.

35. STR, vol. 1: pp. A, 88, 2 1/2:2, R57, R58; SLR, 1 1/2:74.

36. STR, 2 1/2:30, 84–85, R25, R62; SLR, 1 1/2:31, 111, 120, 136, 149, 226–27, 2:6–7, 37–38, 132, 202. See Williams, "The Brittle Thread of Life," 63, for details of Salmon Brook households in 1701. On the phenomenon of "clan" living, see David Freeman Hawke, *Everyday Life in Early America* (New York: Harper and Row, 1988), 61–62.

37. STR, 2 1/2:R4, R55, R58, R66; *Public Records of the Colony of Connecticut*, 4:443; Rev. Charles Wells Hayes, M.A., *George Hayes of Windsor and His Descendants* (Buffalo: Baker, Jones, 1884), 1–8; Barber, *Simsbury*, 126.

38. STR, 2:84, 2 1/2:12, R3, R55–56, R59–60, R75. See tax rate schedules in STR, 2 1/2:3, 7, 11, and on admissions of new freemen, 2 1/2:R4.

39. STR, 1:35–37, 2 1/2:R50, R61; Barber, *Simsbury*, 215; Bushman, *Puritan to Yankee*, 27.

40. *Public Records of the Colony of Connecticut*, 4:463.

41. Phelps, *History*, 32–38; Hayes, *George Hayes*, 8–10; Barber, *Simsbury*, 214; *The Public Records of the Colony of Connecticut*, 5:401, and see also 5:19, 29, 32, 40, 66, 86.

42. STR, 2 1/2:R91; *Public Records of the Colony of Connecticut*, 4:15–16; CA, "War," 3:74b, 118d.

43. SLR, 2:51, 71, 121, 170, 173, 205, 216, 217, 218, 234–35, 238, 239; STR, 2 1/2:47, 71, R59, R70, R95, R99, R121, R126; Phelps, *History*, 105–6; *Public Records of the Colony of Connecticut*, 5:76; Barber, *Simsbury*, 70, 377.

44. Warren R. Hofstra, "The Extensions of His Majesties Dominions: The Virginia Backcountry and the Reconfiguration of Imperial Frontiers," *Journal of American History* 84 (1998): 1281–1312; Henry Bronson, *The History of Waterbury, Connecticut* (Waterbury: Bronson Brothers, 1858), 103–10.

CHAPTER 2. ON PENALTY OF LOOSING OUR FREEHOLDS

1. SLR, 6:R10; Mark Williams, "The Nathaniel Holcomb III House (c. 1720)," National Register of Historic Places Nomination Study, Connecticut Historical Commission, April 30, 1981.

2. STR, 3:15; Hannah McPherson, *The Holcombes: Nation Builders* (Washington, D.C.: the author, 1947), 2, 101, 203, 211.

3. STR, 2 1/2:R81. For other grants in Salmon Brook see also R71–74 and SLR, 2:59, 61, 66, 94, 95.

4. STR, 2 1/2:R83, with an amendment on R100. For other grants, see STR, 2:R101, 105, 106, 123, 124, and SLR, 2:163, 165, 176, 198, 219, 222, 240.

5. *Public Records of the Colony of Connecticut* (Hartford: F. A. Brown, 1852), 4:443, 90, 523; Lucius I. Barber, *A Record and Documentary History of Simsbury, 1643–1888* (Simsbury: Abigail Phelps Chapter, Daughters of the American Revolution, 1931), 121, 26; William M. Vibert, *Three Centuries of Simsbury, 1670–1970* (Simsbury: Simsbury Tercentenary Committee, 1970), 51; STR, 2 1/2:R105, R112, R132; David Freeman Hawke, *Everyday Life in Early America* (New York: Harper and Row, 1988), 170; Howard S. Russell and Mark B. Lapping, *A Long, Deep Furrow: Three Centuries of Farming in New England* (Hanover, N.H.: University Press of New England, 1982), 61, 75, 93–97, 147; William Cronon, *Changes in the Land: Indians, Colonists, and the Ecology of New England*, 1st ed. (New York: Hill and Wang, 1983), 120; Richard L. Bushman, *From Puritan to Yankee: Character and the Social Order in Connecticut, 1690–1765* (Cambridge: Harvard University Press, 1967), 35; J. Hammond Trumbull, *The Memorial History of Hartford County, Connecticut, 1633–1884; Ed. by J. Hammond Trumbull . . . Projected by Clarence F. Jewett* (Boston: E. L. Osgood, 1886), 2:346.

6. STR, 2 1/2:R79; Noah A. Phelps, *History of Simsbury, Granby, and Canton: From 1642 to 1845* (Hartford: Case, Tiffany, and Burnham, 1845), 54–56; Barber, *Simsbury*, 196–98.

7. Bushman, *Puritan to Yankee*, 46; SLR, 1 1/2:1.

8. STR, 2 1/2:R84–85, R101–2, R108–9; Barber, *Simsbury*, 182–84, 196, 225–26, 378; John Langdon Sibley et al., *Biographical Sketches of Graduates of Harvard University, in Cambridge, Massachusetts* (Cambridge,: C. W. Sever, 1873), 4:217.

9. Hartford Probate District, "Estate of Benjamin Dibol" (1712), CSL.

10. "Samuel Willcockson Jr. Inventory" (1713), STR, 2 1/2:1, 22.

11. *Simsbury, Connecticut, Births, Marriages, and Deaths*, transcribed from the town records, and published by Albert C. Bates (Hartford: Case, Lockwood, and Brainard, 1898); Carol Laun, "Ephraim Howard of Windsor, Early Physician and Miller," *Farmington Valley Herald*, May 14, 1987, 3A.

12. STR, 2 1/2:R52, R65, R66, R69, R78, R82, R90, R92, R100, R121; Phelps, *History*, 36.

13. Hartford Probate District, "Estate of John Matson" (1728), CSL; STR, 2 1/2:1 (back), 3; *Genealogy of the Matson Family* (1928), photostat at CSL.

14. *Public Records of the Colony of Connecticut*, 4:401; STR, 2 1/2:71, R125; Phelps, *History*, 44.

15. STR, 2 1/2:R3, R119, R125, R142; Phelps, *History*, 81.

16. *Public Records of the Colony of Connecticut*, 1:100. Bushman, *Puritan to Yankee*, 80, discusses the growing tension throughout Connecticut between speculators and those in need of land.

17. STR, 3:7–9; CA, "Towns and Lands," 4:101. See also Bushman, *Puritan to Yankee*, 46–52, for discussion of these status problems.

18. By 1728, Rev. Timothy Woodbridge collected five tons of turpentine from his neighbors in a year and found a buyer for it in New York City. Hartford County Court Records, Court of Common Pleas, vol. 7, CSL; Russell, *Long, Deep Furrow*, 62, 93–99; Cronon, *Changes in the Land*, 109–18.

19. Bushman, *Puritan to Yankee*, 118–28; Russell, *Long, Deep Furrow*, 99–101.

20. STR, 2 1/2:1, 70, 75, 96, 108, 130, 122, 143, 144, 146, 157, 159, 188, R135, 3:7, 52, 62, 75, 79, 4:26, 94, 101, 145–46, 148, 165–66; SLR, 4:R47–50; Hartford Probate District, "Estate of George Hayes" (1725), CSL.

21. STR, 3:7–9.

22. STR, 3:9; Barber, *Simsbury*, 218–19.

23. CA, "Towns and Lands," 4:102.

24. STR, 3:12, 14–15; SLR, 4:144, 147; Barber, *Simsbury*, 223; *Public Records of the Colony of Connecticut*, 6:173.

25. CA, "Towns and Lands," 4:99–107; STR, 3:15–21.

26. STR, 2 1/2:27, 68, 104, 138; SLR, 4:24, 239, 321, 5:191, 186–87, 217, 286; Hartford County Court Records, CSL, 4:333, 5:32, 114, 190–94, 234, 316, 323, 347, 352, 6:8, 334, 402, 412–13.

27. SLR, 5:59–79, 224–31; *Public Records of the Colony of Connecticut*, 7:290; Hartford County Court Records, 5:942.

28. CA, "Towns and Lands," 4:103.

29. STR, 2 1/2:R219, 3:23, 36, 37. For an indication of the distribution of wealth in Simsbury, see Mark Williams, "The Brittle Thread of Life: The New England Backcountry in the Eighteenth Century" (Ph.D. dissertation, Yale University, 2006), Appendix I-B, 393–94, which is the list of grants of land that were finally made on the basis of size of estate. There was considerable negotiation, so even those differences are probably minimized.

30. STR, 3:23–27.

31. STR, 3:4; CA, "Towns and Lands," 4:103; *Public Records of the Colony of Connecticut*, 6:407.

32. CA, "Towns and Lands," 4:104a, 105, 106c, 107; *Public Records of the Colony of Connecticut*, 6:394. Bushman discusses the impact of this dispute on the

colony in *Puritan to Yankee*, 51–52. The grants are spread out throughout the SLR, vols. 3–7. For proprietor protests, see STR, 3:4.

33. Phelps, *History*, 34, 83; *Public Records of Connecticut*, 4:511–12, 6:407–8; CA, "Wars," 3:199a, 229a. On soldier's pay, see Harold E. Selesky, *War and Society in Colonial Connecticut* (New Haven: Yale University Press, 1990), 67–68.

34. STR, 2 1/2:R152.

35. Bruce Colin Daniels, *The Connecticut Town: Growth and Development, 1635–1790* (Middletown, Conn.: Wesleyan University Press, 1979), 181; Joseph S. Wood and Michael Steinitz, *The New England Village* (Baltimore: Johns Hopkins University Press, 1997), chapters 1–2.

36. STR, 2 1/2:R134, 141, 3:5–6, 22, 36, 37, 39, 41; *Public Records of Connecticut*, 6:563, 7:79; CA, "Ecclesiastical Affairs," series 1, 4:224–25.

37. STR, 3:37, 41; CA, "Ecclesiastical Affairs," series 1, 4:233a, 235.

38. CA, "Ecclesiastical Affairs," series 1, 4:230–31, 235; STR, 3:41; *Public Records of Connecticut*, 7:93, 134; Franklin Bowditch Dexter, *Biographical Sketches of the Graduates of Yale College* (New York: Holt, 1885), 5–7.

39. *Public Records of Connecticut*, 7:146, 197; STR, 3:42, 47–48; CA, "Ecclesiastical Affairs," series 1, 4:237, 241.

40. STR, 3:44–46; CA, "Ecclesiastical Affairs," series 1, 4:241–55.

41. *Public Records of Connecticut*, 7:248; CA, "Ecclesiastical Affairs," series 1, 4:250, 262a.

42. STR, 3:48–50; CA, "Ecclesiastical Affairs," series 1, 4:268, 272–73a; *Public Records of the Colony of Connecticut*, 7:296–97.

43. STR, 3:52, 54; North Association of the County of Hartford Records, CSL, meeting of March 31, 1730; *Public Records of Connecticut*, 7:395–96.

44. CA, "Ecclesiastical Affairs," series 1, 4:305a.

45. STR, 3:57–58; CA, "Ecclesiastical Affairs," series 1, 4:284–85, 289–91, 294a.

46. *Public Records of Connecticut*, 7:553, 8:12, 23, 48, 75–76; STR, 3:66–67; CA, "Ecclesiastical Affairs," series 1, 4:301, 312, 314–15; Barber, *Simsbury*, 239, 254, 256–57; Lawrence Scanlon, "A New Look at Old Maps," talk for SBHS, March 6, 1980.

47. CA, "Ecclesiastical Affairs," series 1, 4:305a.

48. CA, "Ecclesiastical Affairs," series 1, 4:54–59; *Public Records of Connecticut*, 8:274; First Congregational Church of North Granby, *Records*, SBHS, 5:5–6.

49. STR, 3:71, 77, 80, 91; *Public Records of Connecticut,* 8:161, 260–61, 546; SLR, 2:36, 4:R35, 5:82, 105, 223, 283, 332, and part 2 of 5:R6, 6:112, 218, 433, 7:72, 77, 78, 269, 349, 8:255, 10:270, 11:4, 12:92, 437, 14:101, and GLR, 1:133; maps of Granby from c. 1730, 1815, 1855, and 1869, which are at SBHS; Elisha Loomis, *Descendants of Joseph Loomis in America* (n.p.: publ. by the author, 1909), 132, 140–41, 155–56.

CHAPTER 3. ZEAL FOR THE SUPPORT OF THE DARLING LIBERTY

1. Henry P. Johnston, A.M., ed., *The Record of Connecticut Men in the Military and Naval Service During the War of the Revolution, 1775–1783* (Hartford: Case, Lockwood, and Brainard, 1889), x, xi, 448, 472–73; William S. Hart, "For Captain Hays' Company, Kip's Bay Was No Picnic, It Was a Panic," *Granby Drummer,* October 1993, p. 18; Benjamin Williams, "Selective Patriotism: Granby, Connecticut's 'Sunshine Patriots' in the American Revolution," unpubl. paper (March 1998), on file at SBHS. See also [Joseph Martin], *A Narrative of Some of the Adventures, Dangers, and Suffering of a Revolutionary Soldier* (Hallowell, Maine: n.p., 1812); Pearl Steele Cossitt, A.M., Frederic Henry White, and Frederic Briggs Stebbins, *The Cossitt Family* (Pasadena, Calif.: F. M. White, 1925). George Washington is quoted in General George Weedon to John Page, President of the Virginia Council, Morris's Heights, New York, September 20, 1776, in *The Spirit of Seventy-Six,* ed. Henry Steele Commager and Richard B. Morris (New York: Harper and Row, 1959), 467.
2. Edward Thompson, "Sermon on Matthew 5:8," July 5, 1685, in Samuel Thompson, "Notebook, 1678–1695," Manuscript Collection, American Antiquarian Society, as quoted in Harry S. Stout, *The New England Soul: Preaching and Religious Culture in Colonial New England* (New York: Oxford University Press, 1986), 157.
3. Hartford North Association, *Records,* CHS Manuscript Collection, 1:28; Stout, *New England Soul,* 186–96; Richard L. Bushman, *From Puritan to Yankee: Character and the Social Order in Connecticut, 1690–1765* (Cambridge: Harvard University Press, 1967), 184, 258.
4. Franklin Bowditch Dexter, *Biographical Sketches of the Graduates of Yale College* (New York: Holt, 1885), 1:5–7, 58, 98–100, 574; First Congregational Church of North Granby, *Records,* SBHS, 1:1–5.
5. Hartford North Association, *Records,* 1:28.
6. First Congregational Church of North Granby, *Records,* 1:9; Stout, *New England Soul,* 229.

7. *Public Records of the Colony of Connecticut* (Hartford: Case, Lockwood, and Brainard, 1873), 8:454–57; First Congregational Church of North Granby, *Records*, 1:11.

8. First Congregational Church of North Granby, *Records*, 1:12–14; Hartford North Association, *Records*, 1:32.

9. First Congregational Church of North Granby, *Records*, 1:15; Hartford North Association, *Records*, 1:33–34.

10. *Records of Rev. Roger Viets, Rector of St. Andrews, Simsbury, Conn., 1763–1800*, Albert C. Bates, ed. (Hartford: Connecticut Historical Society, 1893). In the Hoadley Collection, CHS Manuscript Collection, Box 12, is a 1743 membership list of the Anglican church at Scotland; Lucius I. Barber, *A Record and Documentary History of Simsbury, 1643–1888* (Simsbury: Abigail Phelps Chapter, Daughters of the American Revolution, 1931), 264–66; *Public Records of the Colony of Connecticut*, 6:87; Stout, *New England Soul*, 16–17; Bruce Colin Daniels, *The Connecticut Town: Growth and Development, 1635–1790* (Middletown, Conn.: Wesleyan University Press, 1979), 116.

11. Mary Coffin Johnson, *The Higleys and Their Ancestry: An Old Colonial Family* (Granby: Grover S. Hayes, 1963); research notes by Ethel Linnell in the "Baptist Church" folder, SBHS "Granby File"; and "Simsbury, Connecticut, Baptist Church Records," Microfilm Roll #607, CSL Church Records; First Congregational Church of North Granby, *Records* in 1765, 5:76.

12. David S. Rowland, "Ministers of Christ Freed from Blood-guiltiness" (Boston: Benjamin Mecom, 1761), CHS Manuscript Collection; Dexter, *Yale Biographies*, 1:744–45.

13. Hartford North Association, *Records*, 1:37–38.

14. First Congregational Church of North Granby, *Records*, 1:21.

15. First Congregational Church of North Granby, *Records*, 1:22–28; Stout, *New England Soul*, 212–23; Bushman, *Puritan to Yankee*, 187.

16. First Congregational Church of North Granby, *Records*, 1:21–29; Dexter, *Yale Biographies*, 1:163–65, 2:148, 201–2; Noah A. Phelps, *History of Simsbury, Granby, and Canton: From 1642 to 1845* (Hartford: Case, Tiffany, and Burnham, 1845), 141.

17. Joseph Strong, "The Duty of Singing Considered as a Necessary and Dutiful Part of Christian Worship" (New Haven: Thomas and Samuel Green, 1773), CHS Imprint Collection.

18. First Congregational Church of North Granby, *Records*, 1:29, 5:69–71; "Salmon Brook Publick Library" folder, Granby File, SBHS; Dexter, *Yale*

Biographies, 2:221–24; Joseph Strong, "That Presbyterian Ministers May Justly Challenge Ministerial Regard, Asserted and Proved" (Hartford: Green and Watson, 1768), CHS Imprint Collection.

19. Charles Wells Hayes, *George Hayes of Windsor and His Descendants* (Buffalo: Baker, Jones, 1884), 6–7; Cossitt, White, and Stebbins, *The Cossitt Family;* W. M. Maltbie, "The Episcopal Churches of Granby," 1959 typescript, "Episcopal Churches: St. Ann's, St. Peters" folder, Granby File, SBHS; *Public Records of the Colony of Connecticut,* 10:167–68; "Simsbury, Connecticut, Baptist Church Records," CSL Church Records.

20. Daniels, *Connecticut Town,* 34–43; William S. Hart, "North Granby-Bedford: The History of 'The Wedge,'" *Collections of the Salmon Brook Historical Society* 3 (1987): 1–21.

21. CA, "Ecclesiastical Affairs," series 1, 4:305a. For a tax list that includes some landless family heads, see Mark Williams, "The Brittle Thread of Life: The New England Backcountry in the Eighteenth Century" (Ph.D. dissertation, Yale University, 2006), Appendix I-C, 395; SLR, 4:R32, R33, R319, 5:26, 6, 168, 7:506, 516; Hartford County, Superior Court Records, CSL, 5:97; Cossitt, White, and Stebbins, *The Cossitt Family.*

22. Vernon Andre Kraft-Nicholson, *The Halladay Family, 1650–1933* (High Wycombe, England: University Microfilms, 1975); SLR, 6:147, 166–68, 7:88, 8:173, 224, 2526, 336, 9:347, 11:R2.

23. *Public Records of Connecticut,* 9:86, 91, 229; Harold E. Selesky, *War and Society in Colonial Connecticut* (New Haven: Yale University Press, 1990), 69–96.

24. SLR, 7:554–55, 613, 662, 8:256, 285, 356.

25. Hayes, *George Hayes,* 15–16; SLR, 8:113, 156, 217, 330, 331, 367, 376, 9:106, 11:R2.

26. SLR, 3:294, 5:1ff, 258, 274, 322, 6:43, 93, 391, 524, 607, 7:5, 34, 35, 120, 296, 314, 436, 449, 468, 588, 637, 640, 650, 680, 8:6, 8, 65, 112, 122, 134, 175, 181, 227, 252, 259, 261, 336, 373, 384–85, 396, 443, 447, 454, 490, 9:46, 261, 262, 326–29, 11:22, 78, 260, 12:94; SPR, 2:130, 133, 162–63, 4:235–38; STR, 4:3; Hayes, *George Hayes,* 14; Oliver Phelps and Andrew Servin, *The Phelps Family in America* (Pittsfield, Mass.: Eagle, 1899), 1:328; *Records of Rev. Roger Viets,* 14, 49; Hannah McPherson, *The Holcombes: Nation Builders* (Washington, D.C.: the author, 1947), 148, 61–63; Harriet Russell Stratton, *A Book of Strattons* (New York: Grafton, 1908), 231–33. For evidence of the Strattons' sawmill business, see Mary Jane Springman, "Revolutionary Era Record: The Seventh Account Book of John Owen, Esq., Simsbury,

Conn.," unpubl. ms., Trinity College, May 7, 1984, Simsbury Public Library, 11–12.

27. Howard S. Russell and Mark B. Lapping, *A Long, Deep Furrow: Three Centuries of Farming in New England* (Hanover, N.H.: University Press of New England, 1982), 80, 88, 106–17; William Cronon, *Changes in the Land: Indians, Colonists, and the Ecology of New England* (New York: Hill and Wang, 1983), 152.

28. STR, 4:5; Phelps, *History*, 93; Stout, *New England Soul*, 244–49; Fred Anderson, "A People's Army: Provincial Military Service in Massachusetts During the Seven Years War," *William and Mary Quarterly* 40 (1983): 499–527.

29. *Collections of the Connecticut Historical Society*, vols. 9, 10 (1903, 1905). CA, "War, Colonial," series 1, 7:12, 55a, b, c.

30. *Public Records of Connecticut*, 11:96, 227, 353; Selesky, *War and Society*, 96–143; "Wars, French and Indian War," Granby File, SBHS.

31. Phelps, *History*, 90–91, 101, 106; Christopher P. Bickford, "The Lost Connecticut Census of 1762 Found," *Connecticut Historical Society Bulletin* 44:2 (April 1979); STR, 3:54, 68, 82, 91.

32. STR, vol. 4: see annual meetings of 1758–1761, 1764, 1765, 1768; Hayes, *George Hayes*, 26, 127; SLR, 8:113, 114, 9:206, 465; First Congregational Church of North Granby, *Records*, 1:50–53.

33. For the last of the grants of the commons, see miscellaneous grants throughout vols. 8–9 of SLR. See also STR, 4:7–8, 15–17.

34. STR, 4:20, 21, 23, 25; *Public Records of Connecticut*, 12:599.

35. STR, 4:5, 14, 16; SLR, 9:343, 344, 10:262, 268, 11:96, 97, 136, 417, 140; Selesky, *War and Society*, 219–28; Phelps, *History*, 92.

36. Carol Laun, "19 Bushy Hill Road" ("Houses—Bushy Hill Road," Granby File, SBHS); First Congregational Church of North Granby, *Records*, 1:54–62.

37. STR, 4:18, 23, 30, 33; *Public Records of Connecticut*, 13:332, 605, 772; Russell, *Long, Deep Furrow*, 81.

38. First Congregational Church of North Granby, *Records*, 5:5–6. On the continuing Baptist congregation see "Baptist Church," Granby File, SBHS; J. Hammond Trumbull, *The Memorial History of Hartford County, Connecticut, 1633–1884* (Boston: E. L. Osgood, 1886), 1103; Simsbury, Connecticut, Baptist Church Records, CSL; Phelps, *History*, 62, 63, 107.

39. CA, "Towns and Lands," series 1, 9:152–53; First Church, *Records*, 5:7; W. M.Maltbie, "The Episcopal Churches of Granby," 1959 typescript, Granby File: "Episcopal Churches: St. Ann's, St. Peters," SBHS.

40. CA, "Towns and Lands," series 1, 9:154–58.

41. See the *Connecticut Courant*, May–August, 1774.

42. STR, 4:36–37.

43. *Connecticut Courant*, August 16, 1774.

44. STR, 4:37; First Congregational Church of North Granby, *Records*, 4:202.

45. *Connecticut Courant*, September 19, 1774, September 4, 1775.

46. STR, 4:50–54; *Connecticut Courant*, April 1, 1776.

CHAPTER 4. IN OUR CORPORATE CAPACITY

1. GTR, 1:62–63.

2. Timothy Dwight, *Greenfield Hill: A Poem in Seven Parts* (New York: Childs and Swaine, 1794), Part 1.

3. Lucius I. Barber, *A Record and Documentary History of Simsbury, 1643–1888* (Simsbury: Abigail Phelps Chapter, Daughters of the American Revolution, 1931), 399; STR, 4:53–56.

4. Hannah Pettibone to Jonathan Pettibone, July 1776, and Jonathan Pettibone Sr. to Jonathan Pettibone Jr., August 5, 1776, CSL Manuscript Collection, American Revolution Box 1a; I. Fayette Pettibone, *Genealogy of the Pettibone Family* (Chicago: Brown, Pettibone, and Kelly, 1885).

5. Franklin B. Dexter, *Biographical Sketches of the Graduates of Yale College* (New York: Holt, 1903), 2:221–24; First Congregational Church of North Granby, *Records*, SBHS, 1:70–72; Howard S. Russell and Mark B. Lapping, *A Long, Deep Furrow: Three Centuries of Farming in New England* (Hanover, N.H.: University Press of New England, 1982), 125.

6. Henry P. Johnston, *The Record of Connecticut Men in the Military and Naval Service During the War of the Revolution, 1775–1783* (Hartford: Case, Lockwood, and Brainard, 1889), 389.

7. STR, 4:3.

8. STR, 4:3, 54, 60; SLR, 9:93.

9. STR, 4:60–84; Mary Coffin Johnson, *The Higleys and Their Ancestry: An Old Colonial Family* (Granby: Grover S. Hayes, 1963), 139–40; SLR, 13:5, 14:230.

10. STR, 4:81–85; Noah A. Phelps, *History of Simsbury, Granby, and Canton: From 1642 to 1845* (Hartford: Case, Tiffany, and Burnham, 1845), 90–91.

11. STR, 4:91–95.

12. GTR, 1:7; CA, "Towns and Lands," series 1, 10:104–5; Phelps, *History*, 110.

13. First Congregational Church, *Records*, 1:88; SPR, 1:500; SLR, 10:284, 13:5, 383, 412, 14:R140; Johnson, *Higleys*, 139–40.

14. CA, "Towns and Lands," series 1, 9:152–53; U.S. Bureau of Census, First and Second Census of the United States (1790 and 1800), Heads of Family manuscript schedules, CSL.

15. For this period, I have drawn from a multitude of records in SPR, GPR, GLR, and deeds, account books, and legal papers in SBHS, CSL, and CHS to get a picture of the changing face of the town after 1786. See also *Granby Town Records, Volumes 1 and 2: 1786–1853*, Mark Williams, ed. (Granby: SBHS, 1986).

16. Guilford Probate District, Estate of John Huggins (1757), CSL; Report of the Adjutant General, *Connecticut Men in the War of the Revolution, the War of 1812, and the Mexican War* (Hartford: Case, Lockwood, 1857), 8, 561; CA, "Private Controversies," rf: Huggins, John; Revolution—series 1, rf: Huggins, James; *Collections of the Connecticut Historical Society* 8 (1901), 12 (1909); SLR, 10:248, 269, 12:24, 265, 270, 348, 461, 465, 486, 560, 13:7, 305, 385, 425, 14:37, 164, 440, 467, 495; GLR, 5:93, 399, 6:25, 398, 7:151; U.S. Census, 1790; STR, 4:90; Nancy Holcomb to James Holcomb, March 23, 1834, private collection.

17. SLR, 12:156, 17:340; Deed of Giles Heacock [*sic*] to Benjamin Hayes, 1793, CHS Manuscript Collection; "Black Families," Granby File, SBHS. All of these people are listed together in the 1800 U.S. Census, Heads of Family Schedule, CSL; SLR, 10:248, 262, 268, 269, 11:136, 148, 12:24, 190, 309, 461, 270, 560, 13:7, 385, 425, 495, 14:37, 467; GLR, 5:147, 347, 6:207, 245, 369–70, 7:160, 170, 242, 368, 533, 534, 8:448, 9:369, 378; Simsbury Probate District, "Estate of Martin Stratton" (1790), CSL; GPR, 1:1ff; STR, 4:90; GTR, 1:27.

18. GTR, 1:43; GLR, 7:235.

19. SPR, 3:341–42; GPR, 1:159–60, 211, 301, 2:63–66, 5:35ff; Seth Holcombe, *The Descendants of Phinehas Holcomb (1759–1833) of New Hartford, Connecticut* (North Granby, Conn.: the author, 1988); SLR, 7:285, 10:212, 11:270; GLR, 1:136, 235; GPR, Granby Town Records, Williams ed., 21, 248.

20. SPR, 2:130, 133, 162–63, 3:83–86, 4:235–38; GLR, 6:174, 191, 296, 428, 8:170, 335, 366, 9:10; GTR, 1:44, 47, 49; Charles Whittelsey, *Ancestry and Descendants of John Pratt* (Hartford: Hartford Press, 1900); SLR, 8:175; Charles Wells Hayes, *George Hayes of Windsor and His Descendants* (Buffalo: Baker, Jones, 1884), 14, 23; "License" for Ozias Higley to Tan (1804), Hartford County Court Records, CSL.

21. GLR, 5:354, 6:271, 8:160, 16:12; Samuel and Seth Hays, Account Book, SBHS; U.S. Manuscript Census of 1800, CSL; Hartford County Court, Dockets, vol. 16, part 3, CHS; SLR, 11:262, 13:85, 14:426; GLR, 5:95, 540; County Court Taverners, vol. 1 (1800–1816).

22. Seth Hayes, Account Book; U.S. Treasury Department, Direct Tax of 1798 (Granby), CHS; GPR, 2:1; First and Second Census of the United States (1790 and 1800); "Inns: Granby," Granby File, SBHS; Russell, *Long, Deep Furrow*, 13; Bushman, *Puritan to Yankee*, 111.

23. "Hillyer Papers," "Industry-Store-Hillyer and Jeptha Curtiss," "Industry-Cider Brandy," Reserve Files, SBHS; "Inns: Granby," Granby File, SBHS; GTR, vol. 1.

24. Holcomb Family Papers, CSL; "Papers—John Ashley," Reserve Legal File, SBHS, and Account Book of "WBC," CHS.

25. Phelps, *History*, 107; Harry S. Stout, *The New England Soul: Preaching and Religious Culture in Colonial New England* (New York: Oxford University Press, 1986), 210.

26. Dexter, *Graduates of Yale College*, 4:614; General Association of the Congregational Churches of Connecticut, *Contributions to the Ecclesiastical History of Connecticut* (New Haven: William Kingsley, 1861), 1:308, 371; First Congregational Church, *Records*, vol. 1, meeting of February 10, 1794, 5:82–88; Timothy Dwight, "On the Duty of Americans in the Present Crisis" (New Haven: T. Greene, 1796).

27. "Miscellaneous Sermons," Reserve File, SBHS.

28. First Congregational Church, *Records*, 2:1–55, 5:82–88. Phelps, *History*, 103, 111; Ann Eliza Edwards, Memoirs, SBHS.

29. Burr, "Story of a Country Parish," in William Maltbie, "Episcopal Churches," Granby File, SBHS; Barber, *Simsbury*, 315; Hoadley Collection, Box 9 and Box 12, CHS Manuscript Collection; *Records of Rev. Roger Viets, Rector of St. Andrew's, Simsbury, Conn., 1763–1800*, Albert C. Bates, ed. (Hartford: CHS, 1893); 1790 "Blodget Map" of Connecticut, History and Genealogy Room, Map Collection, CSL.

30. *Contributions to the Ecclesiastical History of Connecticut*, 1:267–69; Ethel Linstrom Austin, *The Story of the Churches of Granby* (Granby: Holcomb Fund Committee, 1968); West Granby Methodist Episcopal Society, Records, CSL; Phelps, *History*, 111.

31. Sylvanus Holcomb to Nahum Holcomb, September 14, 1800, Holcomb Family Papers, CSL; Arthur G. Sharp, "Exodus to Ohio—A Promised Land," *Hartford Courant*, October 13, 1985.

32. Andrew Hillyer, Justice of the Peace (1793–1824), Account Book, CHS; *Records of Rev. Roger Viets*, 14, 49; Oliver Phelps and Andrew Servin, *The Phelps Family in America* (Pittsfield, Mass.: Eagle, 1899), 1:328; GTR, 1:24; Genealogy Files, SBHS, sf: Joel Buttolph, Hezekiah Phelps, Aaron Post; SPR, 2:95–96, 120–21, 3:341–42; GPR, 1:156ff.

33. Carol Laun's research on black families in early Granby, organized in a genealogical file at SBHS; Selectman's Account Book (1795–1810), SBHS.

34. CA, "Travel, Highways, Ferries, and Bridges," series 2 (1737–1820), 1:82; GTR, 1:7–23, 39–40, 43–70; *Heritage of Granby*, 155; Harold Pinkham, "The Division of Granby, Connecticut: The Evolution of a Separation Minded Area from Its Attempts to Be Annexed to the Neighboring Towns to Its Complete Independence" (Master's thesis, University of Connecticut, 1966), Granby File: "Connecticut, East Granby"; Bruce Colin Daniels, *The Connecticut Town: Growth and Development, 1635–1790* (Middletown, Conn.: Wesleyan University Press, 1979), 104; Barber, *Simsbury*, 378.

35. GTR, 1:46–47.

36. GTR, 1:28; *The Public Records of the State of Connecticut* (Hartford: Case, Lockwood, and Brainard, 1894), 6:224.

37. Selectman's Account Book, especially p. 53, and Carol Laun's notebook on African Americans, SBHS; "Blacks—Foot, Prince," Granby File, SBHS.

38. Pliny Hillyer to Jonathan Humphrey, February 1803, Pliny Hillyer Papers, SBHS.

39. Roger Viets, "Sermon, Preached Before the Lodge of Free and Accepted Masons" (Hartford: Hudson and Goodwin, 1800), CHS, 3. See also "Masons—Granby," Granby File, SBHS.

40. "Salmon Brook Publick Library," Granby File, SBHS; Phelps, *History*, 111; James Kilbourn to Payne Kenyon Kilbourn, December 10, 1844, copy in "Library—Salmon Brook Publick, 1761," Granby File, SBHS.

41. William Maltbie, "Episcopal Churches, St. Ann's, St. Peter's," Granby File, SBHS. The church's doors are now at SBHS.

42. Roger Viets, "A Sermon Preached in St. Peter's Church" (Hartford: Hudson and Goodwin, 1800), CHS; Viets, "Sermon, Preached Before the Lodge."

HUNTSTOWN

CHAPTER 5. SETTLED OUR LAND ACCORDING TO YOUR COMMAND

1. E. R. Ellis, *Biographical Sketches of Richard Ellis, the First Settler of Ashfield, Mass., and His Descendants* (Detroit: Wm. Graham, 1888), 209–10.

2. Ellis, *Richard Ellis*, 410–11; Israel Williams to Governor William Shirley, September 12, 1754, Israel Williams Papers, Massachusetts Historical Society, Boston, Massachusetts.

3. MA, 2:522, 34:164, 236, 239–46, 280, 283, 299, 312, 36:105.

4. MA, 36:134, 169; Howard Henry Peckham, *The Colonial Wars, 1689–1762* (Chicago: University of Chicago Press, 1964), 194nn.15–16.

5. MA, 17:202a, 36:386b, 48:273, 67:49a, 70:26; Massachusetts, *The Acts and Resolves, Public and Private, of the Province of the Massachusetts Bay*, 21 vols. (Boston: Wright and Potter, 1869–1922), vol. 1 for information on taxes. For Ephraim Hunt's land in Weymouth, see SCLR, 13:200, 294, 21:553; *A History of Weymouth, Massachusetts* (Weymouth: Weymouth Historical Society, 1923), 2:528–44, 3:313–14; SCLR, 21:657.

6. *Publick Occurrences*, September 25, 1690; John Walley, "Major Walley's Journal in the Expedition Against Canada in 1692 [*sic*]," Appendix Number 21 in Thomas Hutchinson, *The History of the Colony of Massachusetts Bay* (Boston: Thomas and John Fleet, 1764, reprinted by the Arno Press, New York, 1972), 1:554–56; Peckham, *The Colonial Wars*, 46.

7. Walley, "Journal," 555–58; Robert Leckie, *The Wars of America*, rev. and updated ed. (New York: Harper and Row, 1981), 15–22.

8. Walley, "Journal," 567; MA, 37:48, 61–63, 36:386b, 460; Peckham, *Colonial Wars*, 37; Samuel Adams Drake, *The Border Wars of New England, Commonly Called King William's and Queen Anne's Wars* (New York: C. Scribner's Sons, 1897), 264–65; Ellis, *Richard Ellis*, 209–10.

9. Hutchinson, *History*, 1:399–402; MA, 36:460, 37:61–63; Peckham, *Colonial Wars*, 37–38.

10. Hutchinson, *History*, 1:402, 2:380–82; *Journal of the Honorable House of Representatives of His Majesty's Province of Massachusetts-Bay*, June 14, 1727; Massachusetts, *Acts and Resolves*, 11:701–2, 12:181. See also Roy Hidemichi Akagi, "The Town Proprietors of the New England Colonies: A Study of Their Development, Organization, Activities, and Controversies, 1620–1770" (Ph.D. dissertation, University of Pennsylvania, 1923), 194nn.15–16; United States Bureau of the Census, *Historical Statistics of the United States, Colonial Times to 1970* (Washington: U.S. Department of Commerce, Bureau of the Census, 1976), series Z, 1–19; Brian Donahue, *The Great Meadow: Farmers and the Land in Colonial Concord* (New Haven: Yale University Press, 2004), chapter 7.

11. *Journal of the Honorable House of Representatives of His Majesty's Province of Massachusetts-Bay* (Ford edition), 1:frontispiece, 62, 72ff, 2:116, 123;

Rory Fitzpatrick, *God's Frontiersmen: The Scots-Irish Epic* (London: Weidenfeld and Nicolson in association with Channel Four Television and Ulster Television, 1989), 53–54.

12. Massachusetts, *Acts and Resolves*, 12:105–6, 140–47, 181–82, 289, 341–42, 378, 457.

13. Akagi, "Town Proprietors of the New England Colonies," 103–10.

14. Massachusetts, *Acts and Resolves*, 12:181–82, 278, 299–300, 332.

15. For a breakdown of the original proprietors of Huntstown and their background, see Mark Williams, "The Brittle Thread of Life: The New England Backcountry in the Eighteenth Century" (Ph.D. dissertation, Yale University, 2006), Appendix II-A. For the residences of the proprietors, see specific deed references in "Warren Chase's Notes on Old Deeds," a database compiled by Chase for the Ashfield (Mass.) Historical Society, which database I revised and amended in 2005 and placed on file at the Ashfield Historical Society. See also APR, 17; William L. Chaffin, *History of the Town of Easton, Massachusetts* (Cambridge: John Wilson and Son, University Press, 1886), 432–34; and HCLR, vol. R:272.

16. APR, and HCLR, vol. M:401; Frederick G. Howes, *History of the Town of Ashfield, Franklin County, Massachusetts, from Its Settlement in 1742 to 1910* (Ashfield, Mass.: Town of Ashfield, 1910), 240.

17. APR, 19–25; Howes, *History*, 52.

18. Williams, "The Brittle Thread of Life," Appendix II-B; APR, 17–19.

19. HCLR, vol. M:232, 233, 234, 235, 251, 303, 304, 345, 401, vol. N:513, 2:819, 5:172, 175, 177, 14:286; FCLR, 1:144, 182, 189, 208, 209, 239, 213; APR, 25–30; HCLR, vol. E:224, vol. K:350, vol. M:95, 98, among others.

20. Chaffin, *Easton*, 1–41, 53–56, 796; BCLR, 32:45; Ellis, *Richard Ellis*, 16, 377.

21. Chaffin, *Easton*, 432–34; BCLR, 25:184, 185, 26:509, 575, 53:540; HCLR, vol. R:672; Nancy Gray Garvin, "Who Was Heber Honestman," in "Ashfield Historical Society Newsletter," May 2005.

22. Akagi, "Town Proprietors of the New England Colonies," 92–94.

23. BCLR, 26:44, 28:31, 33, 36, 37; Ellis, *Richard Ellis*, 9–10, 14–16, 297.

24. HCLR, 5:172, 175, 177, 225, vol. R:674; BCLR, 38:31; Hampshire County Court Records, Northampton, Massachusetts (on microfilm), 4:73; Chaffin, *Easton*, 43, 46; Church of Jesus Christ of Latter-Day Saints, Ancestry Files, posted online at www.familysearch.org; Ellis, in *Richard Ellis*, 10–11, 297; Howes, *History*, 60.

25. APR, 31–43; Howes, *History*, 59–60.

26. Hampshire County Court of General Sessions Records, 4:92; HCLR, vol. K:636, vol. M:126, 736, 737, vol. N:126, 264, 2:811 (there are no land records for Chilson in the WCLR); Thomas Baldwin, *Vital Records of Uxbridge* (Boston: Wright and Porter, 1916); Bristol County Land Records, 59:447; SCLR, 34:36, 56:53, 58:256, 62:9, 10, 22, 63:58, 64:173, 218, 65:151, 72:2, 74:240, 75:17, 90:148, 93:111, 99:142, 107:188; Ellis, *Richard Ellis,* 332; Howes, *History,* 240; William S. Pattee, *A History of Old Braintree and Quincy* (Quincy: Green and Prescott, 1878), 60, 86, 586; Church of Jesus Christ of Latter-Day Saints, Ancestry Files, and the International Genealogical Index.

27. MA, 115:1–2; APR, 40–55; Howes, *History,* 60.

28. Warren Chase's database "Notes on Old Deeds" with my revisions at Ashfield Historical Society; APR, 31–62; Howes, *History,* 57–58.

29. APR, 34–67; Hampshire County Court Records, 4:69.

30. APR, 66.

31. APR, 69–71; Ebenezer Smith, "Brief Account of the Life and Trials of Elder Ebenezer Smith of Ashfield, Mass.—Written by Himself" (1820), in Ellis, *Richard Ellis,* 338; Kevin H. Sweeney, "River Gods and Related Minor Deities: The Williams Family and the Connecticut River Valley, 1637–1790" (Ph.D. dissertation, Yale University, 1986), 375–76, 407.

32. Timothy Woodbridge to Capt. Ephraim Williams, May 10, 1751, Israel Williams Papers, Massachusetts Historical Society, Boston, Massachusetts; Ellis, *Richard Ellis,* 11–12, 68; Howes, *History,* 60; FCLR, 1:287, 378; HCLR, vol. X:246.

33. APR, 72–73, 89; Howes, *History,* 75; Ellis, *Richard Ellis,* 302; Alden Gray, "Some Thoughts About a Road that Started at Heber's Fence," in "Ashfield Historical Society Newsletter," May 2005; Hampshire County Court Records, 5:218; Williams, "The Brittle Thread of Life," Appendix II-C.

34. Sylvester Judd, *History of Hadley, Including the Early History of Hatfield, South Hadley, Amherst, and Granby, Massachusetts* (Springfield, Mass.: H. R. Huntting, 1905), 124–29, 138–39, 283–87, 400–403; Ellis, *Richard Ellis,* 72–73, 405, and, in the same, Smith, "Brief Account," 338ff; HCLR, vol. K:350, 8:233.

35. Chileab Smith, *An Answer to Many Slanderous Reports Cast on the Baptists of Ashfield* (Norwich, Conn.: Robertson and Trumbull, 1774), 7–8; Sophia E. Eastman, *In Old South Hadley* (Chicago: Blakely, 1912), 6–111; Isaac Backus, *A History of New England with Particular Reference to the Denomination of Christians Called Baptists,* 2nd ed., 2 vols. (Newton, Mass.:

Backus Historical Society, 1871), 2:149ff; Smith, "Brief Account," 339; William G. McLoughlin, *New England Dissent, 1630–1833: The Baptists and the Separation of Church and State*, 2 vols. (Cambridge: Harvard University Press, 1971), 1:347–49; HCLR, 6:636, 641.

36. Records of the Baptist Church of Ashfield, Ashfield Historical Society, Ashfield, Massachusetts, 1; McLoughlin, *New England Dissent*, 1:454–66; Howes, *History*, 61–62, 149; APR, 72–79; Smith, "Brief Account," 338–39.

37. Ellis, *Richard Ellis*, 68–70; HCLR, vol. X:395, 397, 5:226, 6:41, 14:241, 242; Church of Jesus Christ of Latter-Day Saints, Ancestry Files.

38. Chaffin, *Easton*, 92–105, 793–96; BCLR, 35:440, 36:364, 514, 515, 516, 42:523; HCLR, vol. X:395, 2:854; Hampshire County Court Records, 5:204, 6:217, 7:26.

39. See Christopher Clark, *The Roots of Rural Capitalism: Western Massachusetts, 1780–1860* (Ithaca: Cornell University Press, 1990), 40–41.

40. Howes, *History*, 63, 145; Thomas Shepard, "Sketches of the History of Ashfield, Mass., from Its First Settlement to the Year 1833," in Ellis, *Richard Ellis*, 279; APR, 72–80; Ellis, *Richard Ellis*, 328ff; Mark Williams, "The Brittle Thread of Life," 250.

41. Sweeney, "River Gods and Related Minor Deities," 499–502.

42. Governor William Shirley to Col. Israel Williams, September 3, 1754, and Williams to Shirley September 12, 1754, Israel Williams Papers; Howes, *History*, 64.

43. Col. Israel Williams to Governor Shirley, March 29, 1756, Col. Israel Williams to Col. Pitkin, June 19, 1756, Isaac Wyman to Col. Israel Williams, June 25, 1756, all in Israel Williams Papers; Howes, *History*, 63–65; Smith, "Brief Account," 339; K. David Goss and David Zarowin, eds., *Massachusetts Officers and Soldiers in the French and Indian Wars, 1755–1756* (n.p.: New England Historic Genealogical Society, 1985).

44. Smith, "Brief Account," 339; MA, 117:113–14; Sweeney, "River Gods and Related Minor Deities," 530–38.

45. Israel Williams to William Shirley, March 29, 1756, Israel Williams Papers; Shepard, "Sketches," 280; Eastman, *In Old South Hadley*, 103.

46. *Rex v. Elizabeth Wittium*, Hampshire County Court Records, 6:130.

CHAPTER 6. WE OUGHT TO OBEY GOD RATHER THAN MAN

1. Gregory H. Nobles, *Divisions Throughout the Whole: Politics and Society in Hampshire County, Massachusetts, 1740–1775* (New York: Cambridge

University Press, 1983), 28–34, 65–66, 117–27; Kevin H. Sweeney, "River Gods and Related Minor Deities: The Williams Family and the Connecticut River Valley, 1637–1790" (Ph.D. dissertation, Yale University, 1986), 306–93, 409–19; Christopher Clark, *The Roots of Rural Capitalism: Western Massachusetts, 1780–1860* (Ithaca: Cornell University Press, 1990), 42. For Williams's interests in other settlements, see HCLR, vol. L:33, 139, 310, vol. M:370.

2. MA, 117:115–17.

3. E. R. Ellis, *Biographical Sketches of Richard Ellis, the First Settler of Ashfield, Mass., and His Descendants* (Detroit: Wm. Graham, 1888), 36.

4. Massachusetts, *The Acts and Resolves, Public and Private, of the Province of the Massachusetts Bay*, 21 vols. (Boston: Wright and Potter, 1869–1922), 15:567; Gov. S. Phips, orders to Col. Israel Williams, July 8, 1756, Israel Williams Papers, Massachusetts Historical Society, Boston, Massachusetts.

5. APR, 83; Reports of July 13 and July 16, 1756, from Fort Massachusetts, J. Dwight to Col. Israel Williams, July 26, 1756, Thomas Williams to Col. Israel Williams, July 27, 1756, Josiah Hawley to Col. Israel Williams, July 13, 1756, Seth Field to Maj. Williams, August 12, 1756, all in Israel Williams Papers.

6. Ellis, *Richard Ellis*, 13, 68–70; Ebenezer Smith, "Brief Account of the Life and Trials of Elder Ebenezer Smith, of Ashfield, Mass.—Written by Himself" (1820), in Ellis, *Richard Ellis*, 339; Gov. Shirley's Orders, September 13, 1756, Gov. William Shirley warrant, Capt. John Catlin to Col. Israel Williams, September 6, 1756, all in Israel Williams Papers.

7. Frederick G. Howes, *History of the Town of Ashfield, Franklin County, Massachusetts, from Its Settlement in 1742 to 1910* (Ashfield, Mass.: Town of Ashfield, 1910), 68–69; Lieutenant John Hawks, Diary, Pocomtuck Valley Memorial Association, Deerfield, Massachusetts; Ellis, *Richard Ellis*, 320–21; John Hawks to Israel Williams, May 23, 1757, Israel Williams Papers.

8. Chileab Smith to Israel Williams, May 27, 1757, Israel Williams Papers.

9. Howes, *History*, 69; Ellis, *Richard Ellis*, 374; Sweeney, "River Gods," 564–66; Col. Williams Muster Rolls, one n.d., another 1761, and Receipts, 1761, Israel Williams Papers; HCLR, 1:99, 4:664, 26:334; APR, 84; Ashfield, Proprietors' Treasury Book, Ashfield Town Hall, 15.

10. APR, 89; MA, 117:570; Thomas Shepard, "Sketches of the History of Ashfield, Mass., from Its First Settlement to the Year 1833," in Ellis, *Richard Ellis*, 280–81; Nobles, *Divisions*, 128–30.

11. *Rex v. Eliżabeth Wittium, Rex v. John Abel,* and *Rex v. Wetherell Wittium,* Hampshire County Court Records, Hampshire County Court, Northampton, Massachusetts, 6:110, 130, 218; Records of the Baptist Church of Ashfield, Ashfield Historical Society; Smith, "Brief Account," 338.

12. MA, 117:570; APR, 84; Nobles, *Divisions,* 316.

13. APR, 85, 91, 95, 98; Massachusetts, *Acts and Resolves,* 4:864–65.

14. APR, 85–103; Account Book of Richard and John Ellis, 1765–, Ashfield Historical Society; Clark, *The Roots of Rural Capitalism,* chapter 1.

15. APR, 85–88.

16. Ashfield Baptist Church Records, 2–10; Smith, "Brief Account," 340.

17. APR, 91–94.

18. MA, 14:588; Howes, *History,* 160–61; Isaac Backus, *A History of New England with Particular Reference to the Denomination of Christians Called Baptists,* 2nd ed., 2 vols. (Newton, Mass.: Backus Historical Society, 1871), 2:150–51.

19. Mark Williams, "The Brittle Thread of Life: The New England Backcountry in the Eighteenth Century" (Ph.D. dissertation, Yale University, 2006), Appendix II-D.

20. Baptism records of the First Baptist Church of Ashfield, 17; Hampshire County Court Records, 5:155; Ellis, *Richard Ellis,* 371; APR, 97.

21. APR, 94–95.

22. Williams, "The Brittle Thread of Life," 284; Stafford Land Records, Stafford Town Hall, Stafford, Connecticut, 2:180, 181, 249, 255, 261, 264, 3:195, 246, 360, 436, 437, 497, 499, 546, 564; HCLR, 2:800, 7:737; FCLR, 1:283, 470; Howes, *History,* 311; Nancy Gray Garvin, "David Alden and His Wife Lucia Thomas of Stafford, Connecticut, and Ashfield, Massachusetts: Three or More Generations of Their Descendants," unpubl. ms. (Ashfield, Mass., 2004); Stafford Library Association, *History of the Town of Stafford* (Stafford Springs: The Association, 1935), 8–11; Kendrick Grobel, *History of the Church of Stafford, Connecticut* (Stafford: Women's Council of the Congregational Church, 1942), 5–6, 28–34, 77.

23. Massachusetts, *Acts and Resolves,* 4:782, 818; ATR, 1–2 (these are copies of loose sheets found by Town Clerk H. J. Ranney in the nineteenth century); Ellis, *Richard Ellis,* 13, 78, 308–9; Howes, *History,* 87, 127; APR, 101–3; HCLR, 3:400.

24. APR, 94–98; Account Book of Richard and John Ellis, Ashfield Historical Society.

25. APR, 97–101; Shepard, "Sketches," 288–89; "Manual of the First Congregational Church of Ashfield, Massachusetts" (1895), Ashfield Historical Society; Ellis, *Richard Ellis*, 13, 355; Howes, *History*, 123.

26. HCLR, 6:786; APR, 97–101; Chileab Smith, *An Answer to Many Slanderous Reports Cast on the Baptists of Ashfield* (Norwich, Conn.: Robertson and Trumbull, 1774), 12; *Boston Post Boy*, February 20, 1764; *Boston Evening Post*, February 27 and October 29, 1764; *Boston News-Letter and New England Chronicle*, June 27, 1765; *Boston Gazette*, July 1, 1765.

27. HCLR, 4:889, 6:17, 618, 10:104, 105, 12:753, 14:92, 93, 94, 239; APR, 5; Massachusetts, *Acts and Resolves*, 4:823.

28. For the tax data, see Williams, "The Brittle Thread of Life," Appendix II-E.

29. ATR, 12.

30. For the diminutive description of Ashfield, see Bernard Bailyn, ed., *Pamphlets of the American Revolution, 1750–1776* (Cambridge: Harvard University Press, 1965), 163–64; Ellis, *Richard Ellis*, 287–92; Charles A. Hall, "In Regard to Chileab Smith and His Fight for the Rights of the Ashfield Baptists," paper read before the Pocomtuck Valley Memorial Association, February 26, 1907, reprinted in Howes, *History*, 78ff. For well-told versions of this story that explore other dimensions than social relations, see William G. McLoughlin, *New England Dissent, 1630–1833: The Baptists and the Separation of Church and State* (Cambridge: Harvard University Press, 1971), 1:516–628; and Nobles, *Divisions*, 91ff.

31. APR, 103–5; ATR, 77–78; Shepard, "Sketches," 291; Backus, *History of New England . . . Baptists*, 2:151.

32. Smith, *An Answer*, 13; Smith, "Brief Account," 341–42; Backus, *History of New England . . . Baptists*, 2:151–52; MA, 14:512, 558, 563, 26:473, 27:34; "Summary of Legislation," *Boston Evening Post*, July 4, 1768.

33. Backus, *History of New England . . . Baptists*, 2:152–53; MA, 14:557, 561, 563.

34. MA, 14:556, 563; Backus, *History of New England . . . Baptists*, 2:153–54; HCLR, 9:514, 10:40, 43, 11:2, 11; Smith, "Brief Account," 341.

35. Backus, *History of New England . . . Baptists*, 154–56; MA, 14:592.

36. MA, 14:593–603; *Boston Evening Post*, October 29, 1770, January 7, 1771; *Massachusetts Gazette*, February 7, 1771.

37. MA, 14:593–603; Backus, *History of New England . . . Baptists*, 158.

38. See Smith, "Brief Account," 339ff, and Smith, *An Answer*, for the clarity and depth of their convictions.

39. MA, 14:556.

40. John Davis to Morgan Edwards, September 26, 1770, Isaac Backus Papers, Andover Newton Theological School, Newton Center, Massachusetts; Backus, *History of New England . . . Baptists,* 160; MA, 27:248; Hutchinson to Williams, November 18, 1771, Israel Williams Papers.

41. Smith, "Brief Account," 343–44.

42. Smith, *An Answer,* 15–17; Backus, *History of New England . . . Baptists,* 159–60.

43. Smith, *An Answer,* 17–21; Thomas Hutchinson to Israel Williams, January 8, 1773, Israel Williams Papers.

44. Smith, "Brief Account," 343; Ezra Stiles, *Literary Diary of Ezra Stiles* (New York: Scribners, 1901), 1:333, 2:528, 531. See also Ezra Stiles to Dr. Philip Furneaux, November 20, 1772, in *The Literary Diary of Ezra Stiles,* 2:472–75; Isaac Backus, "Appeal to the Public for Religious Liberty" (1773), in Bailyn, *Pamphlets of the American Revolution,* 163–64.

45. Howes, *History,* 158–59; Records of the First Congregational Church of Ashfield, 9–26; Ellis, *Richard Ellis,* 304; Ashfield Baptist Church Records, 17ff.

46. ATR, 8–26; Ashfield Baptist Church Records, 16–17; Bettye Hobbs Pruitt, *The Massachusetts Tax Valuation List of 1771* (Boston: G. K. Hall, 1978), 442–45.

CHAPTER 7. WE DO NOT WANT ANY GOVINER BUT THE GOVINER OF THE UNIVARSE

1. Massachusetts, *The Acts and Resolves, Public and Private, of the Province of the Massachusetts Bay,* 21 vols. (Boston: Wright and Potter, 1869–1922), 5:228–30.

2. Town valuations for 1766 and 1771 in the ATR, miscellaneous papers transcribed by Town Clerk Henry S. Ranney in 1857; Bettye Hobbs Pruitt, *The Massachusetts Tax Valuation List of 1771* (Boston: G. K. Hall, 1978), 442–45; Edward Cook Jr., *Fathers of the Towns: Leadership and Community Structure in Eighteenth-Century New England* (Baltimore: Johns Hopkins University Press, 1976), 202–6.

3. Lt. John Ellis, Account Book, Ashfield Historical Society; ATR (Ranney transcript), 19–20, 34–35; HCLR, 6:50, 127, 13:149, 708, 709, 14:239, 240, 241, 242, 342; Mark Williams, "The Brittle Thread of Life: The New England Backcountry in the Eighteenth Century" (Ph.D. dissertation, Yale University, 2006), Appendix II-F.

4. ATR (Ranney transcript), 14.

5. For the growing consumer economy, see T. H. Breen, *The Marketplace of Revolution: How Consumer Politics Shaped American Independence* (New York: Oxford University Press, 2004); and James Deetz, *In Small Things Forgotten: An Archaeology of Early American Life,* expanded and revised ed. (New York: Doubleday, 1996), chapters 2–3.

6. Gregory H. Nobles, *Divisions Throughout the Whole: Politics and Society in Hampshire County, Massachusetts, 1740–1775* (New York: Cambridge University Press, 1983), chapter 7; Robert A. Gross, *The Minutemen and Their World* (New York: Hill and Wang, 1976); *Vital Records of Ashfield Massachusetts to the Year 1850* (Boston: New England Historic Genealogical Society, 1942); Hampshire County Probate Records, Hampshire County Probate Court, Northampton, Massachusetts.

7. ATR (Ranney transcript), 24–25.

8. ATR (Ranney transcript), 12–13; APR, 105–12.

9. Pruitt, *Massachusetts Tax Valuation List of 1771*; town valuation for 1771 is in ATR (Ranney transcript), 19–20; Frederick G. Howes, *History of the Town of Ashfield, Franklin County, Massachusetts, from Its Settlement in 1742 to 1910* (Ashfield, Mass.: Town of Ashfield, 1910), 314–15; Church of Jesus Christ of Latter-Day Saints, Ancestry Files, online; E. R. Ellis, *Biographical Sketches of Richard Ellis, the First Settler of Ashfield, Mass., and His Descendants* (Detroit: Wm. Graham, 1888), 311, 373; Charles E. Swift, *History of Old Yarmouth* (Yarmouthport, Mass.: the author, 1884); HCLR, 10:211.

10. ATR (Ranney transcript), 23; Nobles, *Divisions,* 162–70.

11. ATR (Ranney transcript), 19–23.

12. ATR (Ranney transcript), 25–27; Nobles, *Divisions,* 169.

13. ATR (Ranney transcript), 28; Office of the Secretary of State, Massachusetts, *Massachusetts Soldiers and Sailors of the Revolutionary War,* 12 vols. (Boston: Wright and Potter, State Printers, 1896–1908); Howes, *History,* 230.

14. ATR (Ranney transcript), 28. In *Massachusetts Soldiers and Sailors of the Revolutionary War,* I found nearly 180 names of Ashfield soldiers. See also Howes, *History,* 230. To estimate the size of the fighting-age population, I used the 1790 census.

15. ATR, 29–31; Charles Royster, *A Revolutionary People at War: The Continental Army and American Character, 1775–1783* (Chapel Hill: University of North Carolina Press, 1979), chapters 1–2.

16. Barnabas Howes, "Historical Sketches of the Times and Men in Ashfield, Mass., During the Revoutionary War" (1883), as quoted in Ellis, *Richard Ellis,* 304.

17. Nancy Gray Garvin, "Ancestor Research," in *Ashfield Historical Society Newsletter,* May 2006, 3, and the Church of Jesus Christ of Latter-Day Saints, Ancestry Files, for Daniel Lazell; Nahum Mitchell, *History of the Early Settlement of Bridgewater in Plymouth County, Massachusetts* (Boston: for the author, 1890, 1897, 1970), 23–27; *Vital Records of Ashfield, Massachusetts, to the Year 1850,* 223–73; ATR (Ranney transcript), 32–33.

18. ATR, vol. 1, meetings from March 1776 through the end of 1777 that were copied into this book by Jacob Sherwin when he became town clerk; Thomas Shepard, "Sketches of the History of Ashfield, Mass., from Its First Settlement to the Year 1833," in Howes, *History,* 24.

19. ATR, 1:5–6; *Vital Records of Ashfield.*

20. ATR, 1:6; *Massachusetts Soldiers and Sailors* lists a number of men assigned to defend Ticonderoga. See also Barnabas Howes, as quoted in Ellis, *Richard Ellis,* 304; Nobles, *Divisions,* 76–130.

21. Howes, *History,* 229; and Ellis, *Richard Ellis,* 355.

22. ATR, 1:8–27. For an alternate view of backcountry participation, see William Pencak, " 'The Fine Theoretic Government of Massachusetts Is Prostrated to the Earth': The Response to Shays's Rebellion Reconsidered," in *In Debt to Shays: The Bicentennial of an American Rebellion,* ed. Robert Gross (Charlottesville: University Press of Virginia, 1993), 121–44.

23. MA, 156:121–99; the Ashfield response is on p. 131.

24. Oscar and Mary Handlin, eds., *The Popular Sources of Political Authority: Documents on the Massachusetts Constitution of 1780* (Cambridge: Harvard University Press, 1966), 101.

25. ATR, 1:5; *The Massachusetts Spy,* December 4, 1776; MA, 156:200–202, 266–93; Massachusetts, *Acts and Resolves,* 19:932–33.

26. For countywide sentiments, see John L. Brooke, "To the Quiet of the People: Revolutionary Settlements and Civil Unrest in Western Massachusetts, 1774–1789," *William and Mary Quarterly,* 3rd series, 56, no. 3 (1989).

27. MA, 156:304–427, 160:1–32, 125; ATR, 1:18–19; Handlin, ed., *Popular Sources of Political Authority,* 385–431.

28. ATR, 1:21–23; Handlin, ed., *Popular Sources of Political Authority,* 432–40; Ellis, *Richard Ellis,* 304; Ebenezer Smith to Isaac Backus, 1773, quoted in

William G. McLoughlin, *New England Dissent, 1630–1833: The Baptists and the Separation of Church and State*, 2 vols. (Cambridge: Harvard University Press, 1971), 1:767.

29. Handlin, ed., *Popular Sources of Political Authority*, 324ff, 441ff; Leonard L. Richards, *Shays's Rebellion: The American Revolution's Final Battle* (Philadelphia: University of Pennsylvania Press, 2002), 10, 71–72; Michael Lienesch, "Reinterpreting Rebellion: The Influence of Shays's Rebellion on American Political Thought," in *In Debt to Shays*, ed. Gross, 161–84.

30. MA, 276:39. For the reaction of towns that had strong Baptist contingents, see McLoughlin, *New England Dissent*, chapter 33.

31. ATR, 1:28–31.

32. ATR, 1:27–37.

33. Richards, *Shays's Rebellion*, 74–82; Richard Buel, "The Public Creditor Interest in Massachusetts Politics, 1780–1786," in *In Debt to Shays*, ed. Gross, 47–56; ATR, 1:38–46.

34. See the "Lament" of the "Ole Soldier" in *The Hampshire Herald*, March 7, 1786.

35. ATR, 1:46–50; Van Beck Hall, *Politics Without Parties: Massachusetts, 1780–1791* (Pittsburgh: University of Pittsburgh Press, 1972), 187–89; Brooke, "To the Quiet of the People," 430–33; Robert J. Taylor, *Western Massachusetts in the Revolution* (Providence, R.I.: Brown University Press, 1954), 111–21.

36. ATR, 1:50; Shepard, "Sketches," 30.

37. ATR, 1:51–68, 72.

38. Shepard, "Sketches," 30; Howes, *History*, 91–92; "List of Hampshire County Regulators," Robert Treat Paine Papers, Massachusetts Historical Society, Boston, Massachusetts.

39. In addition to the works already cited on Shays's Rebellion, see David P. Szatmary, *Shays' Rebellion: The Making of an Agrarian Insurrection* (Amherst: University of Massachusetts Press, 1980).

40. ATR, 1:26–30, 46, 53, 62, 70, 78; Howes, *History*, 371–73. For statistics on marriages and marriage horizons, see the table in Williams, "The Brittle Thread of Life," 46–47n.47.

41. See Hampshire County Court Records, Hampshire County Court, Northampton, Massachusetts, for debt cases, for example, 14:192, 18:154, 182. For the executions against Samuel Belding see HCLR, vol. B:191, 224, 297, 332, 313, 371; Howes, *History*, 323. See Williams, "The Brittle Thread of Life," Appendix II-G, for analysis of the so-called Shaysites. As indicated

there, I have examined HCLR to determine which of the regulators owned land. For Philip Phillips's appointment, see his own court records in the Ashfield Town Hall. See also Howes, *History*, 373.

42. ATR, 1:71; HCLR, 2:48, 10:290, 12:188, 431, 748, 14:129, 21:373, 377, 22:34, 38, 23:188, 222; Ellis, *Richard Ellis*, 395–96; Howes, *History*, 124–25, 222, 331.

43. ATR, 1:57–72; United States, Bureau of Census, First Census of the United States (1790), State of Massachusetts Manuscript Census, available at HeritageQuest Online; Ellis, *Richard Ellis*, 411; *Vital Records of Ashfield, Massachusetts, to the Year 1850*.

CHAPTER 8. AS THEY SHALL JUDGE NECESSARY

1. "Record of the Planting, Gathering, and Proceedings of the Baptist Church of Christ in Ashfield," Ashfield Historical Society, 25; ATR, 1:65; Frederick G. Howes, *History of the Town of Ashfield, Franklin County, Massachusetts, from Its Settlement in 1742 to 1910* (Ashfield, Mass.: Town of Ashfield, 1910), 150.

2. Baptist Church Records, 13, 17–19, 30–39, 99; E. R. Ellis, *Biographical Sketches of Richard Ellis, the First Settler of Ashfield, Mass., and His Descendants* (Detroit: Wm. Graham, 1888), 398–99, 405.

3. United States Bureau of Census, First and Second Census of the United States (1790 and 1800), Manuscript Censuses for Massachusetts, available at HeritageQuest Online; *Vital Records of Ashfield, Massachusetts, to the Year 1850* (Boston: New England Historic Genealogical Society, 1942).

4. Massachusetts Manuscript U.S. Census schedules for 1790 and 1800; Ellis, *Richard Ellis*, 305.

5. See Howes, *History*, 391ff; Ellis, *Richard Ellis*, 364ff; HCLR, vols. 18–38. I checked these records for deeds for those family heads who are listed on the 1790 or 1800 census but not both. Of the approximately 250 family heads, barely half were grantees of any property prior to 1800. For patterns of estate distribution, see Hampshire County Probate Records, Hampshire County Court, Northampton, Massachusetts, 40:44, 74:59, 145:44.

6. Edward Ellis to Lt. and Mrs. John Ellis of Ashfield [1799 or 1800], in Ellis, *Richard Ellis*, 423–24, among other letters.

7. Account book of an Ashfield Cobbler, 1791–1797, Ashfield Historical Society; Howes, *History*, 92, 126, 131, 222–23, 322, 328–29; Nancy Gray Garvin, "Who Was Selah Norton?" *Ashfield Historical Society Newsletter*, Fall 2003.

8. For land prices, see the database on the first division lots compiled by Warren Chase and supplemented with my additions at the Ashfield Historical Society.

9. ATR, 1:88, 100, 109, 125; Howes, *History*, 93.

10. ATR, 1:78–147. See also a survey of town roads made by Ephraim Williams and Rowland Sears in 1795, a copy of which is at the Ashfield Historical Society.

11. The preceding three paragraphs are based on the ATR, 1:74–147.

12. Leonard L. Richards, *Shays's Rebellion: The American Revolution's Final Battle* (Philadelphia: University of Pennsylvania Press, 2002), 158–59. For probate records see the estates of Aaron Cross, Thomas Howes, Reuben Ellis, and Jonathan Taylor in 1792 and 1793, Hampshire County Probate Records, 40:44, 54:18, 74:59, 145:44; Philip Phillips's court records, 1790–1792, at the Ashfield Town Hall.

13. Account Book of Lt. John Ellis, Ashfield Historical Society; Howes, *History*, 127–29.

14. Norton's advertisement is quoted from a 1793 edition of *The Hampshire Gazette* in Howes, *History*, 131; see also 114, 146. Norton's 1795 advertisements are discussed in Garvin, "Who Was Selah Norton?" For changing household economies in the region, see Christopher Clark, *The Roots of Rural Capitalism: Western Massachusetts, 1780–1860* (Ithaca: Cornell University Press, 1990).

15. Bettye Hobbs Pruitt, *The Massachusetts Tax Valuation List of 1771* (Boston: G. K. Hall, 1978); Ashfield, Massachusetts, Tax Lists for 1793, 1794 and 1795, Ashfield Town Hall. My thanks to Nancy Garvin of the Ashfield Historical Society for getting copies of the latter to me, and for all her help in keeping the comings and goings of various families straight.

16. ATR, 1:78–147; Van Beck Hall, *Politics Without Parties: Massachusetts, 1780–1791* (Pittsburgh: University of Pittsburgh Press, 1972), 222–25.

17. Howes, *History*, 159, 392, which relates the reminiscences of Amanda H. Hall; Nehemiah Porter, Sermon on Hebrews 10:38, first delivered April 26, 1789, Ashfield, Ashfield Historical Society.

18. Howes, *History*, 114; ATR, 1:93–98. I am indebted to Nancy Gray Garvin for telling me the location of Norton's store.

19. Michael Zuckerman, *Peaceable Kingdoms: New England Towns in the Eighteenth Century* (New York: Alfred A. Knopf, 1970), 188.

20. See Mark Williams, "The Brittle Thread of Life: The New England Backcountry in the Eighteenth Century" (Ph.D. dissertation, Yale University,

2006), Appendix II-G, for the Shaysites. Tax list for 1793 and voting list for 1794 are in miscellaneous papers in the Ashfield Town Hall; ATR, 1:74–147; *Vital Records of Ashfield Massachusetts to the Year 1850*.

21. Howes, *History*, 151–52, which cites recollections of Mrs. Lydia Miles; Baptist Church Records, 39–40.

22. Eunice Smith, "Some Arguments Against Worldly Mindedness and Needless Care and Trouble" (Boston: E. Russell, 1791); Eunice Smith, "A Dialogue or, Discourse Between Mary and Martha" (Boston: Printed at Russell's Office, 1797). See also Eunice Smith, "Some Motives to Engage Those Who Have Professed the Name of Jesus" (Greenfield, Mass.: for the proprietor, 1798), "Practical Language Interpreted: In a Dialogue Between a Believer and an Unbeliever" (Boston: E. Russell, 1792), and "Some of the Exercises of a Believing Soul Described" (Boston: E. Russell, 1792), copies of all of which are at the Massachusetts Historical Society, Boston, Massachusetts; Ellis, *Richard Ellis*, 405; *Vital Records of Ashfield*, 192; Sylvester Judd, *History of Hadley, Including the Early History of Hatfield, South Hadley, Amherst, and Granby, Massachusetts* (Springfield, Mass.: H. R. Huntting, 1905), 138–39.

23. Baptist Church Records, 54–55. See also copies of letters of Ebenezer Smith found by David Newell in the Special Collections at Franklin Trask Library, Andover Newton Theological School, a folder of which is on file at the Ashfield Historical Society.

24. *Vital Records of Ashfield*, 263; William G. McLoughlin, *New England Dissent, 1630–1833: The Baptists and the Separation of Church and State*, 2 vols. (Cambridge: Harvard University Press, 1971), 1:649, 688–89; ATR, 1:227–28; Baptist Church Records, 56–68; Thomas Shepard, "Sketches of the History of Ashfield, Mass., from Its First Settlement to the Year 1833," in Howes, *History*, 32; Howes, *History*, 152.

Index